REEL SPIRIT

REEL SPIRIT

A Guide to Movies That Inspire, Explore and Empower

Raymond Teague

Unity House

Unity Village, Missouri

First Edition 2000

To receive a catalog of all Unity publications (books, cassettes, compact discs, and magazines) or to place an order, call the Customer Service Department: (816) 969-2069 or 1-800-669-0282.

The publisher wishes to acknowledge the editorial work of Michael Maday, Raymond Teague, and Medini Longwell; the copy services of Kay Thomure, Thomas Lewin, Deborah Dribben, and Beth Anderson; the production help of Rozanne Devine and Jane Blackwood; and the marketing efforts of Allen Liles, Jenee Meyer, and Sharon Sartin.

Cover design by Karen Rizzo

Interior design by Coleridge Design

Cover photos: All film stills are from Photofest.

Front cover, clockwise from top left—*Forrest Gump*, Paramount Pictures; *The Wizard of Oz*, MGM, Turner Entertainment; *Good Will Hunting*, Miramax; *Star Trek IV: The Voyage Home*, Paramount Pictures; *The Sound of Music*, 20th Century Fox

Back cover, from left—*2010*, MGM/UA; *King David*, Paramount Pictures; *The Secret of NIMH*, MGM, UA

Author photo: Gene King/Unity Photography

The New Revised Standard Version is used for all Bible verses, unless otherwise stated or unless quoted from the movies.

Library of Congress Cataloging-in-Publication Data

Teague, Raymond.
    Reel spirit : a guide to movies that inspire, explore and empower / Raymond Teague.
        p.   cm.
    Includes index.
    ISBN 0-87159-259-2 (hardcover : alk. paper).—ISBN 0-87159-248-7 (softcover : alk. paper)
    1. Motion pictures—Moral and ethical aspects. 2. Motion pictures—Religious aspects. I. Title.
PN1995.5.T39 2000
791.43'653—dc21   99-40045
                                                   CIP

Canada BN 13252 9033 RT

Dedication

. . . .

With love
to my wife Sylvia—truly, madly, deeply
(even if she doesn't like *The Wizard of Oz*)
and
to our daughter Alexandra,
the poet who helped conceive *Reel Spirit* and who knows
there's "No Place Like Monochrome."

Acknowledgments

S pecial thanks to the following people for their wonderful support and assistance during the development and writing of this book:

Michael Maday for encouragement, guidance, editing, and friendship.

Sylvia Teague for ideas, copyediting, and patient movie watching as I repeatedly hit the rewind button on the VCR remote control to double- and triple-check quotations.

Elizabeth Reaves for valuable research and enthusiasm.

Alexandra Teague for inspiration, including the movie card always beside my computer and the owl pen used for hundreds of pages of notes.

Allen Liles, a fellow Texan, for always seeing the potentials.

Joanne Englehart for camaraderie and for the loan of many movies.

Norma Arnold, Pat and Ralph Peterson, Jim and Jerre' Carter, and MaryAnne and David Sturdevant for opening their movie libraries to me.

Rozanne Devine and Phil White for format suggestions.

Marty Cooper and Jan Brown of Cooper Communications, Inc., and Jenee Meyer of Unity House for reel promotional spirit.

Table of Contents

Contents

Contents

Contents

CHAPTER 5
Affirmin' in the Rain   *207*

Main Attractions:

Contents

CHAPTER 6
Lights, Camera—Unity and Peace   251

Main Attractions:

Contents

Contents

CHAPTER 8
Meetings With Remarkable People   *331*

Main Attractions:

Feature Presentation:

CHAPTER 9
The Old *Hollywood* Testament   *375*

Main Attractions:

Contents

CHAPTER 10
Have Yourself a Super Natural Christmas   *399*

Main Attractions:

Ray Bolger, Jack Haley, Judy Garland, and Bert Lahr in *The Wizard of Oz,* MGM,
Turner Entertainment

Photo: The Museum of Modern Art Film Stills Archive

Introduction

· · · · · · · · · · · · · · ·

As the Mask (Jim Carrey) might say, "The movies are spiritually smokin'!"

They're really reeling—reeling with Reel Spirit. And always have been, almost since the emergence of film in the late 1800s. In this age of increased spiritual exploration and renewal, however, the movies have become our cultural storyboard for a great awakening.

Why are we sleepless in Seattle? Why do we crave contact? For what is our good will hunting? Why do we wonder what dreams may come? When is it ever as good as it gets?

Spirit is soaring in the cinema, answering our most fundamental questions, illuminating our consciousness by the light of the silver screen. Reel Spirit is playing now at a movie theater or via a videotape or DVD near you.

A fascinating, enthralling array of films projecting eternal Truth and spiritual principles of life is but a movie ticket or rental away.

Sure, we see mirrored in the movies all of our jumbled thoughts—and there definitely are thoughts and movies that do not reflect higher states of consciousness. Yet throughout the history of the movies, and increasingly today, we find

I

movies that truly matter—movies that uplift our spirits, give us positive role models and directions, make us glad to be alive, put us in touch with our true spiritual nature, and help us understand and love each other more.

People have always gone to the movies for all sorts of reasons—for escapism (such as does the young boy in the movie *Cinema Paradiso,* 1988), for romance (on and off screen), for thrills and frights, for laughs, for tears, and for enlightenment.

Reel Spirit: A Guide to Movies That Inspire, Explore and Empower is for the light-seeking latter.

The modern cinema, says psychotherapist Geoffrey Hill, has become "the collective cathedral of primitive *participation mystique.* It is the tribal dream house of modern civilization."[1]

With open minds in this "collective cathedral," we can participate in learning more about ourselves and our *raison d'etre.* The spiritual messages in the cinematic cathedral are unmistakable today, as they are in other avenues of awareness, for anyone who is willing to look and listen. The messages have become increasingly loud and clear as the populace and filmmakers have become more spiritual-minded.

Infinite Spirit obviously is using the movies, one of our favorite pastimes, to give us clues about our spiritual Selves and help us live up to our innate potential. As individuals, families, and groups in a world that can seem hopelessly impersonal and hostile, we can look to the movies to remember our greatness.

In the Beginning—A Word

This book is a guide to movies that offer inspiration, provide guided exploration into the meaning and fundamentals of reality and being, and suggest the tremendous power which is within each of us as spiritual beings.

There's a marvelous, time-honored word that is perfect for describing thoughts and issues along these lines. That word is *metaphysics.*

Metaphysics, according to *Webster's,* is a kind of philosophy "concerned with the fundamental nature of reality and being . . . a study of what is outside objective experience" (beyond what is perceptible to the senses).[2]

A leading twentieth-century mystic, Charles Fillmore, said metaphysics is the "systematic study of the science of Being; that which transcends the physical," having to do with the laws of Spirit.[3]

Francis Bacon succinctly summed up metaphysics in writing that it deals with the "eternal and immutable."[4]

The province of metaphysical exploration includes the whole world, the vastness of the universe, the unfathomable creations of the mind and imagination, all the realms of existence and experience through those senses we know and those we don't remember, and all spiritual and supernatural dimensions.

Metaphysical Movies

Metaphysical movies, then, explore, expand, and challenge traditional, sense-based, scientific views or concepts of reality. In some way, all the movies in this book transcend the physical and probe the eternal. The book is a guide to such ideas in any kind of movie, not necessarily ones that may be clearly labeled "metaphysical." Some movies are blatantly so, such as *What Dreams May Come,* while others are not primarily concerned with greater issues of life but nevertheless contain valuable insights about life, such as the gangster film *Angels With Dirty Faces.*

Movies are increasingly helping us assimilate an expanded view of reality and new ideas about our inner powers and the nature of matter and energy. Such metaphysical or spiritual topics as angels, life on other planets, reincarnation, and miracles can be vividly depicted in movies. As movie subjects, such topics gradually become more accepted in our culture. Movie watchers who have grown up with *Star Wars*, for example, don't flinch at the concept that there is a Force within the individual that can be summoned.

Basic spiritual principles that underlie the movies in this book include:

1. There is one ever-creating and expanding power and presence of absolute goodness, which may be called God, Universal Spirit, All That Is, or many other names.
2. God is energy, and everything is composed of God-energy and is connected to and by that energy.
3. The essence of God, also called *the Christ* in the New Thought tradition, is within each person. Therefore, despite appearances during our human experiences, we always remain spiritual beings.
4. Through our thoughts and perceptions, we create our world and experiences using God-energy. In other words, we are constantly choosing, through our free will, how to cocreate with God-energy.
5. An awareness of our oneness with God comes through prayer, faith, and direct experience. Our purpose in this life is to remember our unity with God and practice God's presence through love.

These principles are found throughout the dominant spiritual traditions of the world—how significant, and how telling, it is to find them in so many movies for so many years!

Visionary films, made by directors and producers whose inner Forces are using them to try to awaken humankind to Truth, are often labeled as "fantasy," "comedy fantasy," or "romantic comedy fantasy" by studios, publicists, and critics. While these films are fantastic in some respects to ordinary senses and comprehension, they also uniformly contain "higher" ideas just waiting to be discovered.

Mainstream reviewers frequently miss the metaphysical messages because they are looking for more mundane, worldly considerations such as action plots and makeup details. Often the most powerful spiritual movies are called boring and are criticized for not adding up to anything significant, when in fact they can lead to significant realizations about life.

What's Here?

The 400 movies in *Reel Spirit*, including 150 Main Attractions, offer some of the best life-enhancing and thought-provoking lessons for modern viewers as well as much original entertainment.

A metaphysical analysis of a movie is but one lens that can be used to understand a movie's content, and of course, it is the lens of choice for this book. The movies are further divided into ten thematic lenses through which a wide variety of topics may be viewed. Chapter titles include "Angels (and Other Messengers) in Our Midst," "The Force Is With and Within Us" (the innate strength and power of the individual), "Jesus Christ—Superstar," "Seeing the Big Picture" (a potpourri of intriguing subjects), "Affirmin' in the Rain" (inspiring personalities and positive, uplifting views of life), "Lights, Camera—Unity and Peace" (oneness of life and the need for global-cosmic cooperation and understanding), "Loving One Another" (true, unconditional love), "Meetings With Remarkable People" (saints and other notable men and women), "The Old *Hollywood* Testament" (biblical epics), and "Have Yourself a Super Natural Christmas."

The movies spotlighted in these ten chapters span almost the whole length of cinematic history, from 1916 (D. W. Griffith's *Intolerance*) to 1999, and represent a variety of thematic genres from American and foreign film-makers. There are classics and blockbusters, popular favorites, award winners, B-movies, even a few C-movies, and quirky and obscure ones. Only theatrical release movies are reviewed. All movies included are available on video. In addition to video stores, local libraries are excellent sources for videos, especially older titles.

The book certainly does not include all metaphysical movies ever made or all movies that can be given such interpretations. It's probably possible to put some metaphysical spin on just about any movie (although some would be especially challenging). Too, there are movies that fit the genre but aren't well crafted or contain objectionable material (such as unrelenting violence). This book, however, is a substantial guide to some of the most important, potentially life-altering and inspirational movies ever made.

Following in the tradition of all literary criticism, the spiritual interpretations offered may or may not reflect the actual intentions of the film writers, directors, and producers. Many will, of course. However, once they are published or distributed to readers/audiences, creative works take on lives of their own and have meaning for individuals way beyond the thoughts and imaginations of their creators. Analysis, interpretation, and criticism are always in the mind of the beholder. Surely, though, few film writers or creators would object to anyone's finding inspiring, empowering themes and messages in their works. They should be honored to accept the accolades and to know that they, whether intentionally or unintentionally, are offering fellow humans images and examples of inspiration and enlightenment.

In each of the ten chapters, you'll find the following:

Main Attractions

The Main Attraction movies for each chapter have three parts:

1. PREVIEW—A short synopsis of a film's basic story line serves as a teaser for anyone unfamiliar with the film and as a refresher for anyone who is. Principal actors are listed. At the end of the synopsis, parenthetical information includes the film's year of release, country of origin if other than solely the United States, running time, and rating. The rating system of the Motion Picture Association of America is G for General Audiences, PG for Parental Guidance Suggested, PG-13 for Parents Strongly Cautioned (material possibly inappropriate for children under 13), and R for Restricted (children under 17 must be accompanied by a parent or adult guardian). NR means No Rating. Movies especially suitable for young children are marked with an asterisk (*).

2. META VIEW—A review and discussion of the film's main metaphysical ideas are presented in this section. Each Meta View is a minilesson unto itself. The Meta View may be read before seeing the movie to enhance appreciation of the movie's themes (details of endings are generally not discussed unless the film is extremely well known), or it may be read afterward for clarification or comparison of understandings. The discussion centers around specific topics included in the chapter's general subject. Relevant quotations from the film are cited, and every effort has been made to assure their accuracy. The discussions touch on traditional film elements such as acting, direction, and cinematography only when they have particular relevance to the broader import or appreciation of the film. The review does not exhaust the metaphysical content of a movie, nor does it present the only interpretations of topics and plot. Readers/viewers are encouraged to use the discussion to stimulate further thought.

3. YE VIEW—Three questions are given to help viewers begin to draw out themes and issues for discussion. Viewers are asked to discuss and analyze specific details of plot and character as they consider a film's meaning and are given an opportunity to relate a film's issues and themes to their own lives. It is hoped that the questions will spur other questions and observations about the movie.

Main Attraction listings may be followed by two other categories of movies:

IN THE SAME SPIRIT

These films are similar in content and tone to the Main Attraction film. A brief synopsis and analysis, as well as viewing statistics, are offered.

THEME MATES

These films share a common subject or topic with the Main Attraction movie, but differ in tone and manner of presentation. For example, the Main Attraction film may treat a topic humorously, while its Theme Mate may take a dramatic approach to the same topic.

The explication of ideas in a Main Attraction applies also to accompanying films categorized as In the Same Spirit or Theme Mates.

FEATURE PRESENTATION

At the conclusion of each chapter is a special feature that spins off in some way from the chapter title. Most of the Feature Presentations spotlight special thematic implications of additional movies.

How Can the Guide Be Used?

Reel Spirit has multiple audiences and uses.

It is ideal for individuals and groups wanting to explore the spiritual dimensions of life while being entertained or desiring to feel uplifted through the stories of others.

The guide can be particularly beneficial for these:

Families who crave movies of spiritual value—those that inspire, empower, and motivate—to watch together.

Churches that use movies as a teaching tool. Ministers, sponsors, and teachers can select movies for congregational movie nights (popular at many churches—always with popcorn). The youth departments of churches will find the book a handy reference when selecting appropriate movies for teen lock-ins and special events.

Individuals, families, churches, and other groups can make their movie choices by the following procedure:

- Select a general subject, identified by chapter titles, and then
- Read the Previews and the Main Attraction headlines, which indicate specific topics, or consult the Feature Presentations for special themed movies.

Ye View questions are perfect for involving friends, families, and congregants in discussions after the showings.

It is hoped that this book will encourage you to search for the deeper spiritual ideas in all the movies that you see. Pages are provided at the end of the guide to write notes about additional movies.

May you be blessed with Reel Spirit as you explore the movies in this book and as you view all movies and life itself from a higher perspective.

Henry Travers and James Stewart in *It's a Wonderful Life*, RKO
Photo: The Museum of Modern Art Film Stills Archive

Chapter I

Angels (and Other Messengers) in Our Midst

· · · · · · · · · · · · · · ·

Through the ages and throughout the shorter history of film, angels and ghosts and other spiritual and inspirational emissaries have been touching our lives in practical and profound ways. Angels, says Charles Fillmore in his book *Atom-Smashing Power of Mind,* are "divine ideas" in consciousness.[1] Angels are God's messengers to us. They come to or through consciousness as guardians and guides that in some way help each person connect with his or her soul's desires and true Self. These "divine ideas" may take many forms, as seen in the movies in this chapter. You'll see the traditional and not-so-traditional concept of winged humanlike messengers, friendly and supportive ghosts, and other celestial special agents such as Mary Poppins and Bogus. You'll also see humans so filled with "divine ideas" that they become angels in the world.

ANGELS IN THE OUTFIELD

PREVIEW

Believing that he will have a real family again when the California Angels win the pennant, eleven-year-old Roger (Joseph Gordon-Levitt) asks God to help the team—and Roger, team manager George Knox (Danny Glover), the players, and the baseball world are stunned by the miraculous results. (1994, 102 minutes, PG, *)

META VIEW

"The footprints of an angel are love"

"Dad, when are we going to be a family again?" Roger asks just before his father rides away on a motorcycle.

"From where I'm sittin', I'd say when the Angels win the pennant," his dad replies. That means "never," because Roger's favorite baseball team is having a dismal season.

Roger, however, generally lives on the theory that "something good's going to happen," and he believes in heaven. Naturally, then, he tells God that he'd "really, really like a family" and prayerfully suggests "maybe you could help them [the Angels] win a little."

From there, the results may seem fairly predictable as the angels start showing up "in the outfield and in the infield," as Roger says, and the Angels can hit and bat and catch like never before. Only Roger can see the angels helping the Angels, but he tells friend J. P. (Milton Davis, Jr.) and manager Knox about them.

One playful angel—"Just call me Al" (Christopher Lloyd)—tells Roger that the angels have come because he asked for help. Al vaporizes in and out of Roger's days to keep him generally informed about what is going on.

To its major credit, the movie departs from predictability and comes out swinging in defense of angels and the spiritual and the miraculous in everyday life. In a movie so squarely aimed at children, the messages have the potential to score some eternal home runs.

Three main messages come forth:

1. Angels are always around, as Al likes to remind Roger. "Even though you can't see us," Al says, "we're always watching."
2. Angels help humans help themselves. The angels start the manager and team believing in themselves, and their actions help the fans regain their faith in the team. Ultimately, however, individual responsibility comes into play.

During the all-important championship game, Al tells Roger that no angels are coming. "Championships have to be won on their own."

The power of individual responsibility and faith in oneself and a higher power within is seen most clearly in pitcher Mel Clark (Tony Danza). Roger says that Clark can succeed: "All he has to do is believe."

3. There's nothing abnormal about believing in angels and spiritual power.

"There are a lot of amazing things in life that just can't be explained," says Maggie Nelson (Brenda Fricker), who runs the short-term foster care facility where Roger and J. P. live. "I believe in the possibility of miraculous things happening. It's what makes every day of our lives worth getting up for. So . . . I guess I do believe in angels."

Knox tells the news media: "I do believe there are times in life where something stronger, higher, or maybe spiritual is with us. I can't explain it, but something has happened to my players this year, something that's changed the way they play and the way I manage. You could call it faith. You can call it angels. You can call it whatever you want."

Maggie addresses the same cynical and scoffing news conference and of-

13

fers some of the most rational lines ever heard in a film about angels and their role in our lives:

"When a professional football player drops to one knee to thank God after making a touchdown, nobody laughs at that, or when a pitcher crosses himself before going to the mound, nobody laughs at that either. It seems like you're saying it's okay to believe in God, but it's not okay to believe in angels. Now, I thought they were on the same team."

Then Maggie delivers the grand slam: "We all need somebody to watch out for us. Every kid I have ever taken care of has been looking for someone to love—an angel. You've gotta have faith; you've gotta believe; you've gotta look inside yourself. The footprints of an angel are love, and where there is love, miraculous things can happen."

Love—Roger's desire for love and a family—is what brings the angels to the outfield.

✳

Ye View

1. What personality changes do you see in George Knox as a result of his association with Roger and J.P.?
2. All prayers are answered, but not necessarily in the way we think they will be. How is that statement illustrated by the answer to Roger's prayer?
3. Discuss Maggie's speech and give your responses to it.

In the Same Spirit

More helpful angels:

Almost an Angel—God (Charlton Heston) sends a deceased thief (Paul Hogan) back to Earth to do more good deeds. (1990, 95 minutes, PG)

Angels in the Outfield—An earlier version stars Paul Douglas, Janet Leigh, and Keenan Wynn. (1951, 102 minutes, NR)

Charley and the Angel—A man (Fred MacMurray) begins treating his family better after an angel (Harry Morgan) tells him that his earthly days are numbered. (1973, 93 minutes, G, *)

Ghost Dad—A businessman (Bill Cosby) killed in an accident returns to put his finances in order for the security of his three children. (1990, 84 minutes, PG)

ANGELS WITH DIRTY FACES

PREVIEW

Notorious criminal Rocky Sullivan (James Cagney) returns to his old neighborhood and becomes a dubious role model for young boys (The Dead End Kids) and a challenge for his former childhood pal, Father Jerry Connelly (Pat O'Brien), in this classic gangster film. (1938, 97 minutes, NR)

15

META VIEW

Spiritual soap works wonders

> Your world is filled with Angels
> who have lost their way,
> who have forgotten who they are.
> —*Emmanuel's Book III:*
> *What Is an Angel Doing Here?*[2]

We are all angels in human form trying to remember our oneness with God, according to the spirit entity Emmanuel and other channeled friends.

In our earthly experiences, though, sometimes our angelic faces get rather dirty, smudged with too much of the nitty-grittiness of human existence.

Our dirty faces almost obscure our true cleanliness, which is not only next to Godliness but *is* Godliness, as a decent washing reveals.

Angels With Dirty Faces presents a striking contrast between a person (Father Connelly) remembering and attempting to live his unity with God and one (Rocky) generally ignoring his spiritual core. In typical tough-guy fashion, Rocky is out for Number One; his motto is "Don't be a sucker." He wants "dough" and power, and guns and trickery will get them.

Father Connelly and Rocky's friend Laury (Ann Sheridan) are convinced that there is goodness in Rocky, and there are occasional glimpses of a heart Rocky claims not to have. For example, Rocky gives Father Connelly $10,000 to build a recreation center for neighborhood street children.

The priest refuses the money, however, because he doesn't want the children to respect the criminal life. He asks Rocky, "What earthly good is it for me to teach that honesty is the best policy when all around they see that dishonesty is a better policy?"

As one crooked, murderous deed leads to another and the neighborhood boys continue to regard Rocky as a hero, Father Connelly finally must test Rocky's fundamental character. He asks Rocky to make a decision that will require not only a tremendous self-sacrifice to help others but also great courage. "This is a different kind of courage, Rocky, the kind that's—well, it's born in heaven . . . the kind that you and I and God know about."

What Father Connelly is suggesting is a kind of spiritual courage shown by true angels.

Ye View

1. What differences in personalities are seen in the young Rocky and Jerry? How do those differences continue into adulthood?
2. What role do you think society played in creating Rocky's life of crime? Consider his time in facilities for juvenile offenders and criminals.

3. What is your opinion of Rocky at the end of the movie? What do you think is the effect of his decision about Father Connelly's request?

IN THE SAME SPIRIT

Reformed by love:
Angel and the Badman—A Quaker girl (Gail Russell) introduces a Western gunfighter (John Wayne) to the ways of true love, peace, and personal accountability. "You mean nobody can hurt you but yourself?" he asks. (1947, 100 minutes, NR)

THE BISHOP'S WIFE

17

PREVIEW

Bishop Henry Brougham (David Niven) is having trouble raising money to build a cathedral, and his wife Julia (Loretta Young) is feeling neglected and unhappy, when a suave angel named Dudley (Cary Grant) takes charge. (1947, 108 minutes, NR)

META VIEW

Where <u>do</u> those great ideas come from?

Angel ideas rush in where mortal minds fear to tread. They seem to come out of nowhere and won't go away. They lead to momentous inventions and discoveries and works of art as well as to insights and inspirations about everyday life and relationships. Angel ideas are those thoughts that lead us to fulfill our destinies as creative children of God. They are communications of pure Spirit through and to us living and learning here on Earth.

Dudley, an angel who works miracles and creates magical moments with casual elegance, embodies the concept of angel ideas.

"Angels come down and put ideas into people's heads and then people feel very proud of themselves because they think it was all their own idea," he says.

People never remember that they have received angelic help, Dudley says. God works in quiet, subtle ways.

Angel ideas don't take away from an individual's pride of accomplishment. Indeed, a recognition of the Source of great ideas should add to our pride (in the sense of elation) in the knowledge of being connected to God Mind. Angel ideas "come down" from our Higher Consciousness into our create-a-day world.

"You know, Dudley," Julia says, "it's a strange thing. You seem to make me feel as if everything's going to be all right."

"Well, it could be," Dudley replies. "If people could only learn to behave like human beings."

Being in tune or at one with God Mind is our natural inheritance.

The ideas that Dudley gives to people are the awareness and use of the gifts which he lists for the Christ child's stocking in a sermon for Henry— "loving kindness, warm hearts, and the stretched-out hand of tolerance— all the shining gifts that make peace on Earth."

Dudley arrives in response to Henry's prayer: "Dear God, what am I to do? Can't you help me? Can't you tell me? Oh, God, please help me." He also responds to Julia's prayer of longing.

Julia blossoms immediately, as does everyone except the bishop, from the rays of Dudley's charm and warmth. Dudley recognizes special qualities in Julia and tells her: "The only people who grow old were born old to begin with. You were born young. You will remain that way." Having the right attitude about life, Dudley implies, is paramount to the enjoyment of life. Not surprisingly, Henry becomes jealous of the angel. Ironically, the bishop, "a man of God" in the world's eyes, is skeptical that Dudley is an angel and even thinks he may be a demon. Julia, her friend Professor Wutheridge (Monty Woolley), and others, however, are quick to recognize Dudley as extraordinary.

"I know it isn't easy for you, Henry, but you've just got to take me on faith," Dudley says.

The bishop comes to realize that one misses a lot of enjoyment in life by not taking things on faith. He also learns that the answers to prayers are request-specific, and that it is important to pay attention to exactly what one is praying for.

For his part, Dudley is more than an idea man. He is an angel of action, too, and as such is an example of caring and loving. Before he even meets the bishop and his wife, Dudley assists a blind man across a street and rescues a baby in danger. Dudley says such angel aid is common and angels are helping people everywhere. As we're walking through crowded city streets, he says, any stranger we see may be an angel. How often we may be seeing and entertaining angels unawares!

YE VIEW

1. What are your favorite miracles that Dudley performs? For example, what wonders does he bring about while ice skating and directing the choir?
2. What angel ideas does Dudley give to the bishop? to Professor Wutheridge? to Mrs. Hamilton?
3. Discuss Sylvester the cab driver's view that the main trouble with the country is "there are too many people who don't know where they are going, and they want to get there too fast." How does this thought apply to the bishop? in your own life?

IN THE SAME SPIRIT

A not-so-classy remake:

> *The Preacher's Wife*—Denzel Washington is the angel and Whitney Houston is the preacher's wife in this updated *The Bishop's Wife* that at least is aglow when Houston sings. (1996, 125 minutes, PG)

BOGUS

PREVIEW

A big, "amazing, magnificent" Frenchman named Bogus (Gerard Depardieu) appears as the imaginary friend to seven-year-old Albert (Haley Joel Osment), who needs comforting after his mother dies and after he is sent to live with a less-than-motherly godmother, Harriet Franklin (Whoopi Goldberg). (1996, 111 minutes, PG, *)

META VIEW

Figments of imagination are everywhere

Journey Into Imagination is one of my favorite attractions at Epcot at Disney World. A charming purple dragon named Figment leads visitors through the world of imagination. Is the animated character in the ride real? Are the large figures, topiaries, and stuffed animals of him real? Just as real as all the examples of imaginative works and accomplishments to which Figment directs our attention. Just as real as someone's imagination that created Figment.

There are all kinds of figments of our imagination loose in this world to help make our lives more enjoyable and more bearable, and the boundaries of what we call imagination and reality frequently overlap.

Such is often the case with imaginary friends of childhood, and even sometimes of adulthood. Imaginary friends are particularly apt to come into the minds and the worlds of lonely children, and without them life would seem unbearable.

Imaginary friends are figments of the imagination, yet they also are extensions of the self. Bogus fits the concept nicely.

Bogus is imaginary. He says so himself: "I'm not real. I'm imagination." When he is no longer with Albert, Bogus will wait "for someone to make me up again." In a way, then, a person's longing activates the power of imagination, and, voila, a Bogus appears.

Yet Bogus, or any imaginary friend, can't be dismissed as mere imagination, as we know it. Although Bogus is imaginary, he's also a real part of Albert himself that is coming from the soul level to be a friend in need.

"Where you live, I live," Bogus tells Albert. That Bogus is an all-knowing dimension of Albert is suggested by the following lines: "I am your best friend. I know you better than anyone, better than you know yourself."

Bogus knows about Albert's situation and understands his feelings, and he offers Albert comfort and sound advice. When Albert cries over missing his mother, for example, Bogus tells him that a mom is important, but encourages him to see that a godmom could be great. When Albert is upset and feels unwanted, Bogus gently rocks him.

Interestingly, Bogus presents himself as representative of a group of helpers who are as close as a person's imagination and who are always on call, but rarely properly acknowledged.

"When they need us, we are there . . . but when it's done, poof, we disappear," Bogus says. "They never say good-bye. They never see us go. Oh, sometimes they remember us, later. Maybe not."

But, he adds: "I cannot complain. Is my job."

21

To one who remembers a few imaginary friends of childhood, Bogus' job as an imaginary figment seems an extremely worthwhile one.

Ye View

1. Albert is not an ordinary boy, a friend of his mother's says. What factors in Albert's life especially prepare him for the acceptance of an imaginary friend?
2. Discuss Harriet's changing attitude about Bogus. Why is she so resistant to him at first? (Consider Harriet's childhood.) How does Harriet view Bogus by the end of the story? What does Bogus say about Harriet?
3. Have you had a Bogus in your own life? Share your experiences and your thoughts about imaginary friends.

CAROUSEL

Preview

This Rodgers and Hammerstein musical presents the bittersweet but inspiring love story of carousel barker Billy Bigelow (Gordon MacRae) and millworker Julie Jordan (Shirley Jones) in a Maine coast town. (1956, 128 minutes, NR)

Meta View

We never walk alone

In heaven or at least a half-way star-polishing station, Billy receives permission (as everyone does, he is told) to return to Earth for one day. That time for Billy is the high school graduation day for his and Julie's daughter Louise. The Starkeeper tells Billy that Louise needs help and that maybe he could help her. "She's a lot like you," the Starkeeper says.

In the review of the romance between Billy and Julie and in Billy's responses to the Starkeeper, it is obvious that Billy hasn't changed since his tragic death before Louise was born. "I ain't sorry for anything," Billy tells the Starkeeper.

It's also obvious that Billy's tough exterior hides a vulnerable man who never has realized how to express his love and who *does* have regrets ("I let my golden chances pass me by," he sings). Through her brief courtship and marriage and in the years since Billy's death, Julie has loved Billy with a true love that overlooks his bravado and shortcomings and recognizes his quiet strength. As they sing to each other in "If I Loved You," words never come to them in an easy way, but they seem to know the depth of their love nonetheless.

One can't help but believe that Billy's decision to return to Earth to help Louise is a pivotal event in his own soul evolution, because he is unselfishly reaching beyond himself and taking positive action to help another.

How often might such unseen help be with us? Perhaps our loved ones, their spirits, or the energies of their love frequently return in some way to us to guide and direct us. If that is so, then, it's another way that we'll never walk alone, as the words of *Carousel*'s most haunting song "You'll Never Walk Alone," suggest.

The speaker at the high school graduation—a country doctor who looks a lot like the Starkeeper—urges graduates to follow the inspiring and wise words of the song: "Walk on, walk on with hope in your heart, and you'll never walk alone."

YE VIEW

1. During the graduation ceremony, what does Billy tell Louise to

do? Do you think Louise hears and will follow the advice? Why or why not?

2. What does Billy tell Julie when he returns? What indications are there that Julie senses Billy's presence?

3. Discuss the graduation speaker's advice regarding the effects of parents' actions on their children: "It makes no difference what they did or didn't do. You just stand on your own two feet."

THEME MATES

More heavenly love music:

I Married an Angel—It's a playboy's dream, but a lovely excuse for Nelson Eddy and Jeannette MacDonald to sing together. (1942, 84 minutes, NR)

24
✳

CITY OF ANGELS

PREVIEW

A restless angel named Seth (Nicolas Cage) wonders what it would feel like to have a physical body and decides to find out when he falls for an earthly doctor (Meg Ryan). (1998, 116 minutes, PG-13)

REVIEW

Can you be lovesick in heaven?

The angels, not half so happy in Heaven,
Went envying her and me.
—"Annabel Lee," Edgar Allan Poe[3]

Oh, those pining angels! Literature and movies have quite a few angels who yearn for human tenderness—a presentation that always strikes me as a bit chauvinistic on the part of humans. Is it really possible that our conditions and sensual experiences are so marvelous that even beings from a supposedly higher celestial realm go bonkers for them? Perhaps so.

If you accept that premise, then *City of Angels'* Seth is certainly the angel for you. Surely never has there been an angel that longed for human love more persuasively, more languidly, and with larger, more sincere eyes! Seth falls for a heart surgeon named Maggie, who isn't supposed to be able to see Seth hanging around her but can. "Those eyes," Maggie says; she can't get Seth off her mind. Seth finally decides he must experience human sensations. He has no regrets.

This nicely romantic film does open up some questions about the purposes and longings of our souls. It could be that Seth represents the soul's continual searching or creating. Perhaps he is Everysoul searching through spiritual realms for additional opportunities of love to complete itself or creating more opportunities for God to experience all facets of Himself. Perhaps, too, Maggie's spiritual development needs the association with another realm of awareness to further her development in love, which Scripture says is the nature of God.

Angels who don't elect to become human have two important functions, according to the film. They act as guardians, and they also assist humans making their transition to "home," into another realm (beyond what we call death, into a realm that appears to be user-friendly).

YE VIEW

1. How does the presentation of angels in *City of Angels* agree or differ with your concept of angels?
2. Does Seth's decision to become human seem plausible to you? Why or why not?

25

✳

3. What does the character of Nathaniel Messinger, the heart patient, contribute to the film?

IN THE SAME SPIRIT

Earlier angels pondering humans:
Wings of Desire—Angels take to the streets of West Berlin, rather than Los Angeles, and think about being human in this captivating film directed by Wim Wenders that inspired *City of Angels*. (1988, West German-French, 130 minutes, PG-13) Pleasant sequel is *Faraway, So Close!*—involving more angels in "mortal slumming." (1993, German, 140 minutes, NR)

THEME MATES

Also wondering about the earthly experience:
Meet Joe Black—Death, a.k.a. Joe Black (Brad Pitt), satisfies what apparently has been a long pent-up curiosity and gets a life. In becoming involved with the family of media tycoon William Parrish (Anthony Hopkins), Joe discovers unconditional love and peanut butter. (1998, 174 minutes, PG-13) Story originally filmed as *Death Takes a Holiday* starring Fredric March. (1934, 78 minutes, NR)

DAUGHTERS OF THE DUST

PREVIEW

Nana Peazant (Cora Lee Day), the matriarch of a family of the Gullah, descendants of slaves on the Sea Islands of the South, struggles to keep her family together and preserve traditions at the turn of the century. (1991, 114 minutes, NR)

META VIEW

Call upon the ancestors

In the hectic modern world, we tend to busy ourselves so much with the present that we often don't stop to remember the past, much less think about our ancestors and the "old souls" no longer physically with us. But just as there are lessons for us in the past, so perhaps there is guidance available to us from our ancestors. Perhaps we should stop, remember, and listen.

Writer-director Julie Dash's mesmerizing tale of the Gullah directs us to do just that. Her story of the Peazant family, split by those who choose to remain on the islands and those who want to go to the mainland for new adventures, reminds us that there is great soothing and healing value in slowing down and connecting with our roots and our spiritual heritage.

Nana is the anchor of the family and the movie and is the outspoken advocate of preserving the distinctive ways of the Gullah, connecting with the Spirit within and calling upon the spirit of ancestors for guidance and assistance.

Nana encourages her great-grandson Eli (Adisa Anderson) to call upon his ancestors. "It's up to the living to keep in touch with the dead, Eli," she says. "Man's power don't end with death. We just move on to another place, a place where we go and watch over our living family. Respect your elders, respect your family, respect your ancestors."

When Eli, like some other members of the family, resists such seemingly old-fashioned thinking, Nana says, "Eli, I'm trying to learn you how to touch your own spirit." Nana knows that there is always a need to connect with one's spiritual nature, no matter how society changes.

In addition to guidance to help her family know and cherish its traditions, Nana seeks assistance to help Eli make peace with his wife Eula (Alva Rogers) and accept the baby she is carrying. Eula has been raped, and Eli does not think the child is his.

27

Nana prays for something to happen to bring harmony to the family. The spirit world answers and sends "the Unborn Child," the soul that is to be Eula's child. The child, a young girl, is mostly unseen by characters but visible to movie watchers; she runs in and out of scenes and becomes a spiritual force working to unite her parents. Spirits of one generation affecting the lives of other generations is a common African motif, and one in which Nana certainly believes. She feels the child's presence.

The child's voice is heard in narration: "Nana prayed and the old souls guided me into the new world." With the child's appearance, Nana receives a clear and quick demonstration of the power of prayer.

In another voice-over, the child says, "I had to convince my daddy that I was his child." How she goes about doing that involves a telling of the traditional story of the Ibo, a group of Africans who were brought to the islands to be slaves, but who sized up the situation from all time perspectives, turned right around, and *walked* across the water past their ship and all the way back to Africa.

The child also brings strength to her mother-to-be so that Eula is able to give a stirring speech of healing to the other women family members.

"There's going to be all kinds of roads to take in life. Let's not be afraid to take them. We deserve them because we all good women," she says.

"We carry too many scars from the past. . . . We wear our scars like armor for protection. . . . Let's live our lives without living in the fold of old wounds."

YE VIEW

1. "The Unborn Child" says, "In this quiet place years ago my family knelt down and caught a glimpse of the eternal." What do you think the child means?
2. What happens to Eli during Eula's story of the Ibo? What

indication is there that something miraculous has occurred within him?

3. In concrete or abstract ways, do you ever feel a connection with your ancestors? Discuss.

THEME MATES

More supernatural family connections from African-American history and lore:

Beloved—Sethe (Oprah Winfrey), a former plantation slave, comes face-to-face with her haunting past when Beloved (Thandie Newton), the ghost of her daughter, appears in this strong, complex, twisting film based on Toni Morrison's poetic novel. (1998, 175 minutes, R)

He Got Game—Jake Shuttlesworth (Denzel Washington) is temporarily released from prison to try to influence the college choice of his son Jesus (Ray Allen), a high school basketball star. This Spike Lee film ends with a splendid and appropriate testimony to the spiritual dimension of the father-son relationship. (1998, 131 minutes, R)

DEAR GOD

PREVIEW

A personable con man, Tom Turner (Greg Kinnear), ordered by a judge to get a 9-to-5 job, goes to work in the Dead Letter Office of a U. S. Post Office where he begins orchestrating "miracles" in response to "Dear God" letters. (1996, 112 minutes, PG)

29
✳

META VIEW

"The man is an angel"

"I care about myself," Tom says. "Everything else is just an act." He's handsome, clever, and charming, but he's also been conditioned by childhood events not to trust anyone and to fend for himself alone. Tom keeps denying compassion and concern for anyone else, but beneath the surface, his angel nature is eager to take wing.

In this humorous tale full of wacky but believable characters, Tom becomes an angel—as so often happens—in spite of himself or his ego facade. Seemingly by accident, but in a world in which no accidents occur, Tom fulfills the request of a woman who has written to God. Before he knows what heavenly transformation has hit him, Tom has started a wave of kindness and caring that spreads throughout Los Angeles.

"People are helping people. Regular people are doing miracles all by themselves, and you started it. You should be proud," fellow postal worker Abraham (Roscoe Lee Browne) tells Tom.

"The man is an angel. He's an angel," says another coworker, Rebecca (Laurie Metcalf).

Tom's boss (Hector Elizondo) states the obvious: "I do believe that God lives within each of us . . . I believe that God was speaking through Tom. Tom Turner made ordinary people do extraordinary things. We need this."

The feeling of being an angel is too much for the con in him to resist, and Tom himself, speaking in his own defense during a court trial, says, "The letters kept pouring in and I began to believe, to believe that I could really help people—and that being of help was more rewarding than any con that I could pull, and then I found . . . that the less I tried to take advantage of people, the more I got back."

As one of the movie songs states, "Angels gonna find you."

YE VIEW

1. Who are some people helped directly or indirectly by Tom?
2. The postal miracles take team effort. What talents do each of the employees in the Dead Letter Office contribute to the campaign? In what ways are team members altered by the campaign?
3. Do you think Tom will revert to his con ways? Why or why not?

THEME MATES

Other letters and human angels:

Central Station—Dora (Fernanda Montenegro), a woman who writes letters for people in Rio de Janeiro's railroad station and is something of a cynical con artist herself, and Josue (Vinicius de Oliveira), a young boy whose mother is killed in an accident, become angels for each other as they journey to find Josue's father and new directions in life. (1998, Brazilian, 115 minutes, R)

FEARLESS

PREVIEW

After saving some fellow passengers in a devastating plane crash and having a near-death experience, Max Klein (Jeff Bridges) becomes a hero and a changed man—fearless, alienated from his family, and focused on helping another survivor, Carla (Rosie Perez), overcome the loss of her baby. (1993, 122 minutes, R)

META VIEW

"It's like God . . . sent me my own angel"

Mysterious indeed are the ways of the Infinite, and it would certainly appear thus in *Fearless*, directed by Peter Weir from the novel and screenplay by Rafael Yglesias.

During his near-death experience as the plane is going down, Max Klein sees a bright white light and has the thought: "This is it. This is the moment of your death. I'm not afraid. I have no fear." The experience results in feelings of invulnerability and a marvelous ability to soothe others' fears. Max says the crash is the best thing that ever happened to him and brought him "the touch and taste and beauty of life."

However, Max is only able to communicate a feeling of joy for life when he is befriending Carla. Aside from his involvement with her, Max seems tormented and comes across as insensitive and callous toward others, especially his wife Laura (Isabella Rossellini). During the course of the movie, it becomes apparent that Max's obsession with Carla is a divine mission—to help Carla heal the emotional scars from her son's death, resolve her sense of guilt, and regain an appreciation for life. Max tells his wife: "I have a feeling of overwhelming love for her. I've never felt anything like it before."

Carla talks about Max to the jealous Laura: "He's my best friend. It's like God sent him to me. It's like He sent me an angel."

Laura replies that Max is a man, not an angel. However, Max is quite definitely a man being used as an angel of mercy. The divine purpose of Max's near-death experience is apparently to enable him to be a rescuer, a savior. While the experience doesn't give him peace, it gives him an opportunity to face some suppressed emotions and to lead others to safety and perhaps peace. When his mission is accomplished, Max seems to come out from under a spell. Although he had been saying that he was dead in his head, now Max cries out, "I'm alive, I'm alive," with a sense of glee and relief.

32

Max makes several comments to Carla that indicate he doesn't believe in God and doesn't see a purpose in life, but the caption under his drawing of a mystical tunnel suggests otherwise: "The soul comes to the end of its long journey, and naked and alone draws near to the divine." One suspects that the caption suggests Max's own near-death journey.

YE VIEW

1. What effect did the death of his father have on Max? How is Max able to address unresolved feelings about his father?
2. Why do you think it is important to Max that he be saved? How is he saved?
3. Discuss "personal angels" you know or have read about—people who have miraculously and fearlessly helped others in a crisis.

33

THE GHOST AND MRS. MUIR

PREVIEW

An independent-minded widow (Gene Tierney) develops an unusual friendship with and romantic interest in the ghost of the sea captain (Rex Harrison) who once owned the English coast cottage into which she has just moved, in this charming, clever comedy. (1947, 104 minutes, NR)

META VIEW

Outlook opens unseen opportunities

For four years, would-be tenants of Gull Cottage have run away after one night of being terrorized by the ghost of Capt. Daniel Gregg. Lucy

Muir, who comes to the cottage from London with her daughter Anna (Natalie Wood) and her housekeeper, proves that outlook can certainly lead to surprising and unseen opportunities.

"Haunted—how perfectly fascinating!" is Lucy's response. Her attitude opens the way for a friendship to blossom between her and the crusty captain, who has remained around to see that his house is turned into a home for retired seamen.

Both Lucy and the captain want what is best for the house. He decides that she has spunk, and thus can stay, but she is at first shy about having him invade her privacy.

Capt. Gregg tells her, though, "I'm a spirit. I have no body. . . . All you see is an illusion."

They seem perfectly matched in temperament and interests, although his language is more colorful.

"You seem to be very earthly for a spirit," Lucy tells him.

"And you, madam, are enough to make a saint take to blasphemy."

"Capt. Gregg," Lucy responds, "if you insist on haunting me, you might at least be more agreeable about it!"

Yes, they are falling in love, and their relationship deepens when the captain dictates his life story to Lucy so that she can sell it to a book publisher and thus have money to retain the house.

Lucy becomes increasingly confused by her attraction to a ghost and worries what the future will bring with someone who is not real.

"I am real," the captain says. "I'm here because you believe I'm here. And keep on believing and I'll always be real to you."

Later Lucy says to the captain: "I wish you wouldn't be so superior just because you're not alive. It's no crime to be alive."

The captain says that being alive can be a great inconvenience, however, because "the living can be hurt."

Ye View

1. When and why does the captain cease to be real to Lucy? How is Lucy hurt?
2. What do Lucy and her daughter have in common concerning the captain?
3. Do you find the ending of the movie satisfying? Why or why not?

A GUY NAMED JOE

Preview

Pilots don't die but return to help rookie fliers, according to a legend captured in this World War II film, when Pete Sandidge (Spencer Tracy) guides Ted Randall (Van Johnson) in matters of flight as well as love with his own former flame, Dorinda Durston (Irene Dunne). (1943, 120 minutes, NR)

Meta View

No one flies alone

As a war propaganda film, *A Guy Named Joe* is one of the American motion picture industry's finest. Dalton Trumbo's script enunciated to 1940s Americans a clear purpose for the country's involvement in a world war— to give people their natural right to be free. In the movie, the General (Lionel Barrymore), the imposing heavenly commander of pilots, speaks eloquently of the "vision of a free man in a free world."

The country is "fighting for the freedom of the very air we breathe, the freedom of mankind rushing to greet the future on wings," the General says.

On flights high in the sky, he says, it is possible to hear "the music that a man's spirit sings to his heart when the Earth's far away and there isn't any more fear."

Children, he notes, would understand such music because the future belongs to them. "They're going to fly like a generation of angels into the free air and the sunlight." What a beautiful image to motivate freedom fighters in any age!

However, words and images to help individuals connect with their natural states of freedom as free souls, to help them hear their spirits singing of soul liberation, are always timely. The General's message of freedom isn't dated.

The General's message goes even deeper, though. He explains to Pete that our lives are interconnected and that we have responsibilities to each other that affect the present and the future and link the past.

"No man is really dead unless he breaks faith with the future, and no man is really alive unless he accepts his responsibility to it," the General states, adding that the heavenly realm gives people "the opportunity to pay off to the future what you owe for having been a part of the past."

He explains the procedures of his heavenly realm. "We operate on the principle of helping the other fellow," he says. Pilots who have died, or made their transitions, are assigned inexperienced pilots to help.

The General scoffs at Pete's suggestion that he learned to fly by himself. That's not the way it works. "You were helped by every man since the beginning of time who dreamt of wearing wings . . . by every pilot that ever crashed into the ground in order that others could stay up in the sky. And now it's your turn to pass that along to the next man."

We're all pilots guiding each other—that's the marvelous Truth of the General's message. In our earthly experiences and in our continued lives beyond the physical, we are a part of each other and responsible for each other.

As a bit player in a throw-away line in the movie asks, "We're all brothers and sisters, aren't we?"

What Pete discovers is that spiritual, telepathic communication is always going on between souls, and that brothers and sisters in physical bodies can be influenced by spiritual siblings no longer in physical bodies.

As the returned Pete says to an earthly soldier, "Hey, buddy, do you realize there are a lot of things going on around you that you don't know anything about?"

The movie also indicates, through the experiences of Dorinda and her friend Al Yackey (Ward Bond), that extrasensory perception in terms of knowledge and feelings about events and situations can also be a part of the human experience.

YE VIEW

1. What is the meaning of the term *a guy named Joe*? To whom could the term be applied in the movie?
2. The only love that really lives, Pete says, fills one's heart so full that one must give love to someone else. Discuss how Pete, Ted, and Dorinda demonstrate such love.
3. Have you ever felt guided by an unseen presence? Do some of your ideas seem to come out of nowhere? Discuss your experiences.

IN THE SAME SPIRIT

Flattering with imitation:

Always—Director Steven Spielberg paid homage to one of his favorite films by remaking *A Guy Named Joe* with stars Richard Dreyfuss and Holly Hunter. (1989, 121 minutes, PG)

IT'S A WONDERFUL LIFE

PREVIEW

A financial crisis and a wingless Angel Second Class, Clarence, are necessary for George Bailey to come to realize what a wonderful life he has led and how many Bedford Falls citizens he has helped in this beloved classic, the favorite film of both its director, Frank Capra, and star, James Stewart. (1946, 129 minutes, NR, *)

META VIEW

If we only realize and appreciate it!

Sometimes we forget to take time to smell the roses until someone starts to dig up the bushes. We often need an appreciation shock. Life can become overwhelming and unbearable because we lose our perspective and forget, in the midst of challenges, to appreciate the good things about life.

Life's frustrations can reach a danger zone, when we feel so miserable that we wish we'd never been born and suicide seems an attractive alternative—as happens to George Bailey (Stewart) after funds are missing from his building and loan company.

At such times, watching *It's a Wonderful Life* can serve as one of those necessary appreciation shocks or boosters. There is probably a sound psychological reason that the movie has become a Christmas tradition on television in recent years. The holiday season is an extremely trying, lonely, emotional time for many people. It's a time when people especially need the film's message and a guardian angel like Clarence (Henry Travers) to help them appreciate life.

For George, his guardian angel comes, as it does in some form to many people, in answer to prayer: "Dear Father in heaven . . . show me the way. I'm at the end of my rope."

If Clarence successfully saves George, he will finally earn his wings. Well-meaning but not sure how to proceed, Clarence gets an idea when George says it would be better if he'd never been born and he wishes he hadn't been.

"You've got your wish. You've never been born," Clarence says.

"You've been given a great gift, George, a chance to see what the world would be like without you."

George's eyes are painfully opened when he sees what happens if he had never existed: The town is named Pottersville after the county's richest and meanest man (Lionel Barrymore); George's mother runs a boarding house, his uncle is in an insane asylum, his brother dies at the age of nine because George doesn't exist to save him from drowning, his wife Mary (Donna Reed) is an old maid, and his four children are never born.

"Strange, isn't it?" Clarence asks. "Each man's life touches so many other lives. When he isn't around it leaves an awful hole."

George desperately asks to have his life returned to him after he realizes the effects of throwing it away. When his wish is granted, the townspeople rally to George's defense and show their love and respect for him and the many ways he has helped them better their lives.

As for Clarence, of course he gets his wings. He has told George, "Every time you hear a bell ring it means that some angel has just got his wings." We hear Clarence's bell, and it's one of Christmas cheer.

It's a Wonderful Life can serve as a valuable encouragement for people to appreciate their lives more and consider how their lives affect others. Our global village is an incredibly intricate web of touching lives. After a brief discussion of the movie in his book *The Quest for Meaning*, Jim Rosemergy concludes the following about someone who is appreciative and aware:

"A person who seeks to know God, an individual who knows the reason for being, is a stargate through which the divine light comes into the world.

39

Two things are sure. If you had never lived or had never experienced your purpose, the world would be less for it. However, because you live and dance with the question *Why?* the world is a better place."[4]

YE VIEW

1. Identify some other examples of lives altered by George's nonexistence.
2. Do you think George had a wonderful life? Why or why not? Consider early events in his life.
3. Discuss Clarence's note to George: "Remember *no* man is a failure who has friends."

IN THE SAME SPIRIT

Heaven Can Wait—A man (Don Ameche) doesn't think he has led a life worthy enough to gain admission into heaven, but flashbacks tell a different story. (1943, 112 minutes, NR)

MARY POPPINS

PREVIEW

"Practically perfect in every way," Mary Poppins (Julie Andrews) is just the nanny wished for by the Banks children, Jane and Michael (Karen Dotrice and Matthew Garber), to compensate for their neglectful parents in London of 1910 in this superb Disney musical based on the P. L. Travers book. (1964, 140 minutes, NR, *)

META VIEW

She's super-cali-fragilistic-expi-ali-docious!

Descending from the clouds on an east wind by holding onto an umbrella, Mary Poppins is, without a doubt, a heavenly being. Responding to a list of qualifications written by the children and torn up by Mr. Banks (David Tomlinson) and thrown into the fireplace, Mary Poppins is, unquestionably, on a divine mission.

Simply stated, Mary Poppins' job, which represents a wish fulfillment by the children, is to bring the Banks family closer together. The father is a workaholic banker who thrives on consistency, discipline, and rules, and doesn't, in modern terms, spend quality time with his children. The mother (Glynis Johns) is more observant than her husband, but she is consumed with the suffragette movement. The children have acted out their frustrations and loneliness by terrorizing six nannies within four months.

Mary Poppins is all the children wish for, and much more. As they desire, she has a cheery disposition; is kind, witty, nice, loving, and pretty; and plays games, takes them on outings, gives them treats, and sings songs to them. She also produces whatever she needs from her seemingly empty carpetbag, slides up and down the banister, and jumps into a picture with them and takes them on an amazing adventure with real and animated characters, where they learn an exceedingly long word.

With a direct style and "a spoonful of sugar" or kindness, Mary Poppins also manages to pass on quite a few lessons about life to the children, including:

- "Never judge things by their appearances."
- "A thing of beauty is a joy forever."
- "Well begun is half done."

41

- "In every job that must be done there is an element of fun. You find the fun, and snap, the job's a game."
- "Worrying won't help anyone."
- "Sometimes the person we love, through no fault of his own, can't see past the end of his nose."
- "Sometimes a little thing can be quite important."

Through skillful manipulation and character discernment, Mary Poppins also manages to get Mr. Banks to take the children to the bank with him, and the outing has miraculous results.

There are many indications that Mary Poppins has had much experience in her special kind of nanny work, but she never discusses her past or her methods. "I never explain anything," she says simply. In sensing the arrival of Mary Poppins, Bert (Dick Van Dyke) says, "I feel what's to happen all happened before," an observation that suggests Mary Poppins' particular divine appointment. One suspects that she always succeeds because, as Bert sings, "Happiness is blooming all around her."

YE VIEW

1. How does Mr. Banks change? Compare and contrast his personality at the beginning and the end of the movie.
2. Like Mary Poppins, Bert clearly is not a typical human. What are some of his unusual abilities?
3. Uncle Albert (Ed Wynn) literally soars with laughter. In your opinion, why is laughter an important and beneficial part of life?

MICHAEL

PREVIEW

An unusual and uncouth angel named Michael (John Travolta) changes the lives of three writers for a supermarket tabloid. (1996, 106 minutes, PG)

META VIEW

He's a slob with heart—and wings

Michael is not, presumably, your run-of-the-heavens angel. To those expecting "halos, inner light," Michael says, "I'm not that kind of angel." This archangel has long hair, smokes incessantly, drinks beer, scratches, dances, frolics with women, and likes to do battle with bulls and men. He's also a sugarholic and smells like candy and cookies. But he loves Earth and is fascinated with its superlatives, such as the world's largest nonstick frying pan. His most stereotypical angel features are large white wings and an ability to perform miracles, but just "small miracles, only so many." Michael is played mainly for laughs in this Nora Ephron film, but perhaps just as it takes all kinds of people to make a world, it takes all kinds of angels to help that world and its seemingly lost souls.

Michael also is, at least on this final mission to Earth, a matchmaker. He apparently has accepted a project to bring together two lonely writers, Frank (William Hurt) and Dorothy (Andie MacDowell). "It's a difficult case, though," he says, "to give a man back his heart." Michael's only words of wisdom are these: "You've got to learn to laugh. It's the way to true love." From such a nontraditional angel, the message is warmly traditional.

Over the opening credits, Randy Newman performs his song "Heaven

43

Is My Home," whose refrain suggests Michael's work: "You've got to open up your heart."

YE VIEW

1. Why might the script writers have created an angel that is so different from society's typical view of angels?
2. Does Michael succeed in his main mission? If so, how does he succeed?
3. Do you agree with Michael that learning to laugh is "the way to true love"? Why or why not?

TOPPER

PREVIEW

The ghosts of a wealthy, carefree couple, George and Marion Kerby (Cary Grant and Constance Bennett), adopt a mousey, repressed Wall Street bank president, Cosmo Topper (Roland Young), as their "good deed." (1937, 97 minutes, NR)

META VIEW

Accept divine nudges to enjoy life

Have you ever felt trapped in your life and in a rut? You wanted to break out, but just couldn't quite muster the courage. Have you ever identified with the old song "What Did I Have That I Don't Have?" and its description "obsolete in my prime"? Have you ever felt as if life was passing you by, and you weren't experiencing it?

Then you know how Cosmo Topper feels. His wife (Billie Burke) controls every activity. He can't dawdle in the shower or even alter his breakfast menu. He feels "a million years old," yet he has a vague restlessness and a longing to change his routines and break free. He's tired of being a "stuffed egg." He yearns somehow to have fun like he used to and enjoy life.

Topper: "Life is so very short, and we get so *very* little out of it."

Mrs. Topper: "Don't you realize we're middle-aged?"

Topper: "Yes, but why *should* we be middle-aged?"

Sometimes if we really feel that divine discontent welling up inside and we want to alter our lives, as Topper does, but can't make the first move, the Universe takes over and does it for us. An unexpected or unexplained occurrence forces us to change. The catalyst, whatever it is, can be surprising or alarming. (A house fire, though unsettling at the time, provided the impetus for my family to overcome its inertia and be catapulted to a new state, new careers, and new opportunities.)

The Universe sends Topper two ghosts to nudge him. Having recently died in a car accident and realizing that they have a shortage of good deeds perhaps necessary to advance in the celestial realm, George and Marion adopt Topper as their "good deed."

Marion and George had known Topper at the bank, and Marion had recognized Topper's unhappiness. Before the couple die in a car accident, Marion comments to George about Topper: "Something's bugging the man, eating him from the inside." After the dematerialized couple begin leading Topper to looser attitudes and activities, Marion observes, "His whole soul is crying out for self-expression."

This comedy is most delightful when the effects of the good deed kick in and Topper steps out and begins enjoying life.

YE VIEW

1. How do the changes within Topper affect Mrs. Topper?

2. Discuss the validity of one character's observation: "Living with Mr. Topper must be like dancing on dynamite."

3. What do you think usually keeps people who are discontent with their lives from making changes to improve them?

IN THE SAME SPIRIT

Other films in which Topper continues to explore life with a ghosted script:

Topper Takes a Trip—Topper vacations on the Riviera. (1939, 85 minutes, NR)

Topper Returns—Topper assists in a murder case. (1941, 88 minutes, NR)

In need of more good deeds:

The Canterville Ghost—With a little assistance from a descendant (Robert Young), a ghost from the 1600s (Charles Laughton) finally gets a chance to redeem himself. (1944, 96 minutes, NR)

The Return of Peter Grimm—Lionel Barrymore stars as the head of a family come back to right his wrongs. (1935, 82 minutes, NR)

TRULY, MADLY, DEEPLY

PREVIEW

Nina (Juliet Stevenson) loves her boyfriend Jamie (Alan Rickman) truly, madly, deeply, and she can't get over his death—that is, until he returns as a ghost. (1991, 107 minutes, PG)

META VIEW

Ever seen a ghost with a hidden agenda?

That we now see through a glass or mirror darkly and know only in part is a well-known postulate from the New Testament, and one readily accepted by most people. What is especially interesting is the last of that verse, usually overlooked, in 1 Corinthians 13:12: "Then I will know fully, even as I have been fully known." In other words, *we* may not know what we are right now (spiritual beings), but there are those on the other side of the glass or mirror who *do* recognize us for what we really are.

Those in other realms with clearer visions than our own sometimes give us a little needed help. That's what happens to Nina in this tender British film written and directed by Anthony Minghella. Nina is devastated by Jamie's unexpected death, but she feels and hears his presence caring for her. Still, he's not really present, and she tells a psychiatrist: "I'm so angry with him . . . I can't forgive him for not being here, I can't!" She withdraws to her memories and to her flat (which like her life needs major repairs) and basically wallows in her grief and anger.

And then Jamie returns. Or does he? Does his ghost actually return, or is his presence a figment of Nina's imagination, as she suggests at one point? The answer probably depends on whether or not you believe in ghosts, but it doesn't really matter. In some ghostly way, Jamie is once again very real to Nina; that's what is important.

When she first discovers Jamie has come back, she embraces him and sobs with all her pent-up sorrow, longing, and even rage; the scene is uncomfortable to watch because one has the sense of intruding. Jamie won't be pinned down to many specifics about his life after death, but the two start recreating some of their good times in their lives before his death (such as playing music and clowning around together).

Before long, however, it becomes obvious to the viewer (though not ini-

47

tially to Nina) that Jamie is a ghost with an important mission: he has returned to help Nina overcome her grief and her anger, to enable her to forgive him for leaving, and to see that she rediscovers the joy of living and loving.

With Jamie's subtle assistance (including the annoying habit of bringing his ghostly pals home to watch movie videos), Nina comes to a point when she can exclaim, "It's a *life* I want!" She tells her psychiatrist about a book which states that some people get powerful sensations their loved ones have come back to them. "I can imagine it," Nina says, adding, "But then what?" As she begins to see life and her world differently, Nina's world changes and she can see and act on new opportunities—most notably concerning her new friend, an extremely caring and clever teacher and amateur magician (Michael Maloney).

Thank goodness Jamie's ghost doesn't have to look through a glass darkly and can see what needs to be done for Nina. It's great to have friends in high places of vision!

Ye View

1. What are some things that Jamie does to help nudge Nina back into the world of the truly living?
2. Discuss your belief concerning the ability of people who have passed from earthly life to assist those still living here.
3. Have you ever felt, as Nina does, that departed loved ones were giving you guidance or inspiration? Discuss.

In the Same Spirit

A familiar problem:

Dona Flor and Her Two Husbands—A woman (Sonia Braga) has much the same problem as Nina in *Truly, Madly, Deeply*—choosing between a reappearing dead husband and a new boyfriend. (1978, Brazilian, 106 minutes, R) ***Kiss Me Goodbye*** starring Sally Field is a remake. (1982, 101 minutes, PG)

Another helpful returnee:

Ghost—A murdered businessman, Sam (Patrick Swayze), tries to prevent the same fate for his girlfriend (Demi Moore). Sam is a living and then not-so-living example of Job's famous statement (Job 3:25) that attests to the power of our thoughts: "Truly the thing that I fear comes upon me." Sam, happy in love, worries: "I just don't want the bubble to burst. It seems like whenever anything good in my life happens, I'm just afraid I'm going to lose it." And, lo, he does.

Whoopi Goldberg shines as a spiritual advisor who finally lives up to her billing. And that crazy ghost on the subway has some wise words about mind power. Those evil spirits are a bit hokey, though. (1990, 122 minutes, PG-13)

WAITING FOR THE LIGHT

49

PREVIEW

Business at the small-town diner inherited by Kay Harris (Teri Garr) booms when her eccentric Aunt Zena (Shirley MacLaine), a former circus magician, and her two children inadvertently stage a "miracle" for a terrorizing neighbor, Mr. Mullins (Vincent Schiavelli). (1990, 94 minutes, PG)

META VIEW

God and helpers work miracles

As so often stated, God works in mysterious ways—and people are often left wondering about the wonders they have beheld. What many people don't realize, however, is that God can work miracles through *them*.

In this movie, for example, the initial event that Mr. Mullins perceives as a miracle is an act of revenge cleverly staged by Aunt Zena, and subsequent efforts to reinforce that miracle are just as humanly engineered. Does the human involvement preclude the events from being true miracles? Certainly not, as God uses Aunt Zena's magic background and the children's youthful initiative to achieve miraculous effects.

The miracle that Mr. Mullins witnesses may be labeled fraudulent if only the human cause is considered, but when one considers that Spirit is always at work, the event can be seen as divine.

When Mr. Mullins mistakes Kay's daughter Emily (Hillary Wolf) for an angel in a tree in his orchard, he sets in motion a story of faith that reaches around the world.

For Mr. Mullins himself, his miracle is profound. "The Lord has entered my soul. I have been born anew," he tells a church congregation. "A messenger of the Lord has appeared to me and shown me the errors of my ways." He is obviously ready for soul growth.

The events take place during the Cuban missile crisis of 1962—a frightening time in the nation's history during which many people were not only building fallout shelters but also turning to their religions to seek comfort. People in the area of the diner and eventually people around the world interpret the angel's appearance—as well as what some say is an image of Jesus' face created by shadows in the orchard—as a sign of hope.

Is it coincidence that the unusual events in the orchard end at the same time that the missile crisis ends? After the crisis, Walter Cronkite says during a television newscast, "President Kennedy immediately attended mass to give thanks." And people gather at the orchard to give thanks and to speak of the miracle that helped give them faith to get through the crisis. As one man comments, "Miracles can teach us a lot about faith"—however they come about.

Aunt Zena says wisely, "Sometimes the magic works better than you bargained for."

The miracle is never in the tree, but always within the individuals who allow themselves to be open to hope and grace.

YE VIEW

1. The title of the movie has a double meaning. What are the two kinds of light for which people are waiting?
2. What long-range effect does the so-called miracle of the angel's appearance have on Kay Harris and her family? What happens to the diner? What are the family's plans?
3. "Now that's what I call a miracle," Aunt Zena says at the end of the movie. To what is she referring?

THEME MATES

Working miracles:

The Man Who Could Work Miracles—A clerk in a department store (Roland Young) has special powers in this H. G. Wells story. (1936, British, 82 minutes, NR)

Miracle in Milan—The spirit of the woman who raised him (Emma Gramatica) comes from heaven to give Toto the Good (Francesco Golisano) the miracle-working power, and he uses it to help the poor in Vittorio De Sica's social fable. (1951, Italian, 95 minutes, NR)

::: **FEATURE PRESENTATION**

Reality Checks

What, pray tell, do they mean?

Movie characters can say the most intriguing and perplexing things about life, and both muddle our minds and stir our souls.

Think about these words of enlightenment from various movie characters:

- "I was thrown out of N.Y.U. my freshman year for cheating on my metaphysics final. You know, I looked within the soul of the boy sitting next to me."—Alvy Singer (Woody Allen), *Annie Hall,* 1977
- "Every man dies; not every man really lives."—William Wallace (Mel Gibson), *Braveheart,* 1995
- "I wrestled with reality for 35 years, doctor, and I'm happy to state I finally won out over it."—Elwood P. Dowd (James Stewart), *Harvey,* 1950
- "We can't run from who we are. Our destiny chooses us."—Prof. Abe Petrovsky (Martin Landau), *Rounders,* 1998
- "It's against my programming to impersonate a deity."—C-3PO (Anthony Daniels), *Return of the Jedi,* 1983
- "We accept the reality of the world with which we're presented."—Christof (Ed Harris), *The Truman Show,* 1998
- "Retire young, work old—come back and work when I know what I'm working for. Does that make sense to you?"—Johnny Case (Cary Grant), *Holiday,* 1938
- "Go ahead, make my millennium!"—Betelgeuse (Michael Keaton), *Beetlejuice,* 1988
- "Look, you don't know me from Adam, but I was a better man with you as a woman than I ever was with a woman as a man. Know what I mean?"—Michael Dorsey (Dustin Hoffman), *Tootsie,* 1982

- "I've fallen in love with the idea of living."—Shirley (Pauline Collins), *Shirley Valentine,* 1989
- "Even when you know, you never know."—Jay Trotter (Richard Dreyfuss), *Let It Ride,* 1989
- "There are times I almost think I am not sure of what I absolutely know—very often find confusion in conclusion I concluded long ago."—The king (Yul Brynner), *The King and I,* 1956
- "You're only whatever you are once."—Joan (Lynn Redgrave), *Getting It Right,* 1989
- "To infinity and beyond!"—Buzz Lightyear, *Toy Story,* 1995
- "My philosophy is you can do what you like, but the outcome will be the same."—Godbole (Alec Guinness), *A Passage to India,* 1984
- "You've got everything except one thing—madness. A man needs a little madness, or else he never dares cut the rope and be free."—Zorba (Anthony Quinn), *Zorba the Greek,* 1964
- "We're God's animated cartoons."—Steven Gold (Tom Hanks), *Punchline,* 1988
- "Any of you guys ever go to Sunday school?"—Indiana Jones (Harrison Ford), *Raiders of the Lost Ark,* 1981

Sean Patrick Flanery in *Powder*, Hollywood Pictures
Photo: The Museum of Modern Art Film Stills Archive

Chapter 2

The Force Is With and Within Us

· · · · · · · · · · · · · · ·

The most important, popular, and appealing meta physical theme in movies, especially during recent years, is this: What tremendous power is ours as creative expressions of the Infinite! Today's films reflect an increased awareness of our potential as children and heirs of a living, dynamic universal Energy of love, peace, and perfection. Whence cometh the Force that sustains Luke Skywalker, the power that takes Dorothy home, the strength that enables Will Hunting to connect with his good, the faith that brings Shoeless Joe Jackson to the Field of Dreams, the fortitude that serves Mulan well, and the lightning that charges Powder? Each is an example of the mighty spiritual energy that is always with and within us, and that ever awaits our recognition to be used to form and control our world for our greatest good and the good of all life. The characters and movies in this chapter show us how to connect with the Force and give us moving scenarios of what can happen when we do.

CHARIOTS OF FIRE

PREVIEW

The race is on for two members of Britain's 1924 Olympic team—runners Harold Abrahams (Ben Cross), a Jewish law student at Cambridge, and Eric Liddell (Ian Charleson), a missionary from Scotland—in this captivating film based on a true story. (1981, British, 123 minutes, PG)

META VIEW

The fire comes from within

The incredible racing engines of Harold Abrahams and Eric Liddell are fueled from within from different but noble motivations.

Abrahams, who is greatly frustrated and angered by the discriminations he encounters against Jews, runs as a way to prove himself to the world. Anglo-Saxon Christians control the "corridors of power," Abrahams notes, but he intends "to take them on—all of them, one by one, and run them off their feet." He regards running as a weapon "against being Jewish."

Liddell, who joins his sister in continuing their father's missionary work, races in God's name, feels God's pleasure in running, and wins "to honor Him." Liddell never forsakes his missionary role, however, and uses his increasing fame as a runner to spread the Gospel. For example, he tells a group of supporters that having faith is like running in a race: "It's hard; it requires concentration of will, energy of soul."

He continues by saying that the racing analogy has a practical application for the realities of daily living and that each person has the power within to accomplish the race of life.

"Everyone runs in her own way or his own way. And where does the fire come from to see the race to its end? From within. Jesus said: 'Behold, the kingdom of God is within you. If with all your heart you truly seek me, ye shall ever surely find me.' If you commit yourself to the love of Christ, then *that* is how you run the straight race."

Preaching in a Church of Scotland, Liddell quotes the Bible: "They that wait upon the Lord shall renew their strength . . . they shall run and not be weary."

Of Liddell, Abrahams says, "I've never seen such drive, such commitment in a runner."

Liddell attracts international attention at the Olympics by refusing to go against his conscience and his understanding of God's laws. He says it would be going against God's law to run on the Sabbath, and he will not do so. Liddell says that he loves his country, but not more than God. The Olympic Association is perplexed by Liddell's stand, but one member calls Liddell "a true man of principle."

Ye View

1. What do you think their performances at the Olympics mean to Abrahams and Liddell?
2. How do both men get along with and interact with other runners? What does this interaction suggest about their personalities?
3. Do you admire Abrahams and/or Liddell? Why or why not?

Theme Mates

Stories of other athletes fueled from within:

Breaking Away—An Indiana boy, Dave Stoller (Dennis Christopher), is determined to emulate his idolized Italian bike champions. (1979, 100 minutes, PG)

Rocky—A Philadelphia boxer (Sylvester Stallone) attempts to beat the odds in and out of the ring. He goes the distance! (1976, 119 minutes, PG)

A rocket-launching fire:

October Sky—When he sees Sputnik for the first time in October 1957, teenager Homer Hickam (Jake Gyllenhaal) decides that he and his friends in a West Virginia coal-mining town can build their own rockets. This true story of the early life of a noted NASA engineer marvelously shows the power of one individual's spirit to transform lives, communities, and the world. It also illustrates the life-changing effect a believing, inspirational teacher, Miss Riley (Laura Dern), can have on a student. (1999, 108 minutes, PG)

DRAGON: THE BRUCE LEE STORY

PREVIEW

The inner spirit of the "Little Dragon" (played by Jason Scott Lee) explodes in this captivating biography of the young martial arts legend. (1993, 119 minutes, PG-13)

META VIEW

Karate chop those inner demons!

Yes, Lee fights up a showy storm, and, yes, the violence and blood quotients are higher than preferred (zero actually would be a nice level). Still, some of the scenes in which Jason Scott Lee, who is not related to Bruce Lee, uses dazzling moves of kung fu to skillfully zap his opponents right and left and above and beyond are admittedly rather exciting.

However, metaphysical viewers must look past the violence (as well as a few fairly discreet sex scenes) to find the heart of the movie: the *chi* or inner spirit that Lee is able to call forth whenever conflict arises.

When the boy Lee begins taking martial arts lessons in Hong Kong in 1949, his teacher tells him that kung fu is not just a system of fighting but is also a system of thought. And opponents, the teacher declares, are not just people. He states:

"We all have inner demons to fight. We call these demons fear and hatred and anger. If you don't conquer them, then a life of a hundred years is a tragedy. If you do, a life of a single day can be a triumph."

The goal, the teacher says, is to out think an opponent—whatever form the opponent takes. Our thoughts can and do influence outcomes.

Lee's opponents are of the external physical kind—fights with coworkers, fellow college students, and other martial arts champions—but they are also of the internal variety: superstitions, jealousies, and (above all) prejudices and discriminations.

In coming to America, going to college, falling in love and marrying, opening his own martial arts studio, and eventually becoming an international film star, Lee encounters much physical hostility and mental cruelty. Lee more than gets by, however, with an infectious smile and generally upbeat personality, and he seems to have successfully grasped the lessons his first teacher taught him.

Lee tells his own students: "Emotion can be the enemy. . . . Be at one with your emotion because the body always follows the mind. This is not about winning. This is about perfection."

When personal tragedy strikes, however, Lee at first succumbs to inner demons of fear and superstition. His wife Linda (Lauren Holly) gives him his own advice: "Fight back with your mind."

The film's claim to Truth fame is how Lee does indeed fight back with his mind and overcomes inner fears and physical disability.

In his book *The Magic of Conflict*, Thomas F. Crum writes, "When one is willing to see all conflicts—whether physical, emotional, or mental—as dances of energy, and to accept them and to blend with them, options and opportunities for successful resolution emerge, powerfully and elegantly."[1]

Lee's story is a study in learning to dance with the energy of conflict.

Ye View

1. Do you think that Lee uses his martial arts abilities wisely? Why or why not?
2. Identify a situation in which you think Lee conquers his "inner demons" and a scene in which he does not do so.
3. Discuss why you would or would not like to learn to practice kung fu or another martial art.

In the Same Spirit

Also exploring the *chi*:

The Karate Kid—A teenager (Ralph Macchio) becomes empowered through martial arts. (1984, 126 minutes, R)

The Karate Kid, Part II—The boy and his teacher (Pat Morita) travel to Japan. (1986, 113 minutes, PG)

FIELD OF DREAMS

Preview

After hearing a voice that says, "If you build it, he will come," Iowa farmer and baseball fan Ray Kinsella (Kevin Costner) plows his cornfield and builds a baseball diamond that attracts an all-spirit team including Shoeless Joe Jackson (Ray Liotta). (1989, 106 minutes, PG)

META VIEW

If we invite them, healings come

"Are you a ghost?" Ray's daughter Karin asks baseball great Shoeless Joe, who has returned from the great beyond (through the cornfield) to play ball on her father's new field.

"What do you think?" Joe asks.

"You look real to me," Karin says.

"Well, then, I guess I'm real," Joe replies.

The conversation gives us a clue about the origins of the pitching and batting apparitions down on the Kinsella farm. Ray and wife Annie (Amy Madigan) and Karin are the first ones who can see the players at all. They think that the players are real, and their thoughts are based on beliefs that such things are possible.

Although Ray is puzzled by the voice that instructs him and amused by the things he is led to do, he has a childlike faith and wonder. Annie, believing in Ray, supports his deep desires to act on his dreams. They, as former hippies, have raised their daughter in an environment of possibilities and she totally accepts the ghostly players.

Ray partly recognizes the deeper power behind the field and the baseball team. "We're dealing with primal forces of nature here," he tells Annie. He senses an important reason to keep following his voice's direction.

Psychologically, the "primal forces" stem from Ray's subconscious need to make peace with his father, a frustrated would-be baseball player from whom Ray was estranged at the time of his death.

Ray says he has "created something totally illogical," but actually his creation is totally if fantastically logical with the power of faith and reconciliation. He comes to realize that the creation is not simply "unbelievable."

"It's more than that. It's perfect," he says. Psychologically speaking, it is, in one of those marvelous, seemingly miraculous workings of God energy.

61

Ray follows his instincts—his divine revelation through words, visions, and feelings—even though appearances suggest to many that he is crazy and financially irresponsible. One can say that Ray's voice comes from God, but, more specifically, from the place of God within him. He has called forth the players (as we all do on some level).

Ray feels guided to do as his voices direct. It's as if "the universe opens itself up for a few seconds to show you what's possible," Ray quotes his favorite author, Terence Mann (James Earl Jones) to Mann's face.

The universe opens up within Ray. He has the great desire to play ball once more with his father, he is receptive when the universe starts opening, and he senses that he and others are being shown their greater good. Healings of various kinds come to Ray and others when they invite them, by thoughts and feelings, to come. Healings then rush onto the field of dreams like celestial baseball players charging into the game of life.

When invited, healings come in some way, though perhaps not how we envision them, but always for the highest good of all concerned. On a conscious level, Ray never could have imagined healing the relationship with his father by building a baseball diamond and bringing back deceased players.

YE VIEW

1. What, according to one character, is "the place dreams come true"? What, in your opinion, is this place for Ray, Shoeless Joe, Terence Mann, and Dr. Graham (Burt Lancaster)?

2. What reconciliation comes to Ray after the field is built? How will this give Ray greater peace?

3. Why, according to Mann, will people come to Ray's "field of dreams"? Do you agree with him? Explain your answer.

THEME MATES

Playing supernatural ball:

The Natural—Seeing with his heart and doing what comes naturally to him, playing baseball, Roy Hobbs (Robert Redford) has an up-and-down career, but lightning and other divine forces move his destiny in this film based on a Bernard Malamud novel. (1984, 134 minutes, PG)

GOOD WILL HUNTING

PREVIEW

Will (Matt Damon), a young genius troubled by a traumatic childhood, gains attention and the help of a therapist, Sean McGuire (Robin Williams), when he amazes MIT professors with his natural ability to solve advanced mathematical equations. (1997, 125 minutes, R)

META VIEW

"It's not your fault!"

Many of us are seemingly complicated mathematical problems for whom the numbers don't come out even because of minds jammed with odd memories from childhood. Somewhere in the unconscious we stubbornly hold on to the figures of ourselves as victims, usually of parents or guardians, and we are convinced that our problems are unsolvable.

The problems *are* solvable, of course, and we hold the answers within us. All the correct answers stem from this set theory: Our true identity is always a whole and perfect child of God, and nothing that happens to us ever changes that.

Until we truly realize and own this all-important answer, however, our lives can be tormented with painful memories, and emotional barriers around us can keep people from getting close to us. Like Will, those who identify themselves as victims believe that they are not worthy of love, so they push help and love away. The orphaned Will was raised in several foster homes and was removed from three homes because of serious physical abuse. Though he is smart and handsome, he settles for a life of petty crimes and menial jobs because he won't let himself imagine that he deserves more. He can't say "I love you" to his girlfriend Skylar (Minnie Driver) because he didn't have love himself as a child.

Somewhere at some time, though, a person, a circumstance, or some connection will come along to help people realize that they don't have to identify themselves as victims, that they are not defined by the problems of others, and that they are not responsible for what others did to them.

Into Will's life comes Sean McGuire, who has first-hand knowledge of much of what Will is going through and who has the patience and stamina to "crack" the problem and reveal the good Will within.

"Why is he hiding? Why doesn't he trust anybody?" Sean asks, referring to Will. "Because the first thing that happened to him, he was abandoned by the people who were supposed to love him the most."

"He pushes people away before they have a chance to leave him. It's a defense mechanism."

Through his trust, compassion, and understanding, Sean is able to be the catalyst that helps Will solve his problem. Sean gets Will to truly know, not at an intellectual level but deep within his heart and soul, that he is not what happened to him or what others thought of him. "It's not your fault," Sean steadily repeats, referring to Will's childhood traumas, until Will actually knows. That's the breakthrough that will allow Will to more fully reflect the Truth of his being as God's whole, perfect, loving, and lovable child.

Sean tells Will: "You can do anything you want. You are bound by nothing."

Ye View

1. How does Will's friend Chuckie (Ben Affleck) help motivate Will?
2. In what ways does Will give Sean's life new meaning and direction?
3. In your opinion, what does the future hold for Will?

In the Same Spirit

Not their fault either:

Ordinary People—A young man (Timothy Hutton) squirms through painful lessons in love and forgiveness in dealing with a cold mother (Mary Tyler Moore) and the accidental death of his older brother, in this excellent adaptation of Judith Guest's novel directed by Robert Redford. (1980, 123 minutes, R)

Smoke Signals—A Coeur d'Alene Indian youth, Victor (Adam Beach), with the help of friend Thomas (Evan Adams), learns to cope with his father's desertion and hurtful acts. "How do we forgive our fathers?" is a pivotal question in the movie. The insightful Thomas says, "I think we're all traveling heavy with illusions." (1998, 89 minutes, PG-13)

65

JOE VERSUS THE VOLCANO

Preview

A hypochondriac dulled by a dreary job, Joe Banks (Tom Hanks) only begins to live when he is told he has a fatal "brain cloud" and accepts an unusual offer to jump into a volcano as a sacrifice to the fire god of a Pacific island people. (1990, 102 minutes, PG)

META VIEW

Eruptions can be soul-satisfying

Think of Joe as Everyman, and his battle as belonging to all humanity. What is it that he fights? What is the volcano? For Joe, as for all, there in an internal cause of an external volcano, and the latter is but the physical manifestation of the former. Thoughts and feelings naturally tend to work their way to the surface and form what appear to be large mountains in our lives. Obstacles on the exterior must first be overcome in the interior, with a change in thought, perception, or belief.

The internal cause is the disruption in our minds and hearts when we have a belief in separation from God or from our wholeness as God's children. When this pressure builds, we usually have a vague sense that something is wrong in our lives, but we don't know what. We might say that our soul is troubled.

Such is the case with Joe as the movie opens. For years he has been in a boring, life-draining job with a company that makes surgical tools. Over the opening credits we hear the words from the song "Sixteen Tons": "I owe my soul to the company store." Ostensibly referring to his shoe, Joe says, "I'm losing my sole (soul)." Like sometimes attracts like, and Joe is attracted to a woman, Patricia (Meg Ryan), who admits that both she and her sister are "soul sick."

Eruptions can be liberating by spewing limiting beliefs into thin air, and thus making room for belief in the fullness of Life. Eruptions come from deep within the individual but can be ignited by movements from without, such as by surprising or devastating news. For Joe, the news is the doctor's prognosis of his terminal condition. This news and the prospect of only six months to live prompt Joe to discard limiting beliefs and begin to enjoy life.

"I feel great!" he exclaims to a date. Sensing that she is struggling with her own volcano, Joe offers her this previously uncharacteristic advice: "If you want to understand the universe, embrace the universe. The door to the universe is you."

Joe asks another woman, whose beliefs in separation take the form of fearing to do what she really wants in life, "Why not take the leap and do the thing you're scared of doing? . . . You know what you're scared of doing, why don't you do it?"

Joe's volcano has erupted, and he suddenly seems to understand life and the power of internal wisdom and courage. "I'm my only hope for a hero," he says.

Patricia, too, is overcoming her feeling of being "soul sick" and realizing what it means to be truly alive. "My father says that almost the whole world is asleep. . . . He says that only a few people are awake, and they live in a state of constant, total amazement."

Having faced their internal disruptions and a few external ones, the two are now in the right consciousness to face their biggest volcano—literally jumping into a real one.

"We'll take this leap and we'll see," Patricia says. "We'll jump and we'll see. That's life."

Joe asks, "So what are we hoping for here?"

Patricia replies, "A miracle."

So-called miracles happen when we identify with our soul's mission to live life to the fullest extent of our divine nature.

YE VIEW

1. Is there a miracle when Joe and Patricia jump into the volcano? Discuss their jump as a true "leap of faith."
2. Marshall (Ossie Davis), the chauffeur, tells Joe, "You're coming into focus, kid." What does he mean? How does Joe change?
3. At the conclusion of an enchanting scene of bliss at sea, Joe prays, "Dear God . . . Thank You for my life." Have you ever felt such a complete sense of thankfulness? Discuss.

IN THE SAME SPIRIT

Another cleansing eruption:

Little Voice—In a northern English town, Laura Hoff (Jane Horrocks) speaks rarely and softly and tries to avoid her man-chasing mother (Brenda Blethyn), but comes alive through her late father's record collection, in this captivating adaptation of a play by Jim Cartright. We all speak with a "little voice" until we fully realize and utilize our powers and talents. Once she is pushed to the brink, Laura, called Little Voice, is able to purge what has been limiting her and keeping her from expressing her true Self. Here's a reminder for us to examine the strength of our own voices and be sure that we aren't giving our power away to someone or something. (1998, British, 96 minutes, R)

LEAP OF FAITH

PREVIEW

When their "Miracles and Wonders" caravan breaks down, the Reverend Jonas Nightengale (Steve Martin) and company make a fateful decision to stage their elaborate revival show in rainless Rustwater, Kansas, in an attempt to bilk the faithful. (1992, 108 minutes, PG-13)

META VIEW

Whose faith works the miracles?

It's a real leap of faith sometimes just to understand that the faith to work miracles comes from within us, not from an outside source—not even from formally ordained sources (preachers, in other words). At our soul level, we are always connected to God and always have the faith or belief in God that can transform outer circumstances. Working so-called miracles is always a matter of identifying with our God-essence so clearly and strongly that only this God-power manifests in our experience.

Preachers, ministers, teachers, rabbis, and other religious figures are way showers who provide an important service by helping us understand our own God nature and calling forth the faith within us. Jesus, for example, repeatedly told people whom he healed that their own faith had made them whole. He didn't say that *he* made them whole. In fact, we're told that he couldn't do anything if the people did not have faith. Once, in Nazareth, Jesus "did not do many deeds of power there, because of their unbelief" (Mt. 13:58).

Jesus and other ministers are catalysts to bring out the force of faith within us. Some catalysts are sincere, as was Jesus, while others are not so sincere in their own beliefs—and that is a matter of their own faith. In terms of helping others, however, the crucial factor is whether or not the ministers somehow touch people so that the people realize their own faith.

Jonas Nightengale considers himself to be a con man whose only motive is to make money through his traveling revival shows. He preaches wonderful words of inspiration (such as "Be strong in the Lord and the power of His might" and "Never underestimate the power of belief"), but he doesn't practice what he preaches. Even bona fide preachers sometimes don't own and practice the truth of what they preach; Sonny (Robert Duvall) in *The Apostle* (1998) is an example.

However, people are healed at Jonas' services. Is this nonbeliever healing the people? No, he is stirring their own faith. Although he doesn't understand the purpose he is serving, Jonas rightly observes, "Without your faith I cannot deliver the Word" and "Faith—you've got to have it, or you can't get healed." Exactly what Jesus was saying. Jonas considers these thoughts to be merely his "ace in the hole" by placing the "blame" for any lack of healings on the individuals themselves. In Truth, however, there *is* no blame—individual faiths are simply ignited at different times and through different means, in divine order.

YE VIEW

1. What happens to Boyd (Lukas Haas) when he comes to Jonas for healing? Who is responsible, Jonas or Boyd?
2. Do you think Jonas begins to think that there might be some truth to what he has been preaching? Why or why not?
3. What, if anything, do you find appealing about the style of Jonas' revivals? Would you like to attend such a revival? Why or why not?

MULAN

PREVIEW

Disney works animated magic on an ancient Chinese folktale of a young woman, Mulan, who disguises herself as a man to take the place of her honorable but aged father in the emperor's army against the invading Huns. (1998, 88 minutes, G, *)

META VIEW

Confucius would probably be proud

"When we see men of worth, we should think of equaling them."
—Confucius[2]

That goes for women of worth too, as a more politically correct Confucius might say today. Surely the great Chinese sage would have advocated that both men and women should aspire to equal Mulan's strength of character. While he might not totally appreciate Mulan's take-charge spunk, Confucius certainly would applaud her high moral standards and respect for ancestors and the family tradition (and he also might admire Disney's stunningly serene style, reminiscent of traditional Chinese art).

With her own inner fortitude, bravery, and wisdom and with the spiritual help of her ancestors, Mulan proves herself in an established man's world of war and honor. What is so refreshing about Mulan, especially when compared to most other Disney animated heroines, is her strong sense of personal identity and her self-reliance. For the sake of family and society, she attempts to do the dutiful daughter bit of dressing up to be married off, but she fails because she isn't being true to herself. And she knows it, singing, "When will my reflection show who I am inside?"

The question is quickly answered. When the emperor requires one man from each family to fight the Huns, Mulan realizes that her father can no longer stand the physical rigors of being a soldier. Thinking only of saving her father, Mulan decides to take his place. If Mulan had not shone in battle and saved the proverbial day, the movie never would have been made. *How* Mulan shines is the inspiring soul of the movie: by using both her brains and her heart, Mulan makes the right decisions and takes the right actions—actions that win her favor with the emperor and the nation, with her family, and with her ancestors. Mulan accomplishes much by living the words of the movie's best song: be "True to Your Heart."

Mulan's father, who initially thinks that his daughter's actions will disgrace the family name, says, "The greatest gift and honor is having you for a daughter."

Disney's signature comic relief comes mainly in the form of a tiny dragon from Mulan's spiritual, ancestral support system. The feisty, bumbling, but well-intentioned dragon, Mushu (voiced by Eddie Murphy), volunteers to accompany Mulan so that he can redeem himself among his celestial kin.

After the emperor acknowledges Mulan's achievements, the proud Mushu has one of the film's best lines: "Our little baby is all grown up and saving China."

Mulan is truly a worthy role model.

YE VIEW

1. What situations most clearly show Mulan's intelligence and intuition?
2. Why are people upset when Mulan's deception is revealed?
3. Explain the comparison of Mulan to a flower that blooms in adversity. Do you know people to whom the comparison also could apply?

IN THE SAME SPIRIT

More spunk:

Ever After—This Cinderella story is set in beautiful Renaissance France, but its sentiments are decidedly modern. Turning to God for strength, Danielle (Drew Barrymore) is an independent-thinking, idealistic, big-hearted young lady who is passionate about human rights, asks only love from her cruel stepmother (Anjelica Huston), and brings both love and enlightenment to the handsome Prince Henry (Dougray Scott). A clever spin on the familiar folktale is having Leonardo da Vinci (Patrick Godfrey) serve as fairy godfather and actually advise both Danielle and the prince. The point of the story, as a descendent of the couple says, is not that Danielle and Prince Henry lived happily ever after, which they did, but "that they *lived*," meaning that they remained true to themselves and lived with passion. (1998, 121 minutes, PG-13)

THE NEXT VOICE YOU HEAR . . .

PREVIEW

The average American family of Joe Smith (James Whitmore) and people everywhere are, by stages, surprised, fearful, and awed when God begins speaking nightly on the radio throughout the world. (1950, 83 minutes, NR)

META VIEW

We're miracle workers

The Word of God (or of Universal Mind or Energy) or the Truth of All That Is (or of whatever one calls the Ultimate) comes into our lives continuously, but is often ignored because we become so thoroughly embroiled in our human dramas. The Word is revealed through countless channels—friends, churches, publications, movies, intuition, billboards, strangers on the street, and on and on—but we must be willing to receive it.

Joe Smith's family represents the average household, with all its frustrations revolving around home, jobs, and school. While the movie setting is particularly and quaintly the American stereotype of the 1940s and early 1950s, similar situations are still with us: money concerns over "making ends meet," irritable feelings resulting from stressful relationships among family members and between employees and bosses, cars that won't start properly, traffic fines, homework, health worries. Joe and his wife Mary (Nancy Davis), who is pregnant, and their son Johnny (Gary Gray) deal with these issues, which at times begin to overshadow the genuine love that exists in the family.

Into the lives of people such as the Smith family coping with life's many day-to-day challenges unexpectedly comes the actual voice of God. Inter-

73

✸

rupting all regularly scheduled radio programs, a voice declares: "This is God. I'll be with you for the next few days." The idea of God offering such a clear wake-up call is interesting, and certainly many people have wished for just such a divine revelation to clarify aspects of life.

Would people welcome the message that God presents in the movie? It depends on whether or not they are willing to actually assume responsibility for their lives. This God states in no uncertain terms that the power to create a fulfilling life is within the individual.

In one of His nightly broadcasts for a week, God says that all of nature is His miracles. "But," He says, "look now for the miracles that *you* can create—the miracles of understanding and peace and loving-kindness. These are the miracles that are within all of you, whoever you are, wherever you are."

On another night, God emphasizes His purpose: "I have spoken to you these few days to ask you to count your blessings—to create for yourselves the miracles of kindness and goodness and peace. You are like children going to school. You've forgotten some of your lessons. I ask you to do your homework for tomorrow."

The voice of God seems to be speaking to each individual with a heart to hear, and many people actually start doing their homework and improving their relationships and conditions.

Joe notices a personal miracle right away: the stubborn starter on his car, which has put him in a bad mood every morning, suddenly begins working. He asks fellow workers if they think the change *means* anything, and one replies: "It *might* mean you come out of the house griping every morning, jam your foot on the starter, and flood the carburetor. Maybe all you had to do was take it easy."

Joe responds: "Yeah, it could *be,* all right. Maybe that means something. Maybe that's what He has had in His mind all along: just teaching us to take it easy."

How wonderful to imagine what the world would be like if everyone began filling his or her life with such simple miracles and taking it easy!

How the world would change if people would slow their paces and do as God suggests: "Enjoy then the miracles I have given you and the miracles you have given yourselves and each other. In all your many languages, keep alive and strong such simple words as *love* and *faith* and *freedom* and *peace*."

YE VIEW

1. What are some other miracles that Joe creates in his life after God begins speaking?
2. Many people, such as Joe's family, are afraid when God speaks. What do you think they fear?
3. How might you react if God began speaking on the radio? If He suggested that you do your homework, what might you do to improve your life?

75

PHENOMENON

PREVIEW

After being knocked down by a ball of light from out of the night sky, auto mechanic George Malley (John Travolta) possesses amazing mental powers and learning abilities. (1996, 124 minutes, PG)

META VIEW

Each of us is a phenomenon

A telling scene occurs at the library's outdoor fair. It's the type of situation politicians often encounter when they want to talk about issues but the press wants to hear about scandal and trivia. George is trying to tell people about the universal dance of energy in which we all two-step and explain about life expressing as one great, connected organism. The townspeople and reporters don't care to be educated or enlightened. They demand to know how George broke a mirror without touching it and what he can tell them about UFOs. They also want him to perform healing miracles.

Everywhere he goes, people marvel at George's powers, while suspecting and fearing his freak abilities and the man himself. George can learn a language in twenty minutes, read at least four books a day, sense subsonic frequency waves of earthquakes, recite a list of mammals alphabetically in sixty seconds, and move objects by using what he says is our natural energy connection with all objects. He knows the names of flowers, yet significantly says, "It doesn't make them any prettier, though."

The real phenomenon isn't the flash that struck George, and it isn't any of his showy powers, which George indicates anyone who applies the proper focus and clarity of thought has. The real phenomenon is George's spirit for living and loving. Before the flash, George was an extremely popular guy, with a soft heart and caring disposition. After his change, George is still his personable, friendly, helpful, considerate self—only with heightened powers.

The point is that George himself really hasn't changed, but he does come to realize what is important in life and that he is more than his brain and abilities. He says he represents the possibility of what everyone can be. "*Anybody* can get here," he adds, and he says that how doesn't matter. "The human spirit," he says, "that's the challenge; that's the voyage; that's the expedition." George, in effect, has learned to appreciate the phenomenon of his own Self. He understands what many of us fail to appreciate: that each one of us is a phenomenon—an exceptional, unique person or object known by the senses but not fully *explainable* by the senses or by science.

People change toward George, though, and he becomes frantic and frustrated. His hard-to-win girlfriend Lace (Kyra Sedgwick) is appalled at people turning on their friend. She asks her two children: "Can't they just look in his eyes and see who he is? Can't *you*?"

Most of the people in the small California town, however, are not introspective, and they are afraid of George's awakening. Doc (Robert Duvall), who considers George almost a son, does recognize George's true qualities. Also grasping the insecurities of people who don't bother to look within themselves, Doc yells at men talking about George in a bar: "Why do you have to tear him down? What are you so afraid of? What have you got to lose? He wasn't selling anything. He didn't *want* anything from anybody. . . . And you people have to tear him down so you can sleep better tonight, so you can prove that the world is flat."

George would be perfectly content to live the simple, uncomplicated life, without surprises, that Lace desires. He would like nothing better than to share his ideas ("I've got a thousand ideas a day") with people whom they would benefit. Such a genuine spirit with its regard and empathy for others is a phenomenon to be cherished—and nurtured and recognized within ourselves and one another.

77

✳

YE VIEW

1. What do you think George means by the statement "Everything is on its way to somewhere"?
2. What is the significance of the swaying trees at the end of the movie? Of the cornfield?
3. Is it important or necessary to know the cause of George's stimulated brainpower? Why or why not?

PLEASANTVILLE

PREVIEW

The black-and-white world of Pleasantville, the idyllic home of characters in a 1950s TV sitcom, is gradually colorized when modern-teen siblings David (Tobey Maguire) and Jennifer (Reese Witherspoon) are zapped there via a special remote control. (1998, 124 minutes, PG-13)

META VIEW

Look what hue can do!

The Hundredth Monkey Phenomenon swings into the action of Pleasantville. The theory, popularized in the Ken Keyes, Jr. book *The Hundredth Monkey*, holds that mass consciousness changes when the minds of enough individuals within a society change. Keyes bases his theory on an experiment in which monkeys in Japan began washing their food, apparently in mental response to other monkeys in different locations having learned the skill. Keyes reasons that the spiritual consciousness of humankind will be elevated when a certain number of people realize their unity with God.

While the Hundredth Monkey Phenomenon has yet to come to fruition in spiritual dimensions—though many see distinct and hopeful signs that the phenomenon is in process—the theory has been successfully demonstrated in social arenas. Notable twentieth-century examples are the popular changes of consciousness that led to the ending of the Vietnam conflict, the Berlin Wall, and the Soviet Union.

Pleasantville is perhaps more a movie of social commentary than of spiritual commentary, but the spiritual and social climates of a culture are not totally exclusive of each other. On a social level, the film exposes the hypocrisy of post-World War II America, in which life was pictured in the public mind like a TV-family situation comedy, such as *Father Knows Best* or *Leave It to Beaver*. In those shows, as in the movie's Pleasantville, the family is composed of a happy and wise father, a dutiful housewife and mother, one son, and one daughter. There are minor and amusing trials and tribulations, but life's lessons are always learned with a dose of parental wisdom and saccharin.

When David becomes Pleasantville's Bud and Jennifer becomes Pleasantville's Mary Sue, children of George (William H. Macy) and Betty (Joan Allen), they begin imposing more modern enlightened and liberated sensibilities on the Pleasantville population, and the people's pleasant surface-level lives start unraveling. One by one, people begin realizing and living their pent-up feelings and passions, and slowly the emotional and physical landscapes change. Even the weather changes—from clearly pleasant to rainy. Pleasantville literally goes from a black-and-white to a color show, in keeping with the Hundredth Monkey Phenomenon.

From a societal standpoint, it can be argued that the changes in Pleasantville—which have parallels with dramatic changes in American society from the 1940s through the 1970s—simply create new problems and challenges, and that society's "people" issues are never all black-and-white or all bright and distinct colors.

On a deeper level, it can also be argued that the changes in Pleasantville represent an important spiritual advancement, because people are learning to be true to themselves and their life-affirming passions. That this change is occurring is apparent when Bud asks his father if he really wants his liberated wife to be the way she was, and George admits he does not. The developments illustrate Keyes's belief that "the appreciation and love we have for ourselves and others creates an expanding energy field that becomes a growing power in the world."[3]

David, as Bud, articulates the spiritual, human breakthrough that occurs with living one's dreams and passions. Such ability is always within a person, he tells the people. "You can't stop something that's inside you," he says. The implications are profound. As people increasingly get in touch with their own freedoms and potentials, society can change to live the color-filled Truth of its creation. As the characters show, the choice to change from a black-and-white to a color existence is always up to the individual—one person at a time.

YE VIEW

1. Choose one person in Pleasantville, such as George or Betty or the soda-shop owner (Jeff Daniels), and discuss that character's changing consciousness. In what way(s) does the character change?
2. What do the two time travelers, David and Jennifer, learn about themselves and their own values?
3. What do David's final remarks to his mother imply about the nature and purpose of change? Do you agree with him? Why or why not?

POWDER

PREVIEW

An albino teenager called Powder (Sean Patrick Flanery) comes out of the cellar, where he has been protected and isolated from society, and electrifies people with his intelligence and extrasensory abilities. (1995, 111 minutes, PG-13)

META VIEW

Everything is God-energy

What a supercharged image *Powder* presents—the true potential of humankind! The character of Powder is nothing less than the embodiment of our true Selves as God-energy. Is Powder amazing and extraordinary? As lightning rods of God-energy, we *all* are. Does Powder seem strange and frightening to people? It's because we so seldom exhibit the full range of our true Selves. This movie, written and directed by Victor Salva, zaps our consciousness with the energizing possibilities of God's creation.

Science teacher Donald Ripley (Jeff Goldblum) recognizes Powder's significance:

Ripley: It's become appallingly clear that our technology has surpassed our humanity.
Powder: Albert Einstein.
Ripley: I look at you and I—I think that someday our humanity might actually surpass our technology.

What are we truly, stripped of the human (a condition suggested by Powder's physical appearance) and revealed in our God glory? Powder tells and shows us:

81

* We are God-energy—completely, always, and eternally.

Charged with energy himself, Powder feels thunderstorms inside him and senses the lightning wanting to come into him: "Grandma said it was God. She said the white fire was God."

Ripley tells Powder that Einstein said people wouldn't need their bodies if they used all of their brains because they would be pure energy: "*You* are closer to that energy level than one body has ever been."

* We are connected to all life and not separated from any part of God's creation.

Powder is able to communicate telepathically and translate and transfer emotions and thoughts from one being to another. A girl (Missy Crider) who befriends Powder asks him, "What are people like on the inside?"

"Inside most people, there's a feeling of being separate, separated from everything," Powder says. "And they're not. They're a part of absolutely every-one and everything."

If people didn't think they were disconnected, they would know that, he says, "and how beautiful they really are, and that there's no need to hide or lie, and that it is possible to talk to someone without lies, with no sarcasms, no deceptions, no exaggerations, or any of the things that people use to con-fuse the truth."

An important realization about God-energy is that It exists—like elec-tricity—whether people believe in It or not. Powder tells educators, "I don't need you to believe in me." Powder's connection with the energy of the Universe just is, and is not dependent on others' opinions.

- We are childlike in desiring to see the wonders and beauty of creation.
- We are filled with all knowledge.

Powder's IQ scores are off the charts, and he is called the "most advanced intellect in the history of mankind."

Ripley says that people today are "stumbling around in a very dark age, basically, just trying not to kill each other," but that Powder comes along with a mind to which the rest of humankind will not evolve for thousands of years.

- We are the epitome of peace, love, and compassion.

The human mind is often unwilling to accept the Truth of the Christ Mind within. Powder endures all sorts of verbal and physical abuse from his peers and adults, but he understands that people are just insecure, fright-ened, hurt, and lonely. He looks at people with compassion, but also, it seems, with a sense of sadness that they don't understand their God con-nection.

YE VIEW

1. What are some examples of Powder's oneness with and compassion for other people and animals?
2. At the end of the movie, what happens to Powder? Where does he go? What is the implication for humankind?
3. How would you react if someone like Powder walked into your life right now?

THE RAINMAKER

PREVIEW

Starbuck (Burt Lancaster), a traveling con artist, tells a ranch family in a drought-stricken Southwestern town that he can make rain, and helps the unmarried daughter (Katharine Hepburn) find showers of her own. (1956, 121 minutes, NR)

META VIEW

Faith comes before the rain

Refreshing downpours of life-saving, sweet inspiration can come from the most unlikely sources. In this mesmerizing and stagy Hal Wallis production of N. Richard Nash's play, the unlikely source may or may not bring rain, but he does bring much-needed words of faith, hope, and dreams.

The story is soaked with symbolism. The drought is any period in our lives when we feel spiritually dry as a result of not seeing God and our own self-worth as God's whole and perfect children. When such a drought occurs, we need the rain of faith to give us new vitality, purpose, and passion.

Often into our lives comes a "rainmaker," a person who assists in some way in helping us to see our true identity or God-power within. Sometimes we don't do well in accurately seeing ourselves, and we need a "rainmaker" to open our eyes.

Starbuck is such a one. He's a larger-than-life godsend who shows up with insightful words about the value of having faith and dreams. A dreamer himself, he has the talent to help others realize their own dreams—and realize their ability to dream in the first place. He is the catalyst who helps the whole movie family wake up to the potential of dreams. (And, of course, in teaching them, he's also teaching himself.)

Lizzie—the book-smart, industrious, but unmarried daughter in an otherwise male household (father and two brothers)—desperately wants to find love and to "make somebody happy." But she lacks faith in herself and doesn't act on her dreams.

Starbuck shocks Lizzie with the truth. "You're scared to believe in anything," he says. "You've got no faith. You don't even know what faith is. Well, I'm going to tell you: It's believing you see white when your eyes tell you black. It's knowing with your heart."

Lizzie says that her "little, quiet" dreams about a husband and home will never come true, but Starbuck tells her to believe in herself and they will.

Both Lizzie and her brother Jimmy (Earl Holliman) listen too much to the negative comments and outlook of their brother Noah (Lloyd Bridges), and thus their own insecurities are reinforced. In Noah's eyes, Lizzie is plain and Jimmy is dumb. Starbuck tells Lizzie, in no uncertain terms, not to let Noah be her "looking glass."

"It's got to be inside you. Don't be afraid—look!" he encourages.

What valuable advice, because often we tend to define ourselves by accepting how others view us, rather than by knowing the Truth about our worth.

Jimmy, an innocent sort who sees the good in people and situations, instinctively follows Starbuck's advice. Brother Noah is more resistant. The father (Wendell Corey) tells him, "You're so full of what's right, you can't see what's good."

In opening up others to have faith in themselves, Starbuck expands his own awareness and creates the climate in which his own dreams can come true.

Ye View

1. In what ways is Lizzie "beautiful"?
2. Do you think Starbuck's invitation to Lizzie at the end of the movie is sincere? Why or why not?
3. Can you recall an incident in your own life when a "rainmaker" gave you faith and helped you see your own Force within? Discuss.

In the Same Spirit

A familiar face and challenge:

Summertime—Katharine Hepburn plays another spinster suffering from inner drought and longing for romance in this beautiful David Lean film. She's Jane, a lonely secretary on holiday in Venice, where a hotel owner advises that miracles can happen sometimes, "but you must give a little push to help." Renato (Rossano Brazzi), Jane's suitor, suggests, "Relax—relax and the world is beautiful." (1955, 99 minutes, NR)

A ROOM WITH A VIEW

Preview

While on a trip to Florence, Italy, with her exceedingly proper Aunt Charlotte (Maggie Smith), a young Edwardian lady, Lucy Honeychurch

85

(Helena Bonham Carter), falls in love with an impetuous American, George (Julian Sands), but rushes back to England and becomes engaged to an effete snob, Cecil (Daniel Day-Lewis). (1986, British, 115 minutes, NR)

META VIEW

True vision is within

The theme is perfectly set at the beginning of the movie at the Pensione Bertolini, where Charlotte is upset because she and Lucy do not have rooms with a view of the River Arno. While they are discussing the matter at the communal supper table, Mr. Emerson (Denholm Elliott) and his son George readily and unhesitatingly offer their rooms, which have views, to the women.

"I don't care what I see outside. My vision is within," Mr. Emerson says. Pointing inward, he adds, "*Here* is where the birds sing; *here* is where the sky is blue."

The "room with a view" that truly matters and for which everyone yearns has to do with how we look at life. The "room" is our mind, and the "view" is our perception, or outlook on life. The "room with a view" that brings us peace and love is the consciousness or perspective of realizing our oneness with Life, or God. Bliss and joy come from living in the Presence, from that sense of completeness within. With the force of such inner vision, we can look at whatever is in the exterior with appreciation and understanding.

The major characters in the movie represent different kinds of views or perspectives on life. Mr. Elliott clearly has the inner vision, as does the Reverend Mr. Beebe (Simon Callow). Young George almost has it too, but his overreflection and brooding about weighty issues of the universe somewhat cloud his perception.

Charlotte lives life from the perspective of worrying about propriety and what people will think.

Cecil's view is entirely of the shallow aspects of himself—the practical and the literary.

Lucy, about whom the story revolves, is a person denying the potential of her inner vision, and therefore living a rather cautious and soulless life. The "imprisoned splendor" within her is waiting for a way to escape, as the poet Robert Browning would have said.[4]

In the movie, Mr. Beebe says much the same after hearing Lucy play the piano: "If Miss Honeychurch ever takes to live as she plays, it will be very exciting, both for us and for her." Much of the plot, based on the novel by E. M. Forster, is about Lucy releasing her "imprisoned splendor" and learning to live passionately.

YE VIEW

1. What is the significance of the question mark that George makes in his food and draws on the back of a picture? What might George be questioning? What does Mr. Emerson tell Lucy about George's questioning?
2. What events cause Cecil to remark on a "new voice" and a new "force" in Lucy? What does this new "force" indicate is happening to Lucy?
3. Mr. Emerson says that he brought up George to "trust to love" and to "love and do what you will." Do you think this is good advice? Why or why not?

IN THE SAME SPIRIT

Other English women learning to release "imprisoned splendor":
Enchanted April—Four women rent an Italian villa, and the new outlooks and relationships they discover there are beautifully symbolized at movie's end by the sprouting of the walking cane that

Mrs. Fisher (Joan Plowright) puts in the ground. (1991, British, 101 minutes, PG)

Shirley Valentine—A middle-aged housewife (Pauline Collins) rediscovers life when she leaves her husband at home and goes on holiday on a Greek island. (1989, United States-British, 108 minutes, R)

THE SECRET OF NIMH

PREVIEW

Mrs. Brisby, a mouse widow with young children, including one with pneumonia, desperately needs help to move her home to safety, and is instructed by the Great Owl to see the rats near the farmhouse—rats who keep a surprising secret in this animated feature. (1982, 82 minutes, G, *)

META VIEW

We already have the keys

A magic bullet, a rabbit's foot, a special charm, a lucky penny, or a specific article of clothing will give us that added power to bring our dreams into reality, we often tell ourselves. We frequently think we need outside assistance when the help we seek is within us. However, we're more capable than we usually give ourselves credit for being.

In actuality, if any of these devices seem to work, it's a sure sign that we are using our own God-given abilities to bring about desired results.

Mrs. Brisby, the central character with a name slightly altered from Robert C. O'Brien's Newbery Medal-winning novel *Mrs. Frisby and the Rats of NIMH*, is a case in point. Nicodemus, the leader of the rats, gives Mrs. Brisby an amulet that her husband Jonathan, who died in brave service to the rats, wanted her to have.

"When worn by one with the greatest heart, the stone glows red," Nicodemus says. "It becomes a blinding radiance. Courage of the heart is very rare. The stone has a power when it's there."

The amulet contains the inscription "You can unlock any door if you only have the key."

Someone who doesn't know Mrs. Brisby's character might think that the amulet she wears gives her special powers. This is not the case at all. Nicodemus doesn't say that the stone *gives* power, but rather that it glows when worn by one already showing "the greatest heart." Early in the tale, Mrs. Brisby proves her bravery and compassion in approaching Mr. Ages for medicine for her ailing son; in journeying to see the Great Owl; in befriending Jeremy, the clumsy, lovelorn crow; and in visiting the rats in the rosebush.

The inscription on the amulet might suggest to some that one has to seek for the keys to unlock doors of difficulty or lack. The irony of the inscription is that it has a hidden meaning, which is that a person actually already *has* the keys to unlock any doors of difficulty or lack. One must *know* that he or she has the key, however, to use it.

There are some similarities between *The Secret of NIMH* and *The Wizard of Oz*. Both Mrs. Brisby and Dorothy are sent to see powerful figures to receive the aid they desire, but both actually already have the powers within them. Dorothy doesn't need special shoes, any more than Mrs. Brisby needs the amulet. The shoes and the amulet are powered by the faith of the wearer. And just as the Cowardly Lion in Oz already has the courage he seeks, so Mrs. Brisby has the courage to help herself and her family overcome any obstacles.

89

✳

YE VIEW

1. After meeting the rats of NIMH, what does Mrs. Brisby do that reflects her courage?
2. What is the secret of the rats? What does Justin, the captain of the rat guard, say is the shame of the rat colony?
3. Discuss the different outlooks about life contained in the following exchange:
   Jenner: I've learned this much—take what you can, *when* you can.
   Justin: Then you've learned *nothing*.

IN THE SAME SPIRIT

James and the Giant Peach—Roald Dahl's story about a mistreated boy who flies a giant peach across the ocean is deliciously ripe. Combining live action and stop-motion animation, the movie creatively shows that magical experiences happen when you dream and are willing to look at life differently. Doesn't everything start as a dream? James asks. He learns about his own powers, the broader meaning of family, and the value of friendship, bravery, and kindness. (1996, 79 minutes, PG, *)

STAR WARS EPISODE IV: A NEW HOPE

PREVIEW

Freedom-loving rebels battle the evil Galactic Empire "a long time ago in a galaxy far, far away" in George Lucas' imaginative and immensely popular original *Star Wars* trilogy. In this first installment, fully titled *Star Wars Episode IV: A New Hope*, Princess Leia (Carrie Fisher), Luke Skywalker (Mark Hamill), Captain Han Solo (Harrison Ford), Obi-Wan Kenobi (Alec Guinness), and droids R2-D2 and C-3PO race against time and Darth Vader (David Prowse—voice of James Earl Jones) to block the Empire's space station Death Star. (1977, 124 minutes, PG, *)

META VIEW

"The Force will be with you always"

The special effects are dazzling and the old-fashioned "good guys vs. bad guys" adventures are fast-paced and entertaining, but it's the enduring presence of the Force that truly stirs our souls in *Star Wars*. One ad for the movie proclaims, "The Force is forever—for all generations." The great appeal of the Force is a clear indication that our souls themselves are stirring to remember their Source.

The teaching of the Force throughout the *Star Wars* movies is in fact one big lesson about the nature of God. The Force is a name that connotes the omnipresence and omnipotency of a God-power, whatever It may be called. Lucas, who conceived the series and directed the first movie, has discussed the spiritual aims of *Star Wars*. He wanted to create stories with moral lessons for children, and in a medium (film) with which modern children identify.[5]

In his book *Skywalking*, Lucas biographer Dale Pollock writes, "The message of *Star Wars* is religious: God isn't dead, he's there if you want him to be."[6]

What is the God of *Star Wars*? Very much a pantheistic one. Obi-Wan Kenobi, a former Jedi Knight (one trained in the use of the Force for good), tells Luke that the Force is "an energy field created by all living things. It surrounds us and penetrates us. It binds the galaxy together." It is the celestial substance and glue of all life.

The Force can be felt within, Obi-Wan says, and connecting with the Force requires letting go of the conscious self and acting on instinct and feelings. It's the principle of "Let go and let God." Obi-Wan cautions Luke

91

not to use his eyes, because they can be deceptive. In 2 Corinthians 5:7, Paul puts it this way: "We walk by faith, not by sight."

Obi-Wan trains Luke in the use of the Force, which can move minds and objects, and tells him, "You've taken your first step into a larger world." That world of the Force, or God, is always present, but humans must consciously desire to observe it to make it visible and viable to them.

"Remember, the Force will be with you always," Obi-Wan says.

This Force has a dark side, represented in the movie most convincingly by Darth Vader, once a Jedi knight and a pupil of Obi-Wan who "was seduced by the dark side of the Force." Vader still is quite adept at using the Force. Does this mean that the Force, or God, Itself can be what we term both evil and good? Yes and no. On a cosmic level, the Force simply is pure, perfect, and complete energy, the creative and ever-flowing and ever-expanding God-energy of which everything is made. On a human level, the Force can be used however we choose, and then labeled according to traditions and moral standards. This concept of God-energy is often illustrated with an analogy to electricity, which in itself is a power that is neither good nor bad, but one that can be used either beneficially or destructively. Suggesting the role of human free will, Obi-Wan states that the Force "partially controls your actions, but it also obeys your commands." The Force is explored further in the next *Star Wars* movies, and we're told what kinds of thoughts and emotions constitute being "seduced by the dark side."

The main characters in the movie can be seen to represent different responses of people toward God and faith in any kind of invisible force.

Han Solo is the materialistic disbeliever. "I've seen a lot of strange stuff," he says, "but I've never seen anything to make me believe there is one all-powerful force controlling everything. There's no mystical energy field controls my destiny. It's all a lot of simple tricks and nonsense."

The "kid," Luke Skywalker, at the outset represents youth who are more interested in being with friends and having experiences than in considering spiritual or moral issues, but who grow more serious when personally faced with life's more challenging issues.

Princess Leia is the traditional upholder and defender of the faith. She's the type who never doubts and is raised in duty to God and country, and does whatever is required to defend both.

Obi-Wan Kenobi is a person who has discovered or remembered his oneness with God, the Force, and lives with the peace and calmness of spiritual conviction. He is willing to sacrifice his physical life for the Force because he knows that life in the Force continues after what we call death in an even more powerful way. He suggests that the Force is actually quite limited within the physical body.

Darth Vader is the fallen believer who for some reason (never disclosed in the trilogy) turns, with a vengeance, away from God.

93

YE VIEW

1. How would you describe your own response to and belief in the Force?
2. Princess Leia says that Han Solo must choose his own path in life. What evidence is there that Han's outlook is changing?
3. What other religious themes and symbols do you find in *Star Wars*?

STAR WARS EPISODE V: THE EMPIRE STRIKES BACK

PREVIEW

The ancient and wise Jedi master Yoda trains Luke Skywalker; Han Solo and Princess Leia lead further resistance against Imperial troops; and Darth

Vader obsessively scans the heavens for Luke in this exciting sequel, fully titled *Star Wars Episode V: The Empire Strikes Back.* (1980, 128 minutes, PG, *)

META VIEW

"Feel the Force around you"

When the pupil is ready, the teacher will appear, the old saying goes. Luke Skywalker believes that he is ready to become a Jedi knight. Obi-Wan Kenobi tells Luke to go see Yoda, who was his own teacher. Yoda, the captivating 900-year-old, two-foot-tall, green, pointed-ear master (marvelously brought to life by Frank Oz), isn't so sure the pupil is ready, but he agrees to teach him.

Echoing Obi-Wan's advice, Yoda tells Luke, "A Jedi's strength flows from the Force, but beware of the dark side." *Star Wars* author George Lucas calls the stories timeless, and Yoda's advice to Luke about how to be one with the natural God-energy is surely for all of us:

- Know that the "dark side" is not stronger than the "good," and recognize the difference by being calm, at peace, and passive. A Jedi never uses the Force for attack, Yoda says.
- Have patience.
- Remain in the present moment.
- "Clear your mind of questions."
- Concentrate and control the mind. "You must feel the Force around you," Yoda says. "Through the Force, things you will see: other places, the future, the past, old friends long gone."
- Have faith. When Luke says that he is unable to accomplish a feat because he doesn't believe it can be done, Yoda replies, "*That* is why you failed."

- Maintain a can-do attitude and mind-set. When Luke says that he will try, Yoda says succinctly: "No, try not. Do, or do not. There is no try."

YE VIEW

1. What evidence is there that Luke is mastering the use of the Force?
2. Were you surprised by Darth Vader's revelation to Luke? Why or why not?
3. Discuss in what ways Jesus or the Buddha could be called a Jedi.

STAR WARS EPISODE VI: RETURN OF THE JEDI

PREVIEW

Han Solo's rescue from the gangster Jabba the Hutt, the teddy bear-like Ewoks' help in saving the day for the rebellion, and Luke Skywalker's decisive showdown with Darth Vader and the Emperor (Ian McDiarmid) are among the warp-speed events in the third film, fully titled *Star Wars Episode VI: Return of the Jedi.* (1983, 131 minutes, PG, *)

META VIEW

Compassion triumphs over hate

The mystical teacher Yoda again reminds Luke that "a Jedi's strength flows from the Force," but cautions him to beware of what makes up the "dark side"—anger, fear, and depression. In *The Empire Strikes Back,* Obi-Wan Kenobi also tells Luke: "Don't give in to hate. That leads to the dark side."

The hate and anger that well up inside him when fighting his true father, Darth Vader, as well as the Emperor, are exactly what Luke must face. On several occasions, Yoda makes it clear that Luke must confront Vader and his own feelings before he can truly become a Jedi—that is, Luke must be truly one with the Force within.

Time and again the Emperor of the Galactic Empire entices Luke to give in to the hate and anger he clearly has and come over to the "dark side." The Emperor keeps saying that it is Luke's destiny to do so. Yoda, however, in *The Empire Strikes Back*, tells Luke that the future is difficult to see, because "always emotions the future." The Emperor underestimates Luke's emotions and inner strength.

"I'll never turn to the dark side," Luke tells him. Luke also refuses to give up his feelings that there is good within Darth Vader. The Emperor has said that Luke's compassion for his father would be Luke's downfall, but Luke's compassion and Vader's fatherly compassion turn out to be the Emperor's downfall. As Han Solo and Princess Leia and gang are trying to deactivate the energy shield which surrounds the Empire's Death Star, Luke's faith and love are deactivating the dark energy shield which has imprisoned his father for so long. Luke says that his father has "only forgotten" the name of his "true Self."

The theme of sacrifice is a powerful one in *Star Wars*. Obi-Wan sacrifices for Luke and the Force, and Luke's father, moved by Luke's compassion, sacrifices for him. When Luke tells his dying father that he wants to save him, his father replies: "You already have, Luke. You were right. You were right about me." Compassion has led to redemption and triumph over hate and the "dark side" of the Force.

YE VIEW

1. Who appears to Luke during the final celebration? What is the significance of the appearances?

2. Discuss the theme of freedom in the *Star Wars* movies. What role does the value of individual freedom play in the series?
3. Obi-Wan Kenobi says, "Many of the truths we cling to depend greatly on our own point of view." Do you agree? Why or why not?

STAR WARS EPISODE I: THE PHANTOM MENACE

PREVIEW

Going back even a longer time ago in a galaxy still far away, this movie is a prequel to the original *Star Wars* trilogy. It's the first episode in Lucas' eventual six-part series, but is best viewed and discussed as the fourth film produced and released. Here Jedi knight Qui-Gon Jinn (Liam Neeson) and his apprentice Obi-Wan Kenobi (Ewan McGregor) meet the young Anakin Skywalker (Jake Lloyd), destined to grow up to be Darth Vader, while on a mission to save the planet Naboo from the clutches of the evil Trade Federation. (1999, 132 minutes, PG, *)

META VIEW

In the beginning was the Force

"In the beginning was the Word, and the Word was with God, and the Word was God." —John 1:1

In the Gospel According to Lucas (better known as the *Star Wars* movies), the Word has a name—the Force. In the beginning was the Force, and the Force is God.

"I put the Force into the movie to try to awaken a certain kind of spirituality in young people—more a belief in God than a belief in any particular religious system," Lucas said.[7]

The nature of the Force is more developed in the original *Star Wars* trilogy, but the Force is, of course, a towering concept in the first prequel. Writer-director Lucas teases viewers with information about the Force, as he does with details about Anakin's heredity and powers.

Qui-Gon is clearly attuned to and guided by the Force. Reminiscent of preachers who speak of "the living God," Qui-Gon refers to "the living Force." He tantalizingly mentions that there are some sort of microorganisms within human cells that allow people to hear the Force.

We can view the Jedi knights like Jesus in Christianity, as way showers who teach others how to use their inner Force; what they do, all can do with proper training and remembering.

Qui-Gon on several occasions advises about the importance of concentration in connecting to the Force. He tells Obi-Wan, "Keep your concentration here and now, where it belongs." Before the pod race, the movie's most exciting event and a galactic version of the famous chariot race in *Ben-Hur*, Qui-Gon counsels nine-year-old competitor Anakin: "Concentrate on the moment. Feel. Don't think. Use your instincts."

The Force, it can be deduced from Qui-Gon, is an instinctive, emotional power, beyond intellectual abilities; and where and how we place our feelings and our instincts create our world and our experiences. To Anakin, Qui-Gon says, "Your focus determines your reality."

Life has many phantom menaces. Sometimes they hit like a Dark Lord of the Sith. Other times they sneak up on us like a stealth droid. They may be cosmic concerns or character blemishes. They may be Jar Jar Binks-type annoyances or Jabba the Hutt-size headaches. Warding off our phantom menaces may take patience, diplomacy, or laser duels. However they come, our phantom menaces eventually only bow to the concentrated, focused Force within us.

Ye View

1. What signs are there that the Force is with Anakin Skywalker?
2. Yoda senses "much fear" in Anakin. Why might the boy be fearful?
3. Anakin is identified as the possible "chosen one" prophesied to bring balance to the Force. Discuss details of Anakin's early life and character that may be seen to parallel the life and character of Jesus Christ.

WHAT DREAMS MAY COME

Preview

Dr. Chris Nielsen (Robin Williams) goes to a gorgeous, heavenly place after he dies in an accident, but his tormented widow, Annie (Annabella Sciorra), who commits suicide, goes to a hellish place from which Chris is determined to rescue her. (1998, 113 minutes, PG-13)

Meta View

What creative artists we are!

You must read between the lines to catch the metaphysical meaning of many movies. Not so in *What Dreams May Come*, in which the metaphysical ideas jump off the screen and sit (or perhaps squirm) in your mind and heart. You'd expect such straightforward spirituality from a production company named Metafilmics and dedicated to enlightenment.

Neale Donald Walsch, author of the *Conversations With God* books, calls *What Dreams May Come,* based on the Richard Matheson novel, a "metaphysical treat" that presents better than any other movie "the truth that we are all writing our own script—both during this life and after our death."[8] Walsch is a writer, so not surprisingly, he uses a writing analogy to suggest humankind's creative capabilities.

In the movie, Annie is an artist and in the art business, and Chris shares her love of art. It is appropriate then that their depictions of heaven and hell involve artistic concepts. The truth, as Chris and Annie would state it, is that we are all painting our own canvasses, both here and in the so-called hereafter.

"We all paint our own surroundings, Chris," states Albert (Cuba Gooding, Jr.), an "other side" guide. "You're the painter now." To Chris, the art appreciator, heaven is glorious, brilliant colors and elaborate sets that resemble favorite paintings.

Other people who have "died" continue to create their own distinct worlds, based on their particular interests and perspectives, and the creations overlap into others' worlds. There's literally room enough for all creation. "Here is big enough for everybody to have their own private universe," Albert says.

In no unmistakable terms, the movie consistently asserts what Unity calls the law of mind action ("thoughts held in mind produce after their kind") and the belief that we create our lives through our thoughts.

Albert says to Chris: "Thought is real. Physical is the illusion. Ironic, huh?"

The movie's title is from *Hamlet*, Act III, Scene I: "For in that sleep of death what dreams may come, / When we have shuffled off this mortal coil, / Must give us pause."[9]

The nature of hell is explored with graphic allegorical scenes that would do Dante's *Inferno* justice. The scenes of hell are as disturbing in their depiction of human suffering as the scenes of heaven are breathtaking in their beauty and scope. However, the movie makes clear that the same creative principle holds true for hell as it does for heaven.

"The real hell is your life gone wrong," Albert states. Chris observes, "Good people end up in hell because they can't forgive themselves." The tremendous role that unforgiveness (of self and others) and guilt play in placing individuals in personal hells is explored with Annie, who blames herself for the deaths of her two children and her husband. However, it is unfortunate that an otherwise uplifting script should unnecessarily perpetuate a traditional view of suicide as the one "unforgivable sin." Sins are human creative efforts that fall short of the mark of oneness with our God perfection, and don't need to be forgiven but merely corrected by a change of perception and a realization of our unity with an all-loving God who always knows our soul perfection.

When watching this film, pay close attention to the correlation between what is said and thought in physical existence and what is experienced in nonphysical existence, and to the connection between objects in both realms. As Chris tells Annie, "What's true in our minds is true."

What dreams may come are determined by what words and thoughts have previously come. Or, to return to the painting analogy, our paintings (lives) are determined by the paints (thoughts) with which we paint. The movie leaves me with an exciting feeling of responsibility and anticipation to be a universe-class painter!

101

Ye View

1. What does the film have to say about God, death, the mind, the human body, and "soul mates"?
2. What are some comments, characters, and scenes in the movie that reflect the theory of reincarnation?
3. Think about your life and your dreams as an artwork in progress. Make a list of things you like in your painting right now. Make another list of things you would like in your painting.

WHY HAS BODHI-DHARMA LEFT FOR THE EAST?

PREVIEW

At a remote monastery in the mountains, a dying master of Zen Buddhism shares his wisdom with a young monk and an orphaned boy in this exquisite film from director-writer-cinematographer Bae Yong-kyun. (1989, Korean, 135 minutes, NR)

META VIEW

Savor the riddles of enlightenment

The movie is like a slowly opening flower filled with the nectars of Truth. The pace is deliberately slow, contemplative, and reflective, and the tone is gentle and mystical. Approach the film with a patient desire to understand more about the meaning of life, and discover that the meaning is within you.

The film's title is a Zen *koan*, which is a riddle or paradox for meditation. Zen Buddhists are to meditate upon a koan with the purpose of going beyond reason to an intuitive grasp of enlightenment. The koan directs the Truth seeker inward.

The elderly master tells the young monk, "The koan is a tool to cross the sea of passion and illusion so as to discover the roots of the true Self."

The master gives this instruction: "If you succeed in freeing the moon hidden inside you, it will light up the sky and the Earth, and its light will chase away all the shadows of the universe. If you understand that one thing, you will understand everything."

But then the master offers another koan: "Where the moon takes over in your heart, where does the master of my being go?"

Since the universe is deep in the shadows, the master says, "Light the fire in your heart to light the way."

The master is encouraging inner investigation, but beyond the personal sense of self. People have enough heart, he explains, "but it's full of the idea of self."

His own seeking has taken him past the self to a fuller understanding of life. "I am insubstantial in the universe," he says. "But in the universe, there is nothing which is not me."

About human life, the master asks, "Is it dream or reality?" He answers, "The dream gone signifies enlightenment."

The movie offers seeds for thought long after "The End" appears on the screen, for, as the master says, "There is no beginning and no end."

Ye View

1. What lessons do you think the boy learns from the injured bird?
2. Why did the young monk leave "the world"? Why does he return?
3. The young monk says, "What a beautiful world when you know how to love it!" How can you personally love the world more to see its beauty?

In the Same Spirit

Another savoring enlightenment:

Life on a String—A blind man, told as a boy to concentrate on music to restore his sight, shares his spiritual sight. (1991, Chinese-British-German, 110 minutes, NR)

THE WIZARD OF OZ

PREVIEW

A tornado whisks a Kansas farm girl, Dorothy (Judy Garland), to the magical land of Oz, where she and three unusual friends seek help from the mysterious wizard who rules in the Emerald City. (1939, 101 minutes, G, *)

META VIEW

We're really off to see the God within

Generally acknowledged as one of the greatest movies of all time (officially proclaimed so by the American Film Institute), *The Wizard of Oz* is also one of the best metaphysical movies ever made.

Generations have traveled down the Yellow Brick Road to Oz without realizing they were on the spiritual path. I started getting doses of metaphysics at the age of seven when I first saw this MGM classic in a real motion-picture theater. (The Wicked Witch's winged monkeys frightened me so much that I hid under my seat until they were off the screen.) I measured my formative years with annual showings of the movie on television. As a result, I can drive my family crazy by quoting the dialogue (replying to objections, as the Wizard, with, "My dear, you cut me to the quick!") and even crazier by singing the songs ("It really was no miracle; what happened was just this"). What is most interesting (or perhaps scary) is that I am far from alone in these abilities!

The story, based on L. Frank Baum's original American fairy tale *The Wonderful Wizard of Oz* but doctored somewhat for the screen, is a part of our culture. Who doesn't know about Dorothy and her little dog Toto (played by Toto) being carried off from black-and-white Kansas ("and Kansas she said is the name of the star") and deposited amidst the Munchkins in the merry ol' Technicolor land of Oz? You know what follows, right? Glinda, the Good Witch of the North (Billie Burke), tells the already homesick Dorothy that she can ask the wonderful Wizard of Oz (Frank Morgan) for help. Along the way, she is befriended by the Scarecrow (Ray Bolger), who wants to ask the Wizard for brains; the Tin Woodman (Jack Haley), who thinks he needs a heart; and the Cowardly Lion (Bert Lahr), who seems to be short on courage. And, of course, there's that pesky mean, green Wicked Witch of the West (Margaret Hamilton), upset because Dorothy's house landed on her sister and killed her, and because Dorothy is apparently encroaching on her power base.

But, oh, Auntie Em, in a metaphysical sense, where are the home, the brains, the heart, and the courage, really? They're all within, of course! Dorothy and company think that they're "off to see the Wizard," who is projected as a kind of God figure, but then they find out that the Wizard isn't what he is reported to be ("I'm a very good man; I'm just a very bad wizard"). The lesson here is that we are not to turn to a God outside us, in a physical heaven or an Emerald City, but within us. As Jesus said, "The kingdom of God is within you" (Lk. 17:21 NKJV). Unity cofounder Charles Fillmore wrote, "The supreme realization of man is his unity with God."[10]

The Wizard turns out to be a person with some metaphysical understanding of these concepts, however. He helps the Scarecrow, Tin Woodman, and Cowardly Lion realize that what they seek is within, and was always there. He tells the Scarecrow that "anybody can have a brain; that's a very mediocre commodity," and then awards him an honorary Th.D. (Doctor of Thinkology). He inducts the Cowardly Lion into the Legion of Courage for "meritorious conduct, extraordinary valor, and conspicuous bravery against wicked witches." He presents the Tin Man with a heart, and says, "And remember, my sentimental friend, that a heart is not judged by how much you love, but by how much you are loved by others."

Dorothy also learns that the kingdom is within her. Glinda, the Good Witch, who may be seen to represent the ever-loving, gentle Holy Spirit guiding Dorothy toward that "supreme realization," tells Dorothy that she has always had the power to go home. However, "She had to find it out for herself," Glinda says (that's the way it is with an individual's realization of God). Dorothy has only to click the heels of the ruby slippers together three times and repeat, "There's no place like home." The clicks and the repetition are merely focusing tools to aid Dorothy in using the Christ Power within to bring her home (symbolically, to God, to her good).

Dorothy expresses her knowledge that Truth is within with this famous declaration: "If I ever go looking for my heart's desire [God] again, I won't look any further than my own backyard, because if it isn't there [and it always is], I never really lost it to begin with."

Dorothy, the Scarecrow, the Tin Woodman, and the Cowardly Lion represent the different ways in which we *think* that we become separated from God, our good, our wholeness. In actuality, of course, we are *never* separated from God. "In him we live and move and have our being" (Acts 17:28). We all battle forces that seem to come from outside us—our Wicked Witches of the East and West—and others play into our projections (hailing "the Witch's Dorothy" and running for cover), but we all can learn the value of going within to find our God essence. The Holy Spirit is always there to guide us to the right paths and the man-made Wizards (even religions) that will serve to turn us inward to God.

The character of Dorothy also can stand for our inherent state of goodness and purity as God's whole and perfect children. From this simple, innocent state, Dorothy's troubles (the Wicked Witch) literally melt away in Oz. Significantly, earlier (on the farm) Dorothy wistfully sings about a place "where troubles melt like lemon drops."

The movie's dream ending—a Hollywood contrivance, not Baum's—perhaps may seem unnecessary, but from a metaphysical perspective, the ending does make a powerful statement about the value of myth and traditional tales, including many biblical stories: the truth of the events, whether or not they actually happened, is not as important as what the myths and stories represent within the human psyche and to the human spirit. The popularity of *The Wizard of Oz* is not only a testament to filmmaking at its finest but also to the enduring Truth the movie represents.

YE VIEW

1. What metaphysical element of *The Wizard of Oz* most appeals to you?
2. Discuss additional philosophical meanings of the story (what about Dorothy's melting the Wicked Witch?), or perhaps explore sociopolitical interpretations (how about those authority figures in Oz?).
3. Explain humankind's desire or longing to go "over the rainbow."

::: **FEATURE PRESENTATION**

The Tao of Popcorn

Within the heated kernel, moisture erupts
    and the rupture rapturously occurs.
The Treasure of Popcorn explodes to Life.
Heaven's ears popped in ancient Mexico, China, and India,
    in New Mexico 5,600 years ago, in Utah's pueblos.
For the Peruvian Indians, Popcorn was confection;
    to Native Americans, snacks offered to English colonists.
The Way of Movie Popcorn opened through Necessity,
    and it was Good and popular unto Plenty.
Depression-era families thrived on 5- or 10-cent bags,
    and Popcorn sellers boomed.
In Oklahoma, a down-but-not-out banker opened a Popcorn business
    near a movie theater, and there was Success.
Popcorn vendors were drawn to the crowds at movie theaters,
    and audiences ate up the attention.
Americans thrived on popcorn, not candy, during World War II,
    because sugar went overseas for the troops.
While Cagney grimaced, Fred and Ginger danced, and Monroe sizzled,
    movie audiences munched and crunched.
Having the Love of Popcorn, and perhaps an iced drink,
    one could sit Blissfully through double features.
And so it was, and so it is.
By reaching for one salty, buttery handful after another, one can know
    the whole world.
Without taking the eyes off the screen, one can taste the Essence of cinema.

Ted Neeley in *Jesus Christ Superstar,* Universal Pictures
Photo: The Museum of Modern Art Film Stills Archive

Chapter 3

Jesus Christ—Superstar

Whatever personal relationship one may have with Jesus and however one may interpret the Christ, one can hardly deny that the historical/spiritual Jesus Christ is a superstar. The influence of his teachings on world religious and philosophical thought has been enormous for two thousand years. It doesn't matter, as recent scholars have determined in The Jesus Seminar, that Jesus probably said only a fraction of what has filtered to us in translations. The ideas themselves, such as the Golden Rule and the Beatitudes, speak to the highest within us and call on us to express ourselves fully as children of God. The movies in "Jesus Christ—Superstar" follow Jesus' life and teachings as and of the Christ. Also included is *Dead Man Walking,* because the spirit of Jesus is an overwhelming presence in the movie.

BEN-HUR

PREVIEW

During the time of Jesus in Jerusalem, a wealthy Jew, Ben-Hur (Charlton Heston), refuses to betray his people and his religion to boyhood friend Messala (Stephen Boyd), now a powerful Roman tribune, with far-reaching and epic consequences, in this spectacular production of the "tale of the Christ" by General Lew Wallace. (1959, 212 minutes, NR)

META VIEW

The race goes on until we forgive

When Ben-Hur comes to the end of the exciting chariot race against his philosophical rival Messala, he thinks the race is over. He's in for an unpleasant surprise, however.

"It goes on. It goes on, Judah. The race is not over," Messala says, speaking pointedly and broadly.

The general race continues for the two men because it is predicated on revenge, and neither one has forgiven the other. The race can't end until forgiveness takes place. With forgiveness, a race of antagonism or hate screeches to a halt.

This "tale of the Christ" emphasizes the necessity of letting forgiveness into the heart to find peace. Forgiveness is of the Christ, for the Christ is the essence of God within each individual.

True forgiveness is seeing and honoring and loving only the Christ in another person. When one beholds God, one realizes that only the goodness of God exists, and therefore there can be, in actuality, no "wrong" to forgive. God does not know condemnation and therefore does not have a need to forgive.

Such an understanding of forgiveness is difficult for many to comprehend intellectually and, even for those who do, is difficult to practice. Most of us are like Judah Ben-Hur—we come to forgiveness slowly and gradually, and often painfully.

Judah swears revenge against Messala for wrongs to his family, and his life becomes focused on revenge. Judah even prays, "May God grant me vengeance."

It is Esther (Haya Harareet), the woman who loves him, who first introduces Judah to the concept of forgiveness. She has heard of Jesus' discussions of forgiveness.

"I have seen too much of what hate can do," Esther tells Judah. "But I have heard of a young rabbi who says that forgiveness is greater and love more powerful than hatred. I believe it."

Denying his own Christ nature, Judah initially refuses to listen to Esther's talk of forgiveness, although there are signs that he needs to. Challenging Messala in the chariot race, Judah realizes, does not bring him peace. He seems to sense an inner emptiness. "I am thirsty still," Judah says. Even Pontius Pilate advises Judah not to crucify himself on the "shadow of an old resentment."

After hearing Jesus for herself, Esther again speaks to Judah of forgiveness. "He (Jesus) said: 'Blessed are the merciful, for they shall obtain mercy. Blessed are the peacemakers, for they shall be called the children of God.'"

Judah declares that he still wants to wash the land clean with blood, but Esther replies that bloodletting leads to more blood. She adds, "The voice I heard today on the hill said to love your enemy, do good to those who despitefully use you."

She adds, "Hatred is turning you to stone."

Judah makes a long, arduous journey to forgiveness, one that even leads to the slave galleys, but it's a necessary journey, in some manner, for each individual.

In her book *A Return to Love*, Marianne Williamson says, "The practice of forgiveness is our most important contribution to the healing of the world."

113

She acknowledges, however, the difficulties sometimes involved in forgiving. "Few of us always succeed, yet making the effort is our most noble calling. It is the world's only real chance to begin again. A radical forgiveness is a complete letting go of the past, in any personal relationship, as well as in any collective drama."[1]

Judah Ben-Hur's story also illustrates the typical progression of responses that people have to their Christ presence or true God nature. At first, Judah has no knowledge or memory of his real nature. Then (when Jesus gives him water) he glimpses something of the Christ, but he doesn't understand it. Next, he denies that any knowledge of the Christ can be of assistance in his worldly troubles. Finally, he remembers (when he returns the favor to Jesus) and accepts the Truth of the Christ for him and everyone.

YE VIEW

1. List the occasions when Jesus is seen in the movie. Why do you think his face is never viewed?
2. What lessons do Judah's mother and sister learn as a result of turning to Jesus for help?
3. If you or anyone you know is in a revenge race right now, think about the forgiveness necessary to end the race.

IN THE SAME SPIRIT

An earlier view of the story:

Ben-Hur: A Tale of the Christ—There's an eerie, fascinating quality to this silent-screen treatment of Wallace's story, because it has the look and feel of vintage newsreels of actual events and people. The restored print includes black-and-white film, original tinted film, and two-strip Technicolor sequences. The printed dialogue adds to the old newsreel flavor. After Jesus first touches Judah (Ramon Novarro), on-screen are the words, "I am strengthened, O Lord, and

I will live—live to fight for the King when he comes!" The movie was a major spectacle of its day, and holds up superbly, including the sea battle and the chariot race. (1927, 148 minutes, NR)

DEAD MAN WALKING

PREVIEW

When she becomes spiritual advisor to death-row inmate Matthew Poncelet (Sean Penn), Sister Helen Prejean (Susan Sarandon) learns the soul-wrenching pain that crime and capital punishment bring to criminals, victims, and their families in this true story. (1995, 122 minutes, R)

META VIEW

Jesus leads the way

The senselessness and horror of the cold-blooded murder of a young couple, the heartbreaking grief of their parents, and the loving courage of a nun who selflessly helps the poor and needy are powerfully shown in this film.

Director Tim Robbins also fairly presents sympathetic scenes that suggest the arguments for and against capital punishment. Some people call for "an eye for an eye." An attorney pleads on behalf of the murdered couple's parents for "simple justice for their unbearable loss." Contrastingly, Sister Helen doesn't condone Matthew's actions, but offers the classic argument against the death penalty: "I just don't see the sense in killing people to say that killing people is wrong."

The movie has been widely and deservedly praised for all of the above factors, but the real star of the show and the shining light or driving force behind Sister Helen is Jesus.

The term *dead man walking* refers to a person on the way to the execution room. With Sister Helen's involvement, Jesus is there every step of the way. He is never seen in the movie, but his name is invoked often and his presence is felt.

"I'm just trying to follow the example of Jesus, who said that every person is worth more than their worst act," Sister Helen tells the murdered girl's parents, who see their daughter's killer as an animal and as "God's mistake" who deserves to be killed.

Even the prison chaplain communicates an "eye for an eye" philosophy and asks Sister Helen if she is familiar with the Old Testament verses that denounce killing and advocate retaliation.

"Yes, Father," Sister Helen replies. "Are you familiar with the New Testament, where Jesus talks about grace and reconciliation?"

She accepts the chaplain's charge to help Matthew find redemption and to offer him the sacraments of the church before he dies. To this end, Sister Helen encourages Matthew to read the Bible, especially passages in which Jesus is seen facing death. Sister Helen and Matthew have the following insightful exchange:

Matthew: I think me and Jesus had a different way of dealing with things. He's one of them 'turn the other cheek' guys.

Helen: It takes a lot of strength to turn the other cheek. You say you like rebels. What do you think Jesus was?

Matthew: A rebel? He wasn't no rebel.

Helen: Sure he was. He was a dangerous man.

Matthew: What was so dangerous about "love your brother"?

Helen: Because his love changed things. His love changed things. All those people nobody cared about—the prostitutes, the beggars, the poor—finally had somebody who respected them, loved them, made them realize their own worth.

Jesus gave these people dignity, she says. Her goal is to help Matthew die with dignity, and to do that he has to own up to his part in the deaths.

"Matt, redemption isn't some kind of free admission ticket that you get because Jesus paid the price," Sister Helen tells him. "You've got to participate in your own redemption. You've got some work to do. I think maybe you should look at The Gospel of John, Chapter 8, where Jesus said, 'Ye shall know the truth and the truth shall make you free.'"

When Matthew finally tells Sister Helen the truth, she says, "You are a son of God."

"Nobody ever called me a son of God before," Matthew says. How much different Matthew's life and the lives of others would have been and how much misery could have been prevented if Matthew had grown up truly knowing that he and everyone else are children of God! How much different the world would be if everyone possessed such a realization—especially from an early age!

Before the execution, Sister Helen sings a hymn with words referring to Jesus, "Be not afraid. I go before you always. Come, follow me, and I will give you rest."

Jesus' forgiving, Truth-filled love is at the execution when Matthew asks forgiveness of and expresses remorse to the parents of his victims. His presence and the spirit of the Christ are called upon again at the funeral.

This movie bids viewers to see that the Way Shower, though not physically visible, and his teachings, the effects of which can be clearly visible, are very much with us, and are still setting people free.

YE VIEW

1. What actions, words, and events at the time of the execution suggest that Matthew's redemption has been accomplished?
2. What is the significance of the final scene of the movie?
3. Discuss capital punishment in light of Jesus' teachings about love and forgiveness.

THE GREATEST STORY EVER TOLD

PREVIEW

The life of Jesus Christ, from birth to resurrection, receives a full-scale Hollywood telling in this epic based on biblical accounts and starring Max von Sydow. (1965, 195 minutes, NR)

META VIEW

The Truth is mightier than the movie

Fortunately, the greatest story ever told can survive the somberness of 1960s biblical filmmaking, as well as considerable overacting and underacting by a multitude of stars; an inane script, except when derived from actual Scripture (even with Carl Sandburg's creative assistance); and a running time of more than three hours.

As a friend quipped after seeing the film in original release, "It's the *longest* story ever told!"

But in true Christian tradition, producer-director George Stevens can be forgiven the excesses when trying to do justice to a story of such immense importance to humankind. After all, with a story that people take so personally, it would be difficult to please everyone. I, for example, would have preferred a better actor, with more charisma, to play Jesus, and would have beheaded Charlton Heston's laughable portrayal of John the Baptist the second time he yelled "Repent." Still, if you're looking for a grand, old-fashioned (though ponderous) panorama of the story of Jesus' life, this is it.

While the primary focus of this book is not to critique artistic virtues, a film's artistry does have a bearing on the impact of its content. There's a lesson here, though: What we have with this movie is actually a testimonial to the truth that simple spiritual Truth can shine through even the showiest of human packaging.

The movie is at its greatest and is most metaphysically relevant to today's viewers when presenting the actual gospel words of Jesus concerning the natures of God and humankind.

Of course, these "actual" words may not be so actual, according to recent scholars. The evangelists were storytellers, drawing from oral traditions, some 40 to 75 years after Jesus' death, and they, like *all* storytellers, embellished their stories for specific purposes. We must remember that the real importance of our traditional and treasured stories and sayings lies in their spiritual intentions and universal meanings, and what they communicate about our basic identity and yearnings.

While the Romans were getting worked up about Jesus' supposedly leading people to revolution against their empire, Jesus was really trying to incite a revolution in spiritual perspective and thinking within individual hearts and minds. Jesus consistently went against the norm in society and religion with sayings such as these found in the movie:

- "The Lord our God is one God. And thou shalt love the Lord thy God with all thy heart and all thy soul, and with all thy mind and with all thy strength. And the second—thou shalt love thy neighbor as thyself."
- "What does it profit a man to gain the whole world and lose his soul?"
- "You cannot serve both God and money."
- "I tell them to do unto others as they would have others do unto them."
- "Our God is a god of salvation, not of revenge."
- "You are the light of the world. And let your light so shine before men that they may see your good works and glorify your Father, which is in heaven."
- "I am the resurrection and the life."
- "Faith, hope, and love abide . . . but the greatest of these is love."

• "Make it your first care to love one another and to find the kingdom of God, and all things shall be yours, without the asking."

These revolutionary instructions and insights were and are designed to help people realize their eternal oneness with a God of love and with each other. Pearls of wisdom don't get any better than these.

Jesus also emphasizes the value of faith, which is truly knowing God's presence and power, in leading to a realization and manifestation of wholeness as a perfect child of God. Jesus tells a crippled man after his healing: "It is your faith that has made you well. There are many more who can, but will not."

YE VIEW

1. Discuss your own emotional reaction to the character of Jesus in the movie.
2. "The Father is in me; I in the Father," Jesus says. What are some specific actions and words of Jesus in the film that support this statement?
3. Why do you think Jesus' life is called "the greatest story ever told"?

IN THE SAME SPIRIT

The "greatest story" more modestly told:

The Gospel According to St. Matthew—The film is as straightforward as its name. (1966, Italian-French, 135 minutes, NR)

The Gospel Road—Country music stars Johnny Cash and June Carter tour the Holy Land to trace Jesus' life. (1973, 83 minutes, G)

Jesus—The Genesis Project filmed this story of Jesus in Israel. (1979, 117 minutes, G)

INTOLERANCE

PREVIEW

D. W. Griffith's silent movie epic entwines four different stories showing "how hatred and intolerance, through all the ages, have battled against love and charity." (1916, 123 minutes, NR)

META VIEW

Jesus is the antidote

Of the four melodramatic but enthralling stories in *Intolerance*, the life of Jesus Christ is given the least amount of film time. Viewers see much more of the mayhem and intrigue during the fall of Babylon in 539 B.C., the St. Bartholomew's Day Massacre of the Huguenots in France in the 1500s, and an early 1900s crime story.

Yet the example of Jesus and his teachings anchors this early American masterpiece, subtitled *Love's Struggle Throughout the Ages,* and gives it an enduring strength. Jesus is treated as the ideal, the antidote to intolerance, as it were. He is presented as "the Man of Men, the greatest enemy of intolerance."

All of the stories depict characters with unsavory, selfish, and unloving attributes (even in the story about Jesus, where the Pharisees are called hypocrites who pray, "O Lord, I thank thee that I am better than other men"). Returning to the story of Jesus and his ministry provides an historical perspective of humankind's intolerance; it also offers some semblance of hope in humanity, and gives a standard that everyone, in every age, can strive to achieve.

The tolerance of Jesus toward people such as the adulterous woman whom society would scorn ("He that is without sin among you, let him cast a stone at her") and his love for all serve as moral ideals for the other stories. Of

121

course, people certainly were not always tolerant toward Jesus, as the movie clearly shows with his sentencing and crucifixion.

That God's divine order is somehow going on, even in an intolerant world, is suggested by the recurring image (seen between story segments) of "the cradle endlessly rocking." The cradle and the mother (Lillian Gish) are bathed in light, symbolic of their spiritual natures. The scene exemplifies the unity within the human experience: "Today as yesterday, endlessly rocking, ever bringing the same human passions, the same joys and sorrows."

YE VIEW

1. What specific kinds of intolerance are shown in the movie? Other than Jesus, what characters, if any, might be considered loving and tolerant?
2. Does the climax seem optimistic or pessimistic to you? Why?
3. Discuss whether or not, in your opinion, humankind has more or less tolerance now than in the times of the four movie stories.

IN THE SAME SPIRIT

Further intolerance:

The Sign of the Cross—Early Christians struggle against religious intolerance in Rome in this Cecil B. DeMille film. (1932, 118 minutes, NR)

JESUS CHRIST SUPERSTAR

PREVIEW

The hit Broadway rock opera about the last week in Jesus' life, seen from the perspective of Judas, makes a super transition to the screen in this fast-paced, high-energy production. (1973, 103 minutes, G)

META VIEW

Judas sings the blues

When you speak a prayer, the adage goes, you're praying once. When you sing a prayer, you're praying twice. And when you sing and dance a prayer, you're praying three times!

The exuberant singing and dancing ensemble of *Jesus Christ Superstar*, then, is praying to the max. What a joyful, soulful noise to the Lord they are making with the engaging, insightful Tim Rice-Andrew Lloyd Webber score. To borrow an apropos line from another Broadway hit, Fats Waller's *Ain't Misbehavin'*: "The joint is jumpin'!"

And Judas (Carl Anderson) isn't happy about it. Judas gets second billing in the show because it's really the story of his relationship with Jesus (Ted Neeley). Judas, a close friend of Jesus' who has been his "right hand man all along," is upset. While he admires and loves Jesus, Judas wants Jesus to lead a revolution to establish a new earthly kingdom; he doesn't like Jesus' growing popularity as the Messiah. "You've started to believe the things they say of you," Judas sings. "Your followers are blind—too much heaven on their minds." Judas also does not approve of Jesus' association with Mary Magdalene (Yvonne Elliman), who sings the show's most memorable song, "I Don't Know How to Love Him."

After betraying him, Judas says to Jesus, "Our ideals die around us. . . . Every time I look at you I don't understand why you let the things you did get so out of hand."

Judas, like Jesus, has a sense that he is merely playing out his role in a predetermined drama, but he is not comforted—and neither is Jesus—by the idea. Free will does seem to have a place in the drama, though; otherwise, neither Jesus nor Judas would anguish so over what he should do. Their challenge—and ours—is always to bring the human will into alignment with God's will. "God, Thy will is hard, but You hold every card,"

Jesus finally concludes, and chooses to do God's will.

Historically and symbolically, both Jesus and Judas are necessary for the complete story. Jesus is humankind coming to accept the Christ idea of God within, and Judas is humankind attached to the physical and material. A part of the human mind does not want to let go of the material and denies the spiritual (the Christ) so that it can continue the false belief in separation from God. That belief, being false and thus not of God, must destroy itself (Judas' hanging).

As do other films about Jesus' final days on Earth, *Jesus Christ Superstar* makes it clear that being a "superstar" most probably was not easy on Jesus. A depressed Jesus sings to God: "I've tried for three years—seems like thirty." In the garden of Gethsemane, he states: "I'm not as sure as when we started. Then I was inspired; now I'm sad and tired." To the human, such feelings are inherent, but the Christ overpowers them.

A strong appeal of the movie is its depiction of Jesus as more than a tormented soul with a mission. The scenes of him smiling, laughing, and genuinely enjoying being with his followers are refreshing. Anyone who says he has come so that people may "have life, and have it abundantly" (Jn. 10:10) surely must have smiled at times! Surely we should find joy in our spiritual life.

Neeley's Jesus has a magnetic attraction, and people are understandably drawn to him to hear such words as these: "Sing out for yourselves, for you are blessed. There is not one of you who cannot win the kingdom—the slow, the suffering, the quick, the dead. . . . Hosanna!"

Director Norman Jewison shot the film on location in Israel with an easy but effective set that consists of the desert, ruins, and scaffolding. The simplicity accents the universality and timelessness of the story.

Ye View

1. Do you have sympathy for Judas in this film? Why or why not?
2. Compare and contrast the characterizations of Judas in *Jesus*

Christ Superstar and in either *The Last Temptation of Christ* or *The Greatest Story Ever Told.*

3. What do you think is the purpose of blending different historical time periods in the movie? What are some examples of time overlaps?

IN THE SAME SPIRIT

Another rock 'n' roll production from the stage:
   Godspell—The modern Big Apple, New York City, is the setting for this rollicking view of Jesus' life. (1973, 103 minutes, G)

KING OF KINGS

125

⊛

PREVIEW

With Orson Welles narrating, director Nicholas Ray's lavish production details both the ministry of Jesus (Jeffrey Hunter) and the political-religious intrigues that led to his crucifixion. (1961, 168 minutes, NR)

META VIEW

What is the kingdom? Who is the king?

The reaction to Jesus' teaching about the kingdom of God, at the time and throughout the centuries, reminds me of the joke about the parent who keeps saying "No" to a child, but the child doesn't seem to grasp the meaning.

Finally, the exasperated parent asks, "What is there about 'No' that you don't understand?"

How could Jesus be any clearer? When asked about God's kingdom, he says, "The kingdom of God is within you."

The people who heard Jesus preach about the kingdom of God had trouble with the concept because it was so different and because they were expecting Jesus to establish an earthly kingdom to liberate them from Roman persecution and limitations.

Welles notes in narration: "The disciples, like the multitudes, were troubled by the Sermon on the Mount. They had come seeking earthquakes and whirlwinds, the word of Jesus to smite the heavens and drop fiery swords in their upraised hands, drown Caesar's chariots in the sea."

Many Christians still expect much the same with the second coming of Jesus. The image is of a liberating Jesus descending from the skies to found a physical kingdom (or a strong semblance thereof), either in the heavens or on Earth, that will supplant all earthly kingdoms.

In stating that the "kingdom of God is within you," however, Jesus defines God's kingdom, or heaven, as a realm of consciousness in each person. His purpose is to help people realize their own natural connection with the kingdom of God.

What is there about "the kingdom of God is within you" that people don't understand?

As long as people seek the kingdom anywhere other than within, to the depths of their beings as God's whole and perfect children, they will feel imprisoned.

While asking a guard about visiting John the Baptist, Jesus says, "I come to free him within his cell."

The guard snickers at the notion and asks how he can do that.

Jesus responds, "You are free to come and go as you please, and yet you are still prisoner, because you place no faith in anything but your sword."

The sword symbolizes earthly kingdoms, which by their nature are limiting and divisive. Jesus says, "If a kingdom is divided against itself, the kingdom cannot stand." The only kingdom that cannot be divided against itself in some way is the consciousness of pure energy which is God.

The movie reflects the Romans' confusion over Jesus' teaching about the kingdom and its nature. When Pilate and Herod are told that Jesus preaches peace, love, and the brotherhood of man, Herod says, "Is that all?" Herod's vision is so squarely on the earthly kingdom that he cannot see the real kingdom within himself and everyone else.

As far as kingdoms go, Jesus asks, "What does a man profit if he shall gain the whole world and lose his own soul?"

Living in the kingdom of God requires calling forth an attitude or a consciousness from within, Jesus says, to love God and all our neighbors. "Do that and you shall live eternally," he says.

A camel driver asks how he can love his neighbor when he doesn't *have* neighbors. A neighbor, Jesus answers, is "he to whom you show mercy and compassion, whether you know him or not."

Who is the king of the kingdom to which Jesus refers? The title and subject of the movie suggest that it is Jesus, but Jesus says his kingdom is "the kingdom of God" and also says, "Blessed are you, O Lord our God, King of the universe." Jesus never suggests his own deification but rather directs all attention to God and to the God within.

Like *The Greatest Story Ever Told*, also from the '60s, *King of Kings* sags today from a heavy tone, but the messages of Jesus soar above the weightiness.

YE VIEW

1. Discuss the portrayal of Jesus in *King of Kings*. Do you think the many close-ups of Jesus' eyes are effective? Why or why not?
2. Discuss Jesus' statement, "You will be judged by the standards you yourself shall apply." What responsibility does this idea place on the individual?

3. How does your own understanding of "the kingdom of God is within" influence your approach to life?

IN THE SAME SPIRIT

For an earlier version of the story:

The King of Kings—Thanks to director Cecil B. DeMille, the message loses nothing in silent translation. (1927, 115 minutes, NR)

THE LAST TEMPTATION OF CHRIST

PREVIEW

The Passion of Jesus—from early stirrings to ministry to his death on the cross, with a heavy emphasis on Jesus' human torment, struggles, and possible temptations—is magnificently filmed by director Martin Scorsese from the Nikos Kazantzakis novel and powerfully acted by a cast headed by Willem Dafoe. (1988, 164 minutes, R)

META VIEW

A controversial life spurs a controversial film

The video-store owner in conservative Small Town America was obviously uncomfortable with my question: "Do you have *The Last Temptation of Christ?*"

"We're not supposed to have it," she replied.

"Well, do you?" I persisted, with a teasing smile.

We were alone in the store, but she looked around as if agents of the devil or the government might be lurking.

Controversy had been swirling around the movie *The Last Temptation of Christ* for some months, and fundamentalist Christians were leading protests and efforts to ban one of the most notorious movies of the 1980s. No "good Christian" was supposed to see it. Preachers railed against it. Of course, they often hadn't seen it, but that didn't stop them.

The store owner and I had talked off and on during the last year. She knew I could be trusted. She quietly reached under the counter and brought out a movie in a plain brown wrapper.

"Here," she said, not daring to verbalize what she was handing me. She wouldn't write a ticket—not wanting to risk a paper trail. I thanked her, paid her on the sly, and walked out with *The Last Temptation of Christ*! I had been eagerly awaiting its video release.

To think that this is the only movie I have ever rented in a plain brown wrapper—and that it was about the life of Jesus!

When I watched it, I said, "What's the fuss?"

Oh, sure, in the movie Jesus is tormented because he sometimes doesn't know what he's supposed to do, and when he thinks that he *does* know what God wants him to do, he doesn't want to do it. He has doubts. He's afraid. He's penitent and seeks forgiveness. At times he wants an ordinary life with a wife and children. He even lusts after women. Well, don't all Christian denominations admit that Jesus was at least partly human, that he was a man, and that he experienced earthly life to better understand and transcend the human plight?

More than any other movie about the life of Jesus, this one depicts Jesus' struggles (and Everyman's struggles) with the human. The film makes clear its intent at the beginning with a quotation from Kazantzakis' novel about "the dual substance of Christ—the yearning, so human, so superhuman, of man to attain God" and the "merciless battle between the spirit and the flesh." Then there is a disclaimer: "This film is not based upon The Gospels but upon this fictional exploration of the eternal spiritual conflict."

After the third or fourth viewing, I have a great respect for what Scorsese achieves in *The Last Temptation of Christ.* With sets, music, lighting, costumes, camera angles, and editing, Scorsese presents an absolutely riveting picture of Jesus. We see—no, we truly *feel,* in an exciting way—the natural manner in which the compassionate Jesus most probably interacted with people. Examples include Jesus' stunned, heartsick reaction to the crowd's treatment of Mary Magdalene (Barbara Hershey), and his obvious joy when he first answers God's call to speak to people and finds himself telling parables about the kingdom of heaven. Jesus' genuine concern and sorrow for the human condition are heart-wrenching. "I feel pity for everything," he says.

The film enriches many other familiar stories about Jesus such as his gathering of the disciples, his meeting with John the Baptist, his meditation in the desert, his raising of Lazarus, his overturning of the money changers' stands in the temple, his arrival in Jerusalem, his appearance at the Last Supper, his activities in the garden of Gethsemane, his relationship with Judas (Harvey Keitel), and his crucifixion.

Throughout it all, the human element, "the battle between the spirit and the flesh," rages within and about Jesus. He freely admits his fears and his temptations. The "last temptation" to which the title refers occupies about the last thirty minutes of the movie, and is a logical progression in Jesus' internal struggle. From the standpoint of Jesus as a man, it seems perfectly natural that, at the moment of death, he would envision an escape—an escape that consists of a happy life with a wife (and, yes—sex) and children. From the standpoint of man's Christ nature, it also seems perfectly natural that he would reject that escape. Thus, this controversial "last temptation" actually takes Jesus to the traditional conclusion.

The whole story of Jesus that has come down to us through the centuries and many translations appeals to various people in different ways, and people derive from it what they want depending on their own states of consciousness. If, for example, people think that they need their own "sins" absolved by an outside agent, then they take to heart the aspects of the Jesus Christ story in which a tormented figure is crucified by his loving Father for the sins of the world.

Others, especially those in such metaphysical Christian movements as Unity and Religious Science, look at the Jesus Christ story and find an elder brother who points the way to the kingdom of heaven within each individual and to an understanding of God as infinite love. This view, too, is well represented in *The Last Temptation of Christ*.

Before beginning his ministry, a conflicted, agonizing Jesus confides: "Lucifer is inside me. He says to me, 'You're not the son of King David. You're not a man. You're the son of man, and more, the son of God, and more than that, God.'"

Jesus' confusion and fears that the declarations may be coming from his base-ego self are understandable, because this is a revolutionary idea dawning on humankind, an evolving unfoldment of God and humankind's relationship to God. Jesus represents humanity becoming consciously aware of its Christ nature, the essence of God within each person. Jesus emphasized that the "kingdom of God is within you" and reminded people that "you are gods." To some people, this awareness is unsettling, and they shun the idea. But as noted metaphysical writer Eric Butterworth says, Jesus' true mission was to help us realize the divinity of humankind, our oneness with God, and all the possibilities that implies.

In his book *Discover the Power Within You*, Butterworth writes, "We must see Jesus as the great discoverer of the Divinity of Man, the pioneer and way-shower in the great world of the within. We must carefully study and then emphatically reject our historical tendency to worship Jesus. When He becomes the object of our worship, He ceases to be the way-shower for our own self-realization and self-unfoldment."[2]

From this perspective, the movie is mistitled: it should be *The Last Temp-*

131
✳

tation of Jesus. The man Jesus *can* be tempted; the Christ, the "only begotten Son" of God, cannot be tempted. As some teachers are fond of pointing out, Christ is not Jesus' last name. The words *Christ* and *Messiah* mean "anointed" and are titles in recognition of Jesus' awakening to his God Presence and identity.

In *The Last Temptation of Christ,* we hear Jesus uttering these words of guidance and wisdom:

- "Everything is a part of God."
- "Death isn't a door that closes. It opens. It opens and you go through it."
- "Love one another."
- "You'll all be blessed, because heaven is yours."
- "I want freedom for the soul. The foundation is the soul."
- "I'm a heart, and I love, and that's all I can do. We're all brothers."
- "God is inside of us."
- "God's world is big enough for everybody."
- "The world of God is here now."
- "I am the end of the old law and the beginning of the new one. When I say 'I' . . . I'm saying 'God.'"
- "God's an immortal spirit who belongs to everybody, to the whole world."

There is indeed much to tempt the spiritual seeker in *The Last Temptation of Christ.*

YE VIEW

1. Discuss what you like and dislike about the interpretation of Jesus and his life in this film.
2. Were you surprised by the "last temptation"? Why or why not?
3. During the "last temptation," Paul tells Jesus, "I don't care whether you're Jesus or not. The resurrected Jesus will save the world, and that's what matters." Explain why you agree or

disagree with this statement. Is it important whether or not the details of the Jesus Christ story are true? Explain.

LIFE OF BRIAN

PREVIEW

A bumbling peasant named Brian (Graham Chapman), born away in a manger in long-ago Judea about the same place and time as Jesus, is mistaken for the Messiah—with hilarious results—in Monty Python's wacky gospel. (1979, British, 93 minutes, R)

META VIEW

133

Look for the messages in this madness

Life of Brian is more than a search for the hysterical Jesus; it presents some gospel truths along the way. A few words of warning, though: The movie is not for the biblically squeamish or straightlaced. The famed British comedy troupe puts the Jews and Romans of the time under its severe microscope of humor, and the views are most unflattering (a favorite is the speech-challenged Pilate). The MP guys also poke considerable fun at traditional stories and views of Jesus. If you're not into Monty Python's distinctive brand of humor, however, you'll probably find ample reason to be offended. If you like the Monty Python style, you'll love the irreverent social and human commentary as Brian's life is chronicled from birth to— yes—crucifixion.

In telling the story of Brian's life, which parallels and parodies Jesus' in certain key respects, Monty Python gives some fascinating possible insights into Jesus' ministry and following and the development of early Christianity.

The grown-up Brian first comes into view while attending what we would call the Sermon on the Mount in Judea at a time designated as "A.D. 33, Saturday afternoon, about tea time." Brian, his mother, and others are quarreling among themselves at the back of the crowd. Meanwhile, Jesus is talking. He is heard and viewed briefly (for the only time in the movie). The people farthest away from Jesus have trouble hearing. What is Jesus saying? The following exchange occurs:

"I think it was 'Blessed are the cheese makers.'"

"What's so special about the cheese makers?"

"Well, obviously it's not meant to be taken literally. It refers to any manufacturer of dairy products."

The scene is rich satire that shows us how easy it is to mishear and misinterpret information in a crowd. One wonders how holy scriptures have been influenced by just such honest human mistakes.

Through strange circumstances—which are all Brian knows, including a ride with aliens in a UFO—Brian begins speaking to the multitudes, who mistake him for a spiritual leader. Calling him "Master," Brian's followers soon divide into two factions—one cherishing his discarded gourd, and the other revering his lost sandal. Religions have been started over as much.

Friend Judith explains the phenomenon to Brian's amazed mother: "Your son is a born leader. Those people out there are following him because they believe in him, Mrs. Cohen. They believe he can give them hope—hope of a new life, a new world, a better future."

The certainly not-so-holy mother tells the crowd, "He's not the Messiah; he's a very naughty boy."

Brian himself attempts to set the record straight:

"Look, you've got it all wrong. You don't need to follow me. You don't *need* to follow anybody. You've got to think for yourself. You're all individuals. You're all different. You've all got to work it out for yourself. . . . That's the point—don't let anyone tell you what to do."

Brian's words very well could be those of Jesus. There is no indication that Jesus ever set out to form a religion. He didn't want people to follow him personally, the man Jesus, but to use their own minds and hearts to follow the Christ Presence within.

Leave it to comedy to laugh us into facing a mighty spiritual Truth: The power and peace we seek are within; the inner Christ in each of us is "the light of the world."

YE VIEW

1. What personality traits do you think Brian might share with Jesus? Is Brian, for example, patient and gentle?
2. Do you think the ending of the movie and the song "Bright Side of Life" are effective? Why or why not?
3. Consider Judith's explanation of Brian's popularity. Does it still accurately reflect people's longing? Discuss.

IN THE SAME SPIRIT

More religious and social conventions humorously exposed:
Jesus of Montreal—A controversial staging of the Passion play lets director-writer Denys Arcand explore timeless and contemporary themes. (1989, Canadian-French, 119 minutes, R)

THE ROBE

PREVIEW

Marcellus Gallio (Richard Burton), a Roman tribune in command of Jesus' crucifixion, doesn't think much of the prize when he wins Jesus' robe, but the garment and the message of its wearer transform his life in this epic treatment of the Lloyd C. Douglas novel. (1953, 135 minutes, NR)

135

META VIEW

Good news travels fast

Emotionally charged glimpses of how Christianity spread in the Roman Empire make *The Robe* a mighty testament to Jesus' teachings.

First, the power and presence of Jesus are felt through the eyes of Demetrius (Victor Mature). The slave stands transfixed as Jesus rides into Jerusalem on the same day he and Marcellus do. Demetrius knows that Jesus looked into his eyes. "I think he wants me to follow him," he says.

Then there is Judas's appreciation of Jesus, despite the betrayal, which he says happened in part because men "can dream of truth but cannot live with it."

Jesus' own words from the cross convey his compassion: "Father, forgive them, for they know not what they do."

The Roman Emperor Tiberius is afraid of the new Christian movement because it represents "man's desire to be free."

People in Galilee who knew Jesus talk and sing about his message of love for God and all people, and live his principles of sharing and caring.

The effect of Jesus on Marcellus and the tribune's growing awareness of that effect dramatically exemplify the strength of the young Christian movement. Marcellus at first doesn't give any thought to Jesus or to his crucifixion, although he is bothered by literally having Jesus' blood on his hands. Then it becomes obvious, through his reaction to the robe, that Marcellus is also bothered in a psychological sense.

Demetrius helps the tormented Marcellus realize that he has not been bewitched by the robe. "It's your own conscience, your own decent shame. Even when you crucified him, you felt it. The spell isn't in this robe. It's in you, your heart, and your mind."

Marcellus enlists with body and soul in the work of spreading the gospel. "I offer him my sword, my fortune, and my life," he says. Marcellus tells his beloved Diana (Jean Simmons) that Jesus' message "changed my life. In time it will change the world."

YE VIEW

1. Discuss Diana's observation that Jesus' life is "a beautiful story, but it isn't true. Justice and charity—men will never accept such a philosophy. The world isn't like that. It never *has* been, and it never *will* be."
2. What is the mood of the final scene of the movie? How would you describe the faces of Marcellus and Diana?
3. Imagine what would happen if Jesus' robe were discovered today.

IN THE SAME SPIRIT

More adventures of the former slave:

Demetrius and the Gladiators—Demetrius (Victor Mature) is still going strong, and now Emperor Caligula (Jay Robinson) wants Jesus' robe. (1954, 101 minutes, NR)

::: **FEATURE PRESENTATION**

The Twelve Powers in <u>Fantasia</u>

Trip the light *Fantasia,* Walt Disney's 1940 two-hour masterpiece of music and animation, and visually experience the Twelve Powers of man. These twelve faculties, enumerated by Unity's Charles Fillmore, correspond to spiritual power centers in the human body and to attributes of each of Jesus' disciples.

By exercising one of these powers, imagination, so brilliantly used by the Disney creative team to produce the film, we can see the Twelve Powers symbolically dance and twinkle and burst across the screen.

Below is one possible imaginative guide to the Twelve Powers in *Fantasia's* seven segments, which have classical numbers performed by Leopold Stokowski and the Philadelphia Orchestra. Metaphysically, the number *twelve* means "spiritual completion." Use the guide to help complete your appreciation not only of *Fantasia* but also of your own wondrous powers.

TOCCATA AND FUGUE IN D MINOR (JOHANN SEBASTIAN BACH)

1. **ORDER**—the power of harmony blending in what the narrator calls "absolute music" and "abstract images"

THE NUTCRACKER SUITE (TCHAIKOVSKY)

2. **UNDERSTANDING**—spiritual illumination quickened as fairies gloriously light up nature
3. **FAITH**—the perception that sees God's eternal dance, even among the cossack-like flowers and the dreamy-eyed fish

THE SORCERER'S APPRENTICE (PAUL DUKAS)

4. **ZEAL**—Mickey Mouse definitely seen as the epitome of enthusiasm as he magically commands the cosmos, while lacking the following power
5. **WISDOM**—the necessity for good judgment shown in Mickey's creation of bucket-carrying brooms run amok. Moral: A hat does not a sorcerer make

RITE OF SPRING (IGOR STRAVINSKY)

6. **LIFE**—the active, animated power of existence as the planet and its creatures evolve. Stravinsky's stated purpose, according to the narrator, was to "express primitive life"
7. **RENUNCIATION**—the vital releasing element in life's natural progression of evolution and change

THE PASTORAL SYMPHONY (LUDWIG VAN BEETHOVEN)

8. **IMAGINATION**—the divinely inspired conception of a mythological kingdom filled with hosts of fanciful creatures such as unicorns and winged horses
9. **WILL**—choices of love, merriment, and survival in fantasyland

DANCE OF THE HOURS (AMILCARE PONCHIELLI)

10. **STRENGTH**—the stabilizing power of total being, captured with famous dancing hippos and elephants in the home of a Venetian nobleman

139

Night on Bald Mountain (Modeste Moussorgsky)

Ave Maria (Franz Schubert)

11. **Power**—the dominion faculty with its two faces—ego power (in the form of the mountain's frightening Chernobog, ghostly figures, and flames) and spiritual power (in the serene setting and mood of "Ave Maria"). As the narrator says, "Musically and dramatically, we have here a picture of the struggle between the profane and the sacred"

12. **Love**—divine love in the beauty and majesty of the promenade of lights, the peaceful blue hues, and the soothing sounds of "Ave Maria"

Ye Turn

Feeling empowered? After viewing any of the following movies, think about how each of the Twelve Powers is illustrated by characters and events:

1. *Apollo 13*—Moon mission runs into trouble. (1995, 139 minutes, PG)
2. *Doctor Zhivago*—Romance and politics clash during Russian Revolution. (1965, 180 minutes, NR)
3. *Indiana Jones and the Last Crusade*—Indy's father, also an archeologist, is missing. (1989, 127 minutes, PG-13)
4. *Lawrence of Arabia*—This epic is based on adventurer T. E. Lawrence's book *Seven Pillars of Wisdom*. Consider Lawrence's belief that "nothing is written." (1962, British, 216 minutes, NR)
5. *Strike Up the Band*—Here's a rousing entry in the "let's put on a show" genre. (1940, 120 minutes, NR)

Sidney Poitier in *Lilies of the Field,* United Artists
Photo: The Museum of Modern Art Film Stills Archive

Chapter 4

Seeing the Big Picture
● ● ● ● ● ● ● ● ● ● ● ● ● ● ● ● ● ● ●

The movie lenses are open wide in this chapter to examine larger-than-life topics about the spiritual fundamentals of existence and the meaning of life itself. Here are films that take a close look at many topics near and dear to searching hearts. They bravely pose questions that challenge viewers to venture beyond the small frames of their individual routines and think about the Big Picture. Questions include: What does it mean to be truly alive? What is faith? Is there divine order? Why do we fear? If life is a classroom, what are we supposed to learn? What do dreams mean? How do we know what Truth is? Is there life after death? Is reincarnation a fact? What is the nature of time and reality? Where is God? The movies provide *some* answers, but *others* are in your heart.

AWAKENINGS

PREVIEW

An introverted and caring research doctor, Malcolm Sayer (Robin Williams), accepts a job in a hospital for the chronically ill in the Bronx, where he uses an experimental drug to awaken Leonard (Robert De Niro) and other longtime catatonic patients in this film based on the true experiences of Dr. Oliver Sacks in 1969. (1990, 121 minutes, PG-13)

META VIEW

What is it to be truly alive?

How easy it is to lose sight of our divine purpose and heritage—to be the creative, joyful expressions of Infinite Intelligence! We wander off in a mental and physical haze of mundane, petty responsibilities and causes, and forget to truly live. It often takes a loss of some sort, perhaps of a relationship or a physical ability, to awaken us to the value of life itself.

Our knowledge that Leonard has lost thirty years of his life makes his observations and advice so potent. Here is a man with a genuine appreciation of life when it is restored to him, and he issues a challenge to Dr. Sayer and to all humankind to awaken. While Leonard accepts that he and others can lose an awareness of life for medical reasons, he can't understand why people of sound mind and body take life for granted and squander its treasures.

Leonard is almost desperate with the need to tell people how good life is.

"People have forgotten what life is all about," he tells Dr. Sayer. "They've forgotten what it is to be alive. They need to be reminded. They need to be reminded about what they have and what they can lose. What I feel is the joy of life, the gift of life, the freedom of life, the wonderment of life."

He says that people don't appreciate the simple things of life, such as play, friendship, and family.

Dr. Sayer agrees: "What he's saying is absolutely right. We don't really know how to live." The doctor awakens to the realization that "the human spirit is more powerful than any drug, and that is what needs to be nourished."

Ye View

1. What are some of the things that the awakened patients say they missed?
2. How does Leonard change Dr. Sayer's life and outlook? What evidence is there of the doctor's awakening?
3. Make a list of things that bring you joy and that you appreciate about life.

145

In the Same Spirit

Other patients proclaiming the human spirit in unique ways:

Charly—An experiment turns a retarded man (Cliff Robertson) into a genius in this film of Daniel Keyes' *Flowers for Algernon.* (1968, 103 minutes, PG)

One Flew Over the Cuckoo's Nest—Based on a Ken Kesey story, an insane-asylum inmate (Jack Nicholson) incites an inspirational riot. (1975, 133 minutes, R)

Theme Mates

Also learning what it means to be truly alive:

My Life—When an ad executive (Michael Keaton) learns that he is dying, he begins really looking at himself, his family, and life. (1993, 112 minutes, PG-13)

Tender Mercies—A country singer (Robert Duvall) plagued with marital and drinking problems rebuilds his life through love and commitment. (1983, 89 minutes, PG)

COME TO THE STABLE

PREVIEW

Two nuns from France, Sister Margaret (Loretta Young) and Sister Scolastica (Celeste Holm), arrive in Bethlehem, Connecticut, filled with faith and determination to keep a promise to God to build a children's hospital. (1949, 94 minutes, NR)

META VIEW

Have faith in divine order

Sisters Margaret and Scolastica are of The Order of the Holy Endeavor, and they let no obstacles hinder them in their holy endeavor to build a children's hospital. The local bishop says of the two, "Something tells me that an irresistible force has been let loose in New England . . . against which, quite obviously, there is no defense. There hasn't been for nearly 2000 years."

The simple faith that the nuns possess is "really sublime, magnificent," the bishop notes. The sisters need land and money for the hospital, and have no doubt that they will acquire both; they feel that God has led them to the exact spot where the hospital is to be built. With a simplicity that is positively divine, the nuns, in a very orderly and confident manner, go about overcoming what seem to others like insurmountable obstacles to achieving their goal.

Time and again, the way opens miraculously for them. For example, they need a building of their own to use as temporary headquarters. Their borrowed jeep has a flat tire beside the perfect building, on which men are actually putting up the "For Sale" sign. "Oh, dear God, You *do* work in strange ways," Sister Margaret says.

Faith is easiest to have when things are going the way one wants them to, but usually more difficult to have when things are not. The Sisters show the depth of their faith when it looks as if they are not going to be able to achieve their goal. Miss Amelia Potts (Elsa Lanchester), the kind and gentle painter with whom the Sisters live, is upset because the dedicated group has failed. Sister Margaret replies, "Not in God's plan, we haven't failed, even though we don't understand it now."

Sister Margaret is voicing the conviction that God is good and is the only power in any situation, and that, despite any appearances to the contrary, everything is working together for the good in God's orderly universe. That conviction is faith.

"It isn't hard to relinquish a dream if it's God's will," Sister Margaret says.

Faith is, in fact, realizing that God's will is always good for us and is in the *cause* as well as in the *effect* of a situation. It is acknowledging that God is the energy of an orderly universe, and that all things are working together for good—and *only* good—despite appearances to the contrary. Faith is realizing that God's will is in the whole process, from start to finish.

In the Sisters' situation, the time of apparent failure is necessary so that even more good can be accomplished through the spiritual transformation of neighbor Bob Mason (Hugh Marlowe).

147

✳

YE VIEW

1. In what ways do Sisters Margaret and Scolastica bring comfort to Miss Potts, Luigi Rossi, and Bob Mason? How do those characters support the nuns?

2. Discuss the significance of the movie's title. To what does it refer within the story? How does it relate to The Gospels?

3. Sister Margaret tells Mason, "God is the only answer to man's insecurity." Do you think this viewpoint is applicable to today's personal and social challenges? Why or why not?

DEFENDING YOUR LIFE

PREVIEW

After dying in an auto accident, Daniel Miller (Albert Brooks) finds himself in Judgment City for a past-life review—and also finds his true love, Julia (Meryl Streep). (1991, 111 minutes, PG)

META VIEW

Little Brains have big fears

Don't be scared off by this film's rather fundamentalist-sounding title and concept of Judgment City. There is no hellfire and damnation here, but rather love and freedom, along with much humor and wit.

It's important to realize that Judgment City isn't heaven or any other final resting place, but is a resort-like way station where those who have died on Earth come for a short examining period. In Judgment City, they are treated to fancy hotels, all the food they can eat (and it won't make them gain weight—many people's concept of an *actual* heaven!), and perfectly clear weather. Everyone wears white togas and receives VIP treatment. For evening entertainment, they go to clubs, restaurants, and the Past-Lives Pavilion (where Shirley MacLaine is the hostess).

Former Earthlings are in Judgment City on serious business, however. After each lifetime on Earth, the newly departed are required to go through an examining process. They are not being judged for sins, as such, but for whether or not they were finally able to overcome fear. During four days in Judgment City, nine days or episodes of a person's life are reviewed, to look at the fear issue. The most important point of Brooks' cleverly written script is that fear is what stops the progress of life. The TV game show in Judgment City is even called *Your Biggest Fear.*

Each person is assigned a defender. Daniel's defender is no-nonsense Bob Diamond (Rip Torn). It is Diamond who explains to the bewildered Daniel what is going on.

"The point of this whole thing is to keep getting smarter, to keep growing, to use as much of your brain as possible," Diamond says. He is proud that he uses 48 percent of his brain, as opposed to Daniel, who uses only 3 percent (which is about par for people on Earth).

One gets smarter and moves forward, Diamond says, by getting over fears. "Everybody on Earth deals with fear. That's what Little Brains do." "Little Brains" is the pet name of Judgment City folk, themselves former Earthlings, for people on Earth.

"Fear is like a giant fog. It sits on your brain and blocks everything—real feelings, true happiness, real joy. It can't get through that fog. But you lift it, and, buddy, you're in for the ride of your life."

In addition to a defender, each person is assigned a prosecutor, who works for the Universe. Diamond explains that the Universe is "like a big machine, and you and I are parts. Now, they don't want a part to get through unless it's ready. A bad part gets through, and the whole machine breaks down. So that's why we're here—to make sure you're ready."

Daniel's prosecutor is the formidable Lena Foster (Lee Grant), known as "the dragon lady." Daniel's life hasn't been too bad—although he has been divorced and has had his share of childhood and financial challenges and (like most people) has wrestled quite a bit with fear. His defender and prosecutor call up various scenes from Daniel's life to make their cases about whether or not Daniel has overcome his fears.

During his first night on the town, Daniel meets another new arrival in Judgment City, a woman named Julia, who apparently lived an exemplary life in her last go-round and is breezing through her examinations. Daniel and Julia fall in love, in "the pit stop," Daniel notes. But the two lovers seem destined for different places, as Daniel's courage is given a big test.

People who pass the life review go forward, but to where is left rather hazy. The impression is given, however, that it is a desirable place. Those who don't pass return to Earth, although ones who go back too many times, Diamond says, are eventually thrown away (but that rather unsettling concept isn't developed; perhaps it means that the energy is recycled in another form). Diamond does say that there is no hell. God isn't discussed, but is off-handedly referred to several times.

Brooks, who also directed the movie, has written many satisfying one-liners and presents a strange but pleasant little romance. And while his overall views of life after Earth don't lend themselves to much serious scrutiny, Brooks' assertion that life is about getting smarter by the overcoming of fear is itself a fearless and noteworthy presentation.

Indeed, people are constantly seeking to overcome a multitude of fears, until they realize the nothingness of fear. As Franklin D. Roosevelt said, "The only thing we have to fear is fear itself."[1] We are all striving to truly understand the perspective set forth in the Introduction to *A Course in Miracles*: "The opposite of love is fear, but what is all-encompassing can have no opposite."[2] In other words, only love (which is of God) really exists; fear is only that "giant fog," as Diamond says, that we need to lift from our consciousness.

Ye View

1. Do you think Daniel learns his lesson about fear? Why or why not?
2. What are some fears that you would like to overcome?
3. In what way would overcoming these fears improve your life?

THE EDUCATION OF LITTLE TREE

PREVIEW

An eight-year-old orphan boy (Joseph Ashton) learns about his Cherokee heritage and life in the backwoods of eastern Tennessee when he goes to live with his grandparents (James Cromwell and Tantoo Cardinal) in 1935 in this adaptation of Forrest Carter's autobiographical book. (1997, 117 minutes, PG, *)

META VIEW

Learn to use your spirit

Grandma and Grandpa's education of Little Tree includes some of the basics such as reading and ciphering and some practical considerations such as helping with the family still, but mainly involves understanding what it means to be really alive.

Little Tree receives an education many with advanced university degrees might envy! As for Grandma and Grandpa, they don't have teaching certificates, but they sure do know what needs to be taught for a life of inner peace and meaning.

For starters, they put their student in touch with nature. You must feel the ground under you to learn anything, says Grandma from her Cherokee perspective, so she makes Little Tree a pair of moccasins. Grandpa teaches him to honor each day by watching the morning come alive with the sunrise.

Patiently and lovingly watching over Little Tree, the grandparents let him learn about nature and human nature (including racial prejudice). Their friend Willow John (Graham Greene) tells Little Tree about his stalwart ancestors on the Trail of Tears. Very quickly, Little Tree starts to absorb "the way" of the Indian.

When Little Tree is afraid that his grandfather may die following a rattlesnake bite, Grandma gives a valuable lesson about what it means to be dead and, conversely, what it means to be alive.

"There's all kinds of dying, Little Tree," Grandma says. "I seen people down at the settlement walking around like you or me, but they just as good as dead, 'cause they spent their lives in meanness and greed, and the spirit inside of them went and shrunk down to no more than the size of a pea, 'cause the only way to make your spirit big is to work on it. You've got to use it to understand, and the more you try to understand, the bigger it gets, until it gets so big and powerful, you come to understand everything, remember all your past body lives."

Physical death doesn't separate lives, Grandma adds: "That's what I want you to know. We'll all us be together in spirit always. That's the important thing."

Grandma really has a handle on understanding. She knows that true understanding is spiritual understanding, and that spiritual understanding is developed and has to be used to become powerful. Understanding, Grandma herself understands, empowers the spirit.

Spiritual understanding is the realization of our unity or oneness with God—that is, "the way" or the presence of God within us. It is an insight at the depths of our beings, a knowing of Truth in the consciousness of our hearts.

Both the book and the movie nicely follow this advice from Grandma: "When you come onto something good, first thing to do is to share it with whosoever you can find. That way, the good spreads out where, no telling how far it will go."

Ye View

1. Do you think that Little Tree should have been sent to a boarding school? Why or why not?

2. What is the significance of Grandpa's and Grandma's last words?
3. What are some specific things that people might do to, as Grandma would say, make their spirits big?

THEME MATES

Also learning "the way" of family and spirit:
  The Secret of Roan Inish—A young girl named Fiona (Jeni Courtney) explores the legends of her Irish family and the "island of the seals" in this mystical, spellbinding tale for both adults and children directed by John Sayles. (1994, 102 minutes, PG, *)

FORREST GUMP

PREVIEW

While America is losing its innocence during the decades of the '50s, '60s, and '70s, Forrest Gump (Tom Hanks), with a low IQ but high moral fiber, retains his innocence and overcomes physical and economic challenges to become a college football star, a decorated Vietnam hero, a shrimp tycoon, and a famous runner in this astounding adaptation of Winston Groom's novel. (1994, 142 minutes, PG-13)

META VIEW

Enjoy the tour and the chocolates!

My wife went running out of the Peace Chapel at Unity Village one sunny summer evening. Startled out of meditation, I followed to see what was wrong. But everything was *right*. Sylvia had been overcome with the joy of a revelation that life is like a mystery tour. In some cosmic sense, we've signed up for this tour, which has been planned and is conducted for our enjoyment by a benevolent tour director, and we're supposed to relax and enjoy the trip and the discoveries along the way, whatever they are and however they may appear.

What a marvelous analogy for life! Forrest Gump's mother (Sally Field) would like that, I think, because it's a variation of her favorite analogy:

"Life is like a box of chocolates. . . . You never know what you're gonna get."

Our goal in being on the mystery tour or in choosing a candy from the box of chocolates is to enjoy whatever life gives us.

"You have to do the best with what God gave you," Forrest's mother says. Forrest's whole life is a grand, amazing mystery tour in which he experiences miracles, loss, glory, heartache, and joy, and meets paupers and presidents. He greets whatever life brings on his personal odyssey with a steady morality and innocent courage.

Both analogies seem to take into account Forrest's own realization about life that combines a sense of personal destiny and free will. "I don't know if we each have a destiny or if we're all just floating around accidental-like, on a breeze, but I, I think maybe it's both, maybe both happening at the same time."

A sense of childlike wonder and innocence is needed to enjoy either being on the mystery tour or reaching into the chocolate box, and Forrest is the embodiment of innocence. His is an innocence that is associated not with the intellect but with the heart. "I'm not a smart man, but I know what love is," Forrest tells Jenny (Robin Wright), the love of his life.

People may call him simple, but Forrest lives from the viewpoint that the purpose of life is simple: to love one another, to care for one another, and to share with one another. The late Chicago Unity minister Mike Matoin said that Forrest has a "holy innocence," beautifully captured in the following exchange:

Lieutenant Dan (Gary Sinise): Have you found Jesus yet, Gump?

Forrest: I didn't know I was supposed to be looking for him, sir.

The response is not sarcastic; it is totally sincere and honest. That is Forrest's approach to life. You can bet if Forrest had thought that he was supposed to be looking for Jesus, he would have searched the world. Forrest never considers Jesus lost, any more than he ever considers himself stupid, inferior, or lost. With an inner knowing that drives all his actions (much bolstered by his mother's positive teachings), Forrest says simply, "I'm going to heaven, Lieutenant Dan."

Like many ministers, no doubt, Kathy Nelson loves to give sermons based on *Forrest Gump*, which was a box-office smash and an award winner: "He is Christ-like. He was Jesus. He loved the lame and the poor," Nelson said. "He sought first the kingdom of God." Truly, Forrest's intention is always to behold the Christ in everyone, to do good for others, and to say the best of everyone.

At times Forrest's approach to life may seem irrational and deluded, but Forrest has a way of getting to the heart of matters. When Jenny collapses after throwing stones at the old house where she was abused by her father, Forrest says knowingly, "Sometimes, I guess, there just aren't enough rocks."

Ye View

1. What are some actions that illustrate Forrest's desire to help people? What are some situations that show his sympathy for people's plights?

2. Do you think that Lieutenant Dan and Jenny ever come to appreciate and accept Forrest's perspective on life? Why or why not?

3. Discuss your reaction to the concepts of life as a mystery tour and a box of chocolates.

GROUNDHOG DAY

PREVIEW

An unpleasant, self-focused TV weatherman (Bill Murray) goes on continual rerun and keeps reliving Groundhog Day while covering the annual festivities in Punxsutawney, Pennsylvania. (1993, 101 minutes, PG)

META VIEW

Wake up—school has started!

Ask not for whom life's school bell tolls; it tolls for each of us. Here's why, according to one view of existence that seems entirely plausible but has become something of a metaphysical cliche: We're in one big school here on Earth. Our spiritual beings are having their·human experiences as students. The purpose of attending this school (some would call it the School of Hard Knocks) is to learn life's important lessons. We remain in school until we *do* learn.

From appearances, we humans tend to be, if not terrible, at least unobservant students. We stumble through the curricula of life and don't absorb the material. Where are our Cliff Notes? (perhaps the world's sacred writings and holy guides). We have trouble "getting it right" on the first test, on the second, on the third. We're like professional students.

Once when my wife was ill, friends gave her a homemade get-well card that read on the outside, "It's in times like these that we learn and grow." Inside, the card said, "What a stupid system!"

That "system" refers to the educational classrooms of life in which we humans learn and grow from our many lessons. Like all schools, the "system" can indeed seem stupid if we're not paying attention to the teacher.

Groundhog Day is a clever, exaggerated look at the nature of this presumed educational system on Earth. It's about a man faced with repeating the same "school day" over and over—beginning with the same song and chatter on the radio at 6 a.m. and continuing humorously and sometimes painfully through all the encounters of the day—until he learns his lessons. In fact, the name of the movie has become a modern cultural symbol for this whole Earth-as-a-school theory. All someone has to say is, "It's *Ground-hog Day*," and heads nod knowingly.

Phil Connors, the TV weatherman in the movie, obviously has a few major lessons to learn—specifically about caring and loving (someone other than himself). He is rude, condescending, sarcastic, and insulting. He calls people "morons" and "hicks," and even brands Punxsutawney Phil, the famous weather-forecasting groundhog, a "rat." And at the start of his adventures, he certainly doesn't stand much of a chance with the nice, cheery new TV producer Rita (Andie MacDowell).

The Earth-as-a-school theory generally holds that, through a lifetime, a person repeats certain "difficult" scenarios and comes into contact with certain people or types of people until his or her reaction to them becomes one of unselfishness, compassion, and love. Some, bringing in the ideas of karma and reincarnation, say that we may continue the lessons from one lifetime to another. The screenplay by Danny Rubin and Harold Ramis nicely telescopes the basic concept into one hilarious, pointed day of *deja vu*.

Two other maxims also come into play in Phil's situation: "We reap what we sow," and "Our experiences reflect our states of consciousness." Certainly, Phil is reaping the effects of his attitudes and is experiencing, over and over, the results of his "me-me" consciousness.

When he becomes aware of what is going on, Phil at first is confused, angry, and depressed. It is Rita who seems to have the initial insight into the benefit of the repetitions. "Sometimes I wish I had a thousand lifetimes," she says. "Maybe it's not a curse; it just depends on how you look at it."

"Gosh, you're an upbeat lady," Phil replies, and one has a sense that his personal forecast is improving. It's a joy to watch just how much Phil's countenance, actions, and reactions change as his very long "school day" progresses.

YE VIEW

1. At one point in his ordeal Phil states, "I wake up every day right here . . . and there's nothing I can do about it." Do you agree with his statement? Why or why not?
2. Discuss your opinion of the theory that Earth is a school in which we are to learn life's lessons.
3. Can you think of a day that you would like to relive? Explain why.

HAMLET

PREVIEW

Laurence Olivier directs and stars in this most melancholy adaptation of William Shakespeare's tragedy of the Danish prince who seeks to revenge the murder of his father. (1948, British, 153 minutes, NR)

META VIEW

Harken to these truthful words!

Even within the darkest tragedies lurks metaphysical Truth. Shakespeare's tale of *Hamlet* itself, for example, is far from being a spiritual beacon, but it does contain some lines of light and inspiration.

Quotations are frequently pulled out of Shakespearean context, as they are from the Bible, to support all manner of theses. Think not, then, on the murder, revenge, and madness in *Hamlet*, but refresh your mind with these samples of noble ideas embedded in the dialogue:

- "This above all: to thine own self be true, and it must follow, as the night the day, thou canst not then be false to any man."—Polonius, advising his son Laertes

What a marvelous motto by which to live, when one realizes that being true to one's Self is being in harmony with the active God principle within! It is easier to see another's Christ nature when one recognizes one's own Self worth as an expression of Infinite Spirit.

- "And for my soul, what can it do for that, being a thing immortal as itself?"—Hamlet, on not being afraid of his father's ghost

Mortal fears cannot touch the soul, here meaning an aspect of eternal and perfect Spirit. The traumas and tragedies we experience in the world leave our spiritual essence unscathed. They are like scratches on the veneer of an oak table. Underneath the scratched veneer, the oak surface is strong and unscarred. We can learn from these scratches, however, and our greatest lesson is perhaps that we cannot harm our true nature.

- "There are more things in heaven and earth, Horatio, than are dreamt of in your philosophy."—Hamlet

Just as the finger only points to the moon, our most enlightened understandings can only point to God. We can, however, train ourselves to be more open to experiencing God's presence and to realizing that God energy is far more encompassing and wondrous than our sciences, religions, and philosophies.

- "To be, or not to be: that is the question."—Hamlet

We always have the choice of how to respond to the circumstances of

159

✼

our lives. We can choose "to be," or live fully with a positive outlook, or we can choose "*not* to be," or live with a negative outlook. The larger question is, "What kind of outlook brings us peace?"

- "My words fly up, my thoughts remain below: Words without thoughts never to heaven go."—King Claudius, consumed with guilt

Heaven is the consciousness of God within us. Our sincere prayers are thoughts aligned with God's presence; they "work" because they reveal the peace and wholeness of our God-nature. Insincere prayers are thoughts still coming from a belief in separation from God; they don't "work" because they are not synchronized with our God-nature.

- "Lord, we know what we are, but know not what we may be."—Ophelia, after her father's death

The fullness of our identity as children of God does, indeed, await other realms, but in *this* realm, just knowing that we are so much more than we seem is a gigantic step forward for humankind.

- "Good night, sweet prince; and flights of angels sing thee to thy rest!" —Horatio, upon the death of Hamlet

Angel thoughts—our realization of being united with God-energy—bring us completion and peace.

Ye View

1. What qualities of friendship does Horatio show toward Hamlet?
2. Compare Olivier's characterization of Hamlet with another actor's, such as Mel Gibson's or Kenneth Branagh's.
3. Choose a quotation from *Hamlet* other than the ones cited above and give your own metaphysical interpretation of it. You might consider this one: "There is nothing either good or bad, but thinking makes it so."

IN THE SAME SPIRIT

The "sweet prince" lives on:
Hamlet—Mel Gibson leads in a shorter, less dark version (1990, 135 minutes, PG).
Hamlet—Kenneth Branagh directs and stars in an ambitious production extremely true to the Bard and filled with an all-star cast. (1996, United States-British, 242 minutes, PG-13)

JERRY MAGUIRE

PREVIEW

The title character (Tom Cruise), a successful, high-pressure, 35-year-old sports agent with seventy-two clients, loses his job after declaring that his profession has lost its personal touch, so he begins his own company with a new vision; with a secretary, Dorothy (Renee Zellweger); and with one demanding client, Rod Tidwell (Cuba Gooding, Jr.). (1996, 138 minutes, R)

META VIEW

Show me the meaning!

He has had a "breakthrough," not a "breakdown," Jerry Maguire points out. He doesn't use the word *spiritual,* but obviously, what he has had is a spiritual breakthrough, or awakening—a realization of the essential worth and dignity of each individual, and a desire to start caring for people and helping them, rather than merely managing them for profit and prestige.

There had been earlier rumblings leading to the breakthrough. Jerry had begun noticing that he was not responding on a human level to his clients and their families, and that his clients were not treating their fans as real people with feelings. Jerry had begun asking himself, "Who had I become—just another shark in a suit?"

"I couldn't escape one simple thought—I hated myself," Jerry says, or more specifically, "I hated my place in the world."

With this awareness, Spirit takes over. "I had so much to say and no one to listen, and then it happened. It was the oddest, most unexpected thing," Jerry recalls. He began writing a 25-page mission statement for the future of his company. Recalling the words of his own mentor, "The key to this business is personal relationships," Jerry advocates fewer clients and less money. He also says that agents should begin actually caring for themselves, their clients, and the games.

Jerry admits, "What I was writing was somewhat touchy-feely." He didn't care, because he had lost the ability to be insincere: "I was the me I had always wanted to be."

Spirit never promised Jerry a rose garden or a Rose Bowl, but Jerry's breakthrough begins a path of personal enlightenment that touches all those with whom he comes in contact and leads to the highest good for all involved.

Dorothy is immediately impressed. "I think in this age, optimism like that is a revolutionary act," she tells Jerry.

Jerry is at first understandably shaken when his career falters ("God, what did I do?" he asks himself) and talks sarcastically about the breakthrough that came when he "went to bed and grew a conscience." But he quickly bounces back and remains true both to his sense of self-worth and to his new vision. "I am a valuable commodity. . . . I make miracles happen," he declares.

Jerry helps other people get past the greedy, self-serving "show me the money" philosophy that Rod espouses, and he himself becomes a testimonial to the fact that the meaning of life is more than money.

How marvelous when that realization comes earlier in life! For example, if the newspaper tycoon of *Citizen Kane* (1941) had experienced a breakthrough such as Jerry had at an early age, he perhaps would not have been wistfully contemplating "Rosebud" at his death.

YE VIEW

1. How does Jerry change as a result of his awakening? What changes occur in his personal life and relationships?
2. If the heart is empty, the head doesn't matter, Jerry's mentor says. What happens when Jerry applies this philosophy to Rod's football playing? What has been Rod's focus?
3. Discuss some businesses today that you think especially need to read Jerry Maguire's mission statement. In what ways are these businesses not meeting people on a personal level?

163

THEME MATES

Also searching for meaning:

The Arrangement—An executive with an ad agency (Kirk Douglas) suddenly scurries out of the rat race in this adaptation of Elia Kazan's novel. (1969, 120 minutes, R)

THE LAST WAVE

PREVIEW

The life and nightly dreams of an attorney named David (Richard Chamberlain) in Sydney, Australia, become frighteningly entangled in the Dreamtime, rituals, and prophecies of tribal Aborigines when he defends a group of Aborigines accused of murder. (1977, Australian, 106 minutes, PG)

META VIEW

Embrace dreams and mysteries

Director Peter Weir has a special talent for taking viewers beyond the ordinary comfort zones of their sense-based existence. In this engrossing, disturbing, artfully eerie movie, Weir not only enters the eternal Dreamtime of the Aborigines, but also brings that supernatural realm of creation into play in the modern world.

As David investigates the murder charges, he learns about the Aborigines' tribal sorcery, ancestral traditions, sacred objects and places, and myths. He also slowly becomes aware that his own dreams, his very identity, and the many occurrences of freak weather and strange phenomena are somehow connected to the Aborigines' Dreamtime and to humankind's immediate future.

One of the accused men, Chris (Gulpilil), tells David that a dream "is a shadow of something real." He says that David is dreaming about secrets, and adds, "It is death to know them."

David seeks out an expert on Aboriginal mythology, who tells him that Aborigines believe in two forms of time, or "two parallel streams of activity." One is the daily objective world of which people are aware. "The other," she says, "is an infinite spiritual cycle called the 'Dreamtime'—more real than reality itself. Whatever happens in the Dreamtime establishes the values, symbols, and law of Aboriginal society."

She informs David that some people with unusual spiritual powers have contact with the Dreamtime through their dreams and through ceremonies involving sacred objects. David has a recurring dream about a stone that is one of the sacred objects, and it becomes clear that his spirit is linked to the

Dreamtime and that his dreams foretell an impending apocalypse which occurs at the end of a cycle when nature needs to renew itself and prepare for a rebirth.

The Last Wave, from an original story by Weir, gives viewers a fascinating look into the supernatural beliefs and mythology of Australia's early nomadic inhabitants, but it also suggests the importance for us today to pay attention to dreams and mysteries in our lives.

In *The Encyclopedia of Dreams: Symbols & Interpretations,* Rosemary Ellen Guiley writes that dreams have meaning, and are not just illusions. "Dreams have a reality of their own—they are just as real as our waking consciousness. In dreams, we transcend the boundaries of our waking consciousness" and go beyond "the objective reality we experience with our five physical senses."

Guiley adds, "By delving into our dreams, and attuning ourselves to their subjective reality, we stand to learn much about ourselves and our relationships to others and to the cosmos." People of ancient times understood the value and validity of dreams, she says.[3]

David, superbly portrayed by Chamberlain, comes to understand not only the value of dreams but also of mystery in dreams and in life.

He asks his stepfather, a minister, "Why didn't you tell me there were mysteries?"

The stepfather replies, "David, my whole life has been about a mystery."

"No," David says, "you stood in that church and explained them away."

If we learn to pay attention to our dreams and the many mysteries unfolding in the world around us and to connect those dreams and mysteries to our "waking" activities and thoughts, we can experience more of the richness and totality of life as creative expressions of Universal Spirit. When that happens, Dreamtime meets Greenwich time in the recognition that all is God time.

Ye View

1. What is your opinion of the outcome of the trial?
2. Do you think that "the last wave" could have been prevented? Why or why not?
3. Have you ever had recurring dreams? What interpretations did you give to them? What effect did they have on you?

In the Same Spirit

Other films of dreams and mystery:

Akira Kurosawa's Dreams—Writer-director Kurosawa creates a splendid, thought-provoking roller coaster ride of dreams in eight segments. (1990, Japanese, 120 minutes, PG)

Dead of Night—Guests at a country house share their dreams, and the results are thrilling and chilling. In one episode, Michael Redgrave is a standout as a ventriloquist. This movie is good, scary Halloween fare. (1945, British, 102 minutes, NR)

Dreamscape—A man (Dennis Quaid) has the ability to go into the dreams of other people. (1984, 99 minutes, PG-13)

LILIES OF THE FIELD

Preview

Traveling through the Arizona desert, Homer Smith (Sidney Poitier) stops to get water for his car and is practically kidnapped by Mother Maria (Lilia Skala), who oversees a small group of German-speaking nuns, and commandeered to build a chapel. (1963, 93 minutes, NR)

META VIEW

Stop, pray, and build

Homer keeps trying to move on in this allegory about answered prayers and divine appointments. "I'm just passing through," he says repeatedly to Mother Maria. Many people, like Homer, consider themselves merely "passing through" one stage of life on the way to something better, and they don't pay attention to bettering the present.

But then their car runs out of water or breaks down—Spirit dictates an unexpected stop, a new course, and new opportunities to grow and learn (to build a chapel, as it were). It's as if God says, as Mother Maria does to Homer, "I have something you do" and "Come, follow me." People can protest and declare that there must be some mistake ("I don't think He sent a black Baptist to a Catholic nun," Homer says). And they can run away, as Homer does, but sooner or later they must stop running from themselves and become aware of their divine purpose to be of service to others. "He will return," Mother Maria says.

"What bugs me is she [Mother Maria] was so positive I was coming back," Homer says. Prayer—tuning consciousness to God Presence within—can send people in unplanned and surprising directions. "God is good. He has sent me a big, strong man," Mother Maria says, in answer to her prayers for someone to build a chapel on their farm.

"Everything works out. It's God's will," she says. When doubts set in and work on the chapel is stilled because more materials are needed, Mother Maria's response is always, "We pray some more."

Spirit gently triumphs despite human will or ego emotions. Homer initially refuses to let anyone help him build the chapel because "all my life I really wanted to build something." He has pictured himself working alone, without thinking that the lasting and most rewarding work is done with others and with God. Mother Maria keeps her focus on the real builder. "God is building out there the chapel," she says.

When the chapel building really gets under way, more and more people are drawn to it and become involved in it. "Everybody wants to give," Homer says. And everybody receives. When we connect with our divine purpose, whatever it is, as creative expressions of God, all sorts of marvelous "chapels" take shape in our lives.

YE VIEW

1. The Bible verse from which the title is taken (Matthew 6:28) is quoted in the film. What is its significance to the story?
2. Juan (Stanley Adams) explains why he is working on the chapel: "To me it is insurance. To me life is here on this Earth. I cannot see further, so I cannot believe further, but if they are right about the hereafter, I have paid my insurance." What is your response to such thinking?
3. Do you have a project, or a "chapel," that you would like completed and have been praying about? Discuss.

LOST HORIZON

PREVIEW

A plane containing five passengers, including Robert Conway (Ronald Colman), a famous English soldier, diplomat, and hero, is hijacked and crashes in the Tibetan mountains, where the passengers discover the paradise of Shangri-La. (1937, 132 minutes, NR)

META VIEW

This dream never grows old

Based on James Hilton's novel, this vintage movie opens with all-too-modern sentiments: "In these days of wars and rumors of wars—haven't you ever dreamed of a place where there was peace and security, where living was not a struggle but a lasting delight?

"Of course you have.

"So has every man since Time began. Always the same dream. Sometimes he calls it Utopia—Sometimes the Fountain of Youth—Sometimes merely 'that little chicken farm.'"

The dream is embedded in the human psyche because it is our longing to remember our home in God; it is our innate desire for heaven or *nirvana*. Our search for a paradise is actually a quest to know our Source at the core of our being.

169

"Everyone's search is for God, because we are searching for something that will make us whole," says Ernest Holmes, founder of the Science of Mind philosophy. "But what everyone does not realize is that we really *are* searching for God."[4]

Shangri-La is a representation of our eternal longing—the closest to the Infinite that our human imaginations can conceive. It is a place of serenity, peace, beauty, health, blissful isolation, courtesy, moderation, and longevity. It is a land without crime. "There can be no crime where there is a sufficiency of everything," says resident Chang (H. B. Warner).

The High Lama (Sam Jaffe) foresees a time when the outside world's "orgy of greed and brutality" will devastate modern civilization. "When that day comes, the world must begin to look for a new life," he tells Conway, a peace-loving man. "And it is our hope that they may find it here, for here we shall be . . . with a way of life based on one simple rule—be kind."

He continues, "When the strong have devoured each other, the Christian ethic may at last be fulfilled and the meek shall inherit the Earth."

YE VIEW

1. Why is Conway deemed a good prospect for Shangri-La? In what ways has his life been empty? How are Lovett (Edward Everett Horton), Barnard (Thomas Mitchell), and Gloria (Isabel Jewell) changed by Shangri-La?
2. What dream comes true for Conway? Why do others gain inspiration from Conway's story?
3. Discuss what most appeals to you about living in a Shangri-La.

THEME MATES

Shangri-La in space:

Star Trek Insurrection—Captain Jean-Luc Picard (Patrick Stewart) leads the *Next Generation* Starfleet crew in efforts to save the Ba'ku, 600 people who live on a planet reminiscent of Shangri-La, where regenerative radiation keeps them perpetually young. In their "sanctuary of life" without technology, the Ba'ku have learned the power of the moment and the importance of living in the now. A Ba'ku woman, Anij (Donna Murphy), tells Picard, "You explore the universe. We have discovered that a single moment in time can be a universe in itself, full of powerful forces. Most people aren't aware enough of the *now* to even notice." (1998, 103 minutes, PG)

MINDWALK

PREVIEW

A physicist (Liv Ullmann), a politician (Sam Waterston), and a poet (John Heard) go on a spiritual "talkabout"—discussing the nature and meaning of life—as they stroll around the French island of Mont Saint Michel. (1991, 110 minutes, PG)

META VIEW

The "talkies" get serious

In a metaphysical movie, the characters just talk about life's big issues, and not much else happens, right?

Wrong, of course! A metaphysical movie, like any other movie, contains an obvious (and one hopes, interesting) story that unfolds with action and surprising or intriguing plot developments.

Well, true 99.9 percent of the time. And then there's *Mindwalk*.

From the beginning to the end of this intellectual movie, the three principal characters really do just talk about life's big issues, and nothing much happens in the outer. Inside, though, where all true change occurs, the characters grow and change, and viewers who stick with this all-talking, all-thinking marathon may find themselves altered too.

This is definitely the film for viewers who say that they turn to the movies not just for entertainment but also for enlightenment and understanding. The movie offers minilessons in a gamut of abstract but immensely relevant ideas, including the scientific method of Descartes and the resulting mechanistic worldview, the opposing male and female principles of aggression and nurturing, theories about the makeup of matter and so-called solid objects, a unified view of nature and all living organisms, the ethical responsi-

171

bility of scientists, and the ultimate essence of life. We're talking heavy-duty dialogue here!

The movie, based on the book *The Turning Point* by Fritjof Capra, takes place during one day in the 1980s. Jack, a sincere and optimistic United States senator who failed to excite voters in a recent presidential primary, is brought to Mont Saint Michel by his friend Tom, a former speechwriter and professional poet, who is divorced and lives in France.

The two meet Sonia, an obviously brilliant but disillusioned scientist. Sonia, whose specialty is X-ray lasers, has exiled herself to the island after discovering that the U.S. Defense Department used her work to further the Star Wars program rather than medical breakthroughs. It is Sonia who leads the men down intricate pathways of reasoning.

Sonia argues that modern science has made obsolete the old notion that the world is a machine, and that science and technology have tortured the planet. What is needed, she states, is a "new vision of the world," a new perception that recognizes the "interconnectedness" of all life.

At the subatomic level, Sonia explains, there are no solid objects, and all subatomic particles manifest a "strange existence between potentiality and reality."

"The essential nature of matter lies not in objects but in interconnections," she says.

Surely, Jack maintains, human bodies are separate and not illusions.

Sonia smiles in understanding and succinctly states one of the film's main messages: "At the subatomic level, there is a continual exchange of matter and energy between my hand and this wood, between the wood and the air, and even between you and me. I mean a real exchange of photons and electrons. Ultimately, whether we like or not, we are all part of one inseparable web of relationships."

Like many hearing such ideas for the first time, Jack reacts with a sliver of understanding and a mass of confusion. "I get it," he says. "Well, I don't *get* it, but I get it."

Sonia repeatedly brings the conversations back to a need for science and all aspects of society to embrace a "theory of living systems" in which it is recognized that life is a "web of relationships." The nature of all life, she says, is creatively self-organizing, self-maintaining, and self-transcending.

Jack does grasp this theory. "We don't evolve *on* the planet," he says. "We evolve *with* the planet."

Tom the poet appreciates Sonia's lofty ideas, but doesn't like being reduced to a system. Life, he says, is also about family, love, and personal relationships.

All three characters are still mulling over such issues at the end of the movie. Discussions after this one could go on for hours!

As the characters converse, they are constantly roaming, and director Bernt Capra gives viewers a special treat: a visual travelogue of one of the world's spiritual meccas and pilgrimage sites, Mont Saint Michel. It's the fourth star of the show.

Mont Saint Michel is an almost six-acre rock in a bay between Brittany and Normandy. On the tiny island is a medieval town topped by an imposing abbey. The island has been associated with the Archangel Michael since 708. Benedictines came to the island in 966, and an abbey was built there in the early eleventh century. Today, some two million tourists and pilgrims come to the island each year. Take it from one who has been to Mont Saint Michel several times and even walked a six-mile pilgrimage to its gates: the movie faithfully captures the island's haunting mystique.

YE VIEW

1. How have Sonia's ideas influenced Jack's perspective? Your own?
2. Do you think Sonia will accept Jack's offer to become involved in politics? Why or why not?
3. From your own knowledge of current scientific research, discuss Sonia's reasoning concerning the interconnectedness of all life.

IN THE SAME SPIRIT

Eavesdropping some more:

> *My Dinner With Andre*—Two men (Wallace Shawn and Andre Gregory, the authors) meet at a New York restaurant for an insightful visit about matters of life, spirit, philosophy, history, and culture. (1981, 110 minutes, PG)

NIGHT OF THE HUNTER

PREVIEW

Harry Powell (Robert Mitchum), who calls himself a preacher, marries a widow (Shelley Winters) to locate $10,000 that her previous husband robbed from a bank, and then terrorizes her children, John and Pearl (Billy Chapin and Sally Jane Bruce), who know where the money is hidden, in this eerie, haunting film *noir*. (1955, 93 minutes, NR)

META VIEW

"Beware of false prophets"

In spiritual discussions and conversations about news reports, the question often surfaces, "How do I know if so-and-so is really doing God's work?" As do most questions about spirituality, the question prompts a multitude of answers, but one response is that someone who is doing God's work is motivated by love and goodness, and the effects are the greatest love and the greatest good for all concerned.

Discernment is necessary in matters of the Spirit. It is the better part of spiritual valor to decide for yourself whether or not a person, organization, or cause is truly acting out of love and increasing love or acting out of a consciousness of separation from God.

Night of the Hunter is a parable about such discernment—especially the lack of discernment. The film, the only one directed by famed actor Charles Laughton, begins with the face of Mrs. Rachel Cooper (Lillian Gish) in a star-filled sky. She is talking to children about Bible stories she has told them, and children's faces soon appear on the screen too.

Mrs. Cooper reads from the Bible: ". . . and then the good Lord went on to say 'Beware of false prophets which come to you in sheep's clothing, but inwardly they are ravening wolves. Ye shall know them by their fruits.'"

Powell looks, talks, and sings the part of a preacher, and townspeople are generally fooled by his "sheep's clothing" and manner. They don't know that he believes God dislikes women and approves of killing. They don't know of his murderous past, or that he is a "ravening wolf," after the money Ben Harper left with the children. They don't suspect the true motives of this man who repeatedly (chillingly) sings, "Leaning, leaning, leaning on the everlasting arms."

"The Lord God Jehovah will guide my hand in vengeance," Powell proclaims.

He meets his match in Mrs. Cooper, a woman strong in faith, fortitude, love, and the ability to recognize "false prophets."

She exemplifies a subtheme of the movie—the innocence and endurance of children. "Lord, save the little children," Mrs. Cooper says. "My soul is humble when I see the way little ones accept their lot. . . . They abide and they endure."

Ye View

1. What are the "fruits" by which Powell is known?
2. What is John's reaction to Powell? What is his mother's reaction? Why do you think they react as they do?

3. Mrs. Cooper says of herself, "I'm a strong tree, with branches for many birds." What do you think she means?

ON A CLEAR DAY YOU CAN SEE FOREVER

PREVIEW

Daisy Gamble (Barbra Streisand), a young woman with extrasensory powers but a dull, addictive personality, is hypnotized by Dr. Marc Chabot (Yves Montand), a professor of psychiatry, who then falls in love with her flamboyant, sophisticated personality from a past life. (1970, 129 minutes, G)

META VIEW

Reincarnation—sing it again, Barbra!

Frequent theater and movie buffs are well aware that a musical can be made about anything. Alan Jay Lerner and Burton Lane melodically and lightly tackle an age-old, provocative, and controversial topic—reincarnation—in the musical *On a Clear Day You Can See Forever*, directed by Vincente Minnelli.

The humdrum but vocally endowed Daisy sings about being "obsolete in my prime, out of date and outclassed by my past." That past is Melinda Tentrees, a psychic who lived in England from 1787 to 1850. She was convicted of conspiracy and executed. Melinda may have had a shady past and been a bit indiscreet in love, but the conservative Dr. Chabot finds her enchanting, especially in contrast to her modern counterpart.

At the beginning of his association with Daisy, who has sought hypnotic assistance to quit smoking to please her square boyfriend, Dr. Chabot calls ESP "pure, unadulterated rubbish." He dismisses Daisy's abilities to know others' thoughts, to know when the telephone will ring, and to grow flowers quickly. He calls Daisy's Melinda memories "shadows and echoes of things that never were," and labels reincarnation "fantasy."

Dr. Chabot says there have been thousands of cases such as Daisy's, all traced back to something in the people's present lives, and he intends to find the answers in Daisy's boring life.

Dr. Mason Hume (Bob Newhart), the president of the medical school where Dr. Chabot teaches, represents reincarnation's skeptics: "I think reincarnation is appalling. It kills ambition, perpetuates human misery, and propagates false hopes, and is obviously a pack of lies." But then he adds, "I *may* be wrong."

Dr. Conrad Fuller (Simon Oakland) is much more open to the study of extrasensory powers, but recognizes their threat to conventional psychiatric theories. He tells his friend Dr. Chabot, "If reincarnation is ever proven, do you know who will be hardest hit? The sweethearts of Sigmund Freud."

For thousands of years Eastern thought has embraced reincarnation, and the idea is closely associated with Buddhism and Hinduism. In the movie *A Passage to India*, the Brahmin Godbole (Alec Guinness) says, "Life is a wheel with many spokes—a continuous cycle of life, birth, death, and rebirth, until we attain *Nirvana*."

Belief in a cycle of births and rebirths historically has had Western proponents as well. Many citizens of the ancient Western world believed in reincarnation, as have mystics within Western religions, including Christianity. In the last few decades, case studies and near-death experiences have supplied a wealth of evidence suggesting reincarnation as a plausible natural law that hints at mysteries of the human plight and gives us pointers about living our present lives.

Dr. Christopher M. Bache, author of *Lifecycles: Reincarnation and the Web of Life*, writes of the concept's profoundness: "Reincarnation weds our individual evolution to the larger evolution of the universe, and we become more significant participants in everything that is taking place around us.

This inevitably will cause us to raise our philosophical estimate of the purpose of human existence."[5]

Both Dr. Chabot and Daisy become more aware of purpose in life as a result of their brushes with reincarnation. Daisy grows more self-assured and assertive. Dr. Chabot, who even uses extrasensory perception to contact Daisy, helps Daisy know her strengths. He sings, "On a clear day, rise and look around you, and you'll see who you are./ On a clear day, how it will astound you that the glow of your being outshines every star."

Dr. Chabot's own worldview enlarges: "I used to be in love with answers, but since I have known you, I'm just as fond of the questions. I think the answers make you wise, but the questions make you human." He learns that his opportunities to explore questions and answers may not be confined to one lifetime.

Ye View

1. In her final hypnosis, what does Daisy say about her other lives? At this point, what are Dr. Chabot's feelings about the possibility of reincarnation?
2. Referring to Daisy, Dr. Chabot asks, "How did you ever become this little nothing of a creature?" From a reincarnational view, why might Daisy differ so much from Melinda?
3. What is your personal belief about reincarnation?

In the Same Spirit

Meeting themselves coming and going in other comic-romantic films about reincarnation and soul-hopping:

All of Me—The spirit of a deceased wealthy woman (Lily Tomlin) inhabits a young lawyer (Steve Martin). (1984, 93 minutes, PG)

Chances Are—Returning in the body of a younger man (Robert

Downey, Jr.), the spirit of a widow's husband calls upon his former wife (Cybill Shepherd). (1989, 108 minutes, PG)

Heart and Souls—A young man (again Robert Downey, Jr.) finds himself the physical host of four victims of a bus accident. (1993, 104 minutes, PG-13)

Heaven Can Wait—"Are you kidding? You're going to put me into the body of another man? I just got *my* body back in shape," says a disbelieving Joe Pendleton (Warren Beatty), a football player, to a celestial official (James Mason) attempting to correct an error that caused Joe to die before his time. Joe returns in the body of a wealthy businessman not previously noted for his good heart. (1978, 100 minutes, PG) This is a remake of *Here Comes Mr. Jordan,* with Robert Montgomery as a prizefighter. (1941, 93 minutes, NR)

Made in Heaven—Mike (Timothy Hutton) and Annie (Kelly McGillis) are a perfect match in heaven, but can they be reunited on Earth? Of particular interest is the depiction of heaven as a creative launch pad for Earth life. Annie, a new soul who was born in heaven, tells the recently deceased Mike, "Anything that you can imagine *is*, and anything that is in heaven will eventually find its way back to Earth. Nothing is lost." Of course, she adds, you can imagine only good things in heaven. (1987, 103 minutes, PG)

THEME MATES

Serious twists on reincarnation:

Dead Again—A detective named Church (Kenneth Branagh) and a woman with amnesia, Grace (Emma Thompson), are linked to a long-ago murder. (1991, 107 minutes, R)

The Search for Bridey Murphy is an intriguing look at a woman with past-life recall. (1956, 84 minutes, NR) Compare her story with the present-day multiple personalities seen in *The Three Faces of Eve* with Joanne Woodward. (1957, 91 minutes, NR)

THE PURPLE ROSE OF CAIRO

PREVIEW

Cecilia (Mia Farrow), a waitress who escapes the Depression and her depressing marriage by going to the movies, is surprised when the handsome character Tom Baxter (Jeff Daniels) literally walks out of a film and into her life. (1985, 82 minutes, PG)

META VIEW

Illusions meet illusions in the cinema of life

Really, who's to say what is real anyway? Many spiritual teachings suggest that life as we know it is, in some way, an illusion, and that our waking world is no more real than our dream world. The Hindus, for example, use the word *maya* to suggest our tricky world of appearances that only *seems* real. Everything is as real as we believe it is. *A Course in Miracles* maintains that everything in this world, including space and time, is an illusion. Such outlooks don't mean, however, that the illusions, which do appear very real to us, aren't meaningful within the grand design of creation and the journeys of our souls.

Our minds, it has been suggested, are powerful image makers. How fascinating is the analogy that life is like movies our minds are playing as we ourselves make up the scripts and operate the projectors! Movies then become illusions within illusions. Actors and actresses in movies are themselves illusions, projections of the soul, pretending to be other illusions. To adapt Shakespeare, the world is a movie, and men and women are the players and producers.

Into such a backdrop of cosmic screening comes *The Purple Rose of Cairo*. Writer and director Woody Allen skillfully and wittingly toys with the whole concept of reality, on-screen and offscreen. He creates his own illusionary world in which the characters in the movie *The Purple Rose of Cairo* (the name of the movie within the movie of the same name—another illusion within an illusion) talk to audiences and can even mingle with them, argue among themselves, and worry about having the projector turned off and their being annihilated. Audiences are generally upset because they don't want their well-defined bubble of reality to burst: movie characters are supposed to follow the script and stay on the screen!

One irate moviegoer says, "I want what happened in the movie last week to happen this week; otherwise, what's life all about anyway?"

One character on the screen—among those just sitting around because the Tom Baxter character has run out of the film and run off with Cecilia—finally reasons:

"Let's redefine ourselves as the real world, and *them* [the audience] as the world of illusion and shadow. You see, *we're* reality and *they're* a dream."

A fellow character quips: "You'd better calm down. You've been up on the screen flickering too long."

Allen has some great fun and one-liners at reality's expense, but he also gives us a heartbreaking story of a poor, plain, lonely, mistreated, unloved woman who suddenly finds herself loved both by a dashing screen character and the actor who plays that character (the latter gets into the picture to persuade the character he "fleshed out" to return to the screen). She is romanced and wined and dined like a movie star herself.

How does Cecilia feel? "I'm confused. . . . I just met a wonderful new man. He's fictional, but you can't have everything."

Tom Baxter says he loves Cecilia and wants to learn about the "real world" with her, but he knows only what has been written into his character, and he has trouble acclimating in a world where he needs real money and a key to start a car.

Cecilia tells him that in her world "people get old and sick and never find true love."

Tom replies, "You know, where I come from people don't disappoint; they're consistent; they're always reliable."

Cecilia says, "You don't find that kind in real life."

Tom thinks that God must be the movie writer who created his "real world." Cecilia explains God as "a reason for everything. Otherwise, it would be like a movie with no point—and no happy ending."

It seems to be a topsy-turvy world where, as a movie honcho says, "The real ones want their lives fiction, and the fictional ones want their lives real." Perhaps it's all the same, anyway, although I for one *know* that Madison, the mermaid in the movie *Splash,* truly exists, Yoda is no figment of imagination, and Indiana Jones is as real as I am—however real *that* is.

YE VIEW

1. "The most human of all attributes is your ability to choose," one movie character says. Discuss crucial choices that Cecilia must make.
2. Why is Cecilia attracted to the movie world? Why is Tom attracted to the "real world"?
3. Recall some times when you have felt as if life were not "real." What is your view of the nature of reality?

IN THE SAME SPIRIT

Other flicks that creatively play with the idea of the illusory nature of reality:

Benny and Joon—A strange young man (Johnny Depp) lives in his own world of silent film comedy, but he has a profound effect on a brother and sister. (1993, 98 minutes, PG)

Don Juan DeMarco—The spirit of love—and perhaps the legendary Spanish lover himself—is alive and well in an enigmatic young man

(Johnny Depp again) who gives his psychiatrist (Marlon Brando) a new perspective on life. (1995, 97 minutes, PG-13)

Harvey—Elwood P. Dowd (James Stewart), an extremely likable but rather eccentric man, insists, much to his family's chagrin, that he has been befriended by an invisible rabbit named Harvey who is 6 feet 3 inches tall. Mary Chase's play makes a delightful transition to the screen. (1950, 104 minutes, NR)

Who Framed Roger Rabbit—It's a dizzying, highly animated world of people and cartoon characters interacting in this inventive work from the Disney Studios and Steven Spielberg. Robert Zemeckis directed the humorous antics, in which a detective (Bob Hoskins) tries to clear Toon star Roger Rabbit of a murder rap. (1988, 103 minutes, PG, *)

THEME MATES

For a darker look at illusion and reality:

Who's Afraid of Virginia Woolf?—Professor George (Richard Burton) and his wife Martha (Elizabeth Taylor), with strong language and piercing dialogue, illustrate how frightening it can be to abandon our illusions and try to understand reality and illusion in this Edward Albee drama. (1966, 129 minutes, NR)

RASHOMON

PREVIEW

Each of the four people involved in a rape-murder in a forest tells a greatly different story about what happened in this internationally acclaimed film by Japan's preeminent filmmaker, Akira Kurosawa. (1950, Japanese, 88 minutes, NR)

META VIEW

We create our own realities

My reality is not the same as *your* reality or anyone else's. No matter how much overlap there is in experiences and observations, what one individual perceives as reality—as the truth, if you will—is not identical with what another individual perceives. Each of us is a spiritual being constantly creating our own life through an individual, unique perspective. Each person's perspective is formed by his or her specific personality traits and values, background, and intentions.

Such a viewpoint of many metaphysical thinkers is dramatically captured in the events surrounding the rape of a noblewoman (Machiko Kyo) by the infamous bandit Tajomaru (Toshiro Mifune) and the death of the woman's husband (Masayuki Mori). The woman, the bandit, a firewood dealer (Takashi Shimura), and the woman's dead husband (through a medium) offer their own interpretations of what happened.

Each version is different, because each person sees and recounts from his or her own perspective. Actions that mean one thing to one participant mean something entirely different to another participant. One person offers an explanation of an act, while the same act is viewed differently by another person. For example, the firewood dealer and the woman have different slants as to why Tajomaru tells the woman that he is a famous bandit. One person has cause to remember and describe an event one way, but another person has a different motive for describing the same event in another way. For example, Tajomaru tells of the woman's strength and fierceness following the attack, but her husband recounts the woman's weakness.

Which stories are true? What really happened? It becomes difficult to decide about details, because each person has an individual viewpoint. Each person's perspective is derived from personality factors, and may include deliberate attempts, either consciously or subconsciously, to fashion events into a preferred pattern. A priest (Minoru Chiaki) who is attempting to understand how the stories can be so divergent says, "Because men are weak, they lie . . . to deceive themselves." Each person is constantly creating his or her own reality, but sometimes that reality includes deceptions for the individual and for others. These are complex stories that we create, and the truth about an individual's reality is within the individual.

The movie's title has become synonymous with the elusiveness of truth.

YE VIEW

1. What are some of the other major discrepancies among the four stories about the events in the forest?
2. How do the firewood dealer's actions help the priest keep his "faith in man"? Why is the priest's faith in jeopardy?
3. Think about a recent event in your life in which participants disagreed about details of what happened. What factors went into your own perception of the event? Single out one other person in the event and give several reasons why that person's perspective may have differed from yours.

THEME MATES

Another serious matter of perception:

A Passage to India—A young British woman (Judy Davis), in India for the first time during the 1920s, makes alarming accusations about events during a pleasure outing, and sends cultural shock waves throughout the community. The truth is as mysterious as the country in this David Lean film of the E. M. Forster novel. (1984, British, 163 minutes, PG)

185

And now, a humorous matter of perception:

The Englishman Who Went Up a Hill, but Came Down a Mountain—Welsh villagers become irate when mapmakers (including Hugh Grant) classify their mountain a hill. A small survey issue becomes a large perception issue because the people are perceiving the truth of their own worth in relation to their landmark. (1995, British, 99 minutes, PG)

THE RAZOR'S EDGE

PREVIEW

Returning from World War I, Larry Darrell (Bill Murray) leaves his fiancée and job prospects, and travels to France and India in search of life's meaning. (1984, 128 minutes, PG-13)

META VIEW

Just keep calmly walking!

Do you ever think about walking out on the life you know? Are there times when you don't want to keep up with the Joneses anymore? Do you ever think that your values are shallow and that your life has no meaning?

Then you, like many, can identify with the character of Larry Darrell. It takes the horrors of war to open the eyes of the hero of W. Somerset Maugham's novel. Tragedies and challenges have a way of making us see things differently and leading us to start spiritual journeys and reevaluate priorities.

"I got a second chance at life," the unhappy Larry says in breaking off his engagement to Isabel (Catherine Hicks). "I am not going to waste it on a big house and a new car every year and a bunch of friends who want a big house and a new car every year."

Admirably, Larry wishes to think about life. When he shows that initial willingness and desire necessary to connect with the Universe, he is guided to where he needs to be. He works as a fish packer and then as a coal miner. He saves the life of a fellow miner, who gives him a book of the Upanishad, Vedic scripture, and tells him to go to India for answers. In India, he immediately meets a man who volunteers to take him to a holy place in the mountains, where he serves as a cook, and studies and contemplates.

When Larry leaves, a lama suggests that Larry is close to being a holy man, but cautions, "The path to salvation is narrow and as difficult to walk as a razor's edge."

Back in Paris, Larry discovers just how difficult the walk on the razor's edge can be. Old friends have been going through rough times (the Depression, personally and globally), including the woman he has always loved, Sophie (Theresa Russell). Because of his time of spiritual renewal, however, Larry has become centered and is able to respond to events with control, compassion, healing, and understanding. He walks the walk calmly, apparently from the perspective that life has meaning, but the answers are part of a Big Picture we don't always see.

187

YE VIEW

1. What are some examples of Larry's control and compassion?
2. What is Larry talking about when he says, "There is no payoff— not now." How does the comment apply to Sophie? To his own life?
3. Larry says, "It is easy to be a holy man on the top of a mountain." Why might it not be so easy to be a holy man in a city?

IN THE SAME SPIRIT

For an earlier search:
The Razor's Edge—Tyrone Power and Anne Baxter star in the first movie version of the novel, and it's a sharp image. (1946, 146 minutes, NR)

THEME MATES

Questing for meaning too:
The Muppet Movie—Kermit, from the swamps of Georgia, and the rest of the Jim Henson gang on their way to Hollywood are representative of life's eternal quest for stardom in this enjoyable feature. (1979, 94 minutes, G, *)
The Treasure of the Sierra Madre—Three prospectors (Humphrey Bogart, Walter Huston, and Tim Holt) illustrate the baser routes of the human quest for something that will bring lasting fulfillment (and that something is *not* gold, folks). (1948, 124 minutes, NR)

THE REVOLT OF JOB

PREVIEW

During the Nazi takeover of Hungary, an elderly Jewish couple, Job and Roza (Ferenc Zenthe and Hedi Temessy), adopts a Christian boy, Lacko (Gabor Feher), to carry on their spiritual values. (1983, Hungarian-German, 97 minutes, PG-13)

META VIEW

Where is God?

At first it seems that Job and Roza have made a poor trade for their two calves—a wild boy from an orphanage. Roza thinks they've made a mistake, but Job is confident. Seeing God's work in everything, Job says: "You don't choose offspring. The Lord gives them."

It soon becomes apparent that the Lord has given them a most sensitive and inquisitive boy to replace their seven natural children, who have all died.

Lacko is especially curious about God, a new concept to him. "Who is God?" he asks. Told that God is locked in the Jewish services on the Sabbath and in the Christian church on Sunday, Lacko says that he will free God.

"I'm looking for God," Lacko says as he roams the countryside. Job teaches him that God is in everything and is everywhere, and Lacko does begin to see God in all situations and happenings, such as in a writhing dance that a young man brings back from the front. Dealing with the political climate of the time, the young Lacko also must learn to see God's goodness and love in the midst of heartbreak and human cruelty.

An intensely religious man, Job gives Lacko much spiritual advice (such as telling him that a man isn't "bad," although he can do a "bad thing"). However, Job asks a Christian friar to instruct Lacko about the "lamb of God," who takes away the sins of the world. The friar says that Lacko needs to know only that. In addition to looking for God, Lacko starts looking for the Messiah.

Townspeople call Jews "rotten," but the values and actions of Job and Roza strongly contradict this description.

The movie was inspired by director Imre Gyongyossy's childhood experiences. Sobering statistics at the end of the movie reveal that between May

189

✳

and October of 1944, more than 600,000 Jews were deported from Hungary, and that 500,000 never returned.

YE VIEW

1. What is Job's revolt? What does Job mean by saying that he has outwitted Hitler?
2. Does Papa Job in the movie have any character traits in common with Job in the Old Testament story? Compare the two characters.
3. This adage recurs in the movie: "Everyone's plate has a different flower." What does the saying mean to you?

A RIVER RUNS THROUGH IT

PREVIEW

Two brothers—Norman (Craig Sheffer) and Paul (Brad Pitt)—both learn about fly-fishing and spirituality from their minister father (Tom Skerritt) but cast widely different life lines. (1992, 124 minutes, PG)

META VIEW

Fish for the Big One

"In our family there was no clear line between religion and fly-fishing," states narrator Norman at the beginning of director Robert Redford's adaptation of Norman Maclean's autobiography. Norman and Paul grew up experiencing their father's devotion to God and to fly-fishing in the beautiful wilderness of Montana during the early 1900s.

What is this connection that Reverend Maclean finds between God and fly-fishing? We begin to understand by examining the two words. The English word *religion* comes to us from the Latin root *religare*, meaning "to retie" or "rebind." Religion, then, is about reconnecting with the presence of God that is our true Self. The concept of tying is also vital to fly-fishing: fishing flies are tied or bound when made and then tied or fastened to the hook; the term for making the flies is *tying*. Clearly, though, fly-fishing means more than the sport to Reverend Maclean; the activity itself is an act of being a part of "the natural side of God's order" (Norman's phrase). To Maclean, fly-fishing, like life itself, requires diligence, patience, and skill, and those who succeed at either connect with some inner spark of divinity. Fly-fishing can be seen as a metaphor for life and the proper way to live life.

What, then, is the proper way to live life, as represented by fly-fishing? Reverend Maclean seems to believe that fly-fishing represents becoming one with the rhythm of God. Although Reverend Maclean, a Presbyterian minister, thinks that humans come into life messed up, he does think that they regain power and beauty by picking up "God's rhythms." Norman says about his father, "To him, all good things, trout as well as eternal salvation, come by grace, and grace comes by art, and art does not come easy." The art of life, then, is reconnecting with the presence and rhythm of God—religion's purpose.

"Eventually," Norman says, "all things merge into one, and a river runs through it."

Fly-fishing is the art of life, and the river that runs through life is God-life or God-energy. Sometimes, however, what we have to wade through while we are fishing isn't all that pleasant. It is probably easier to connect with a sense of God's peace and presence while fishing or hiking in the gorgeous, serene Montana mountains than while coping with some of life's more unpicturesque environments and more unsettling times. The movie meets these times in our artistic pursuits head-on, and the family must deal with fighting, drinking, gambling, and killing. Norman says that he and Paul understood, even as children, that the world is tough "and admired it."

191
✳

It's all a part of the art form. Norman notes, however, that "life is not a work of art," in the sense that it is perfect.

The brothers represent two different types of artists and varying ways of experiencing life: Norman is steady and traditional in his approach to life; Paul is daring and seems to actually taunt the presence of God. Yet both boys, in their own ways, become accomplished artists on life's palette.

We may not always understand how others are pursuing the art of life (and the Maclean family certainly doesn't always understand Paul), but Reverend Maclean says there *is* something we can always do: "We can still love them. We can love completely, without complete understanding." Calling up such love is a real art too, but we know that love is the essence of the river which runs through it all.

Ye View

1. What do you think Reverend Maclean means when he calls Paul "beautiful"? Explain.
2. What are some other metaphors for life that seem appropriate to you? Discuss.
3. Describe your own artistic techniques for living or your philosophy of life.

THE SEVENTH SEAL

Preview

In fourteenth-century Sweden, where the black plague roams, the knight Antonius Block (Max von Sydow) returns from ten years in the Crusades, and enters into a chess game with Death while trying to fathom life. (1957, Swedish, subtitled, 96 minutes, NR)

META VIEW

Checkmate: Death doesn't have the answers

Ingmar Bergman's hypnotic allegory may at first seem dark, depressing, and foreboding. The people talk and sing of virtually nothing but the black plague, omens, and death; and Death himself shows up periodically to play chess, claim another person, and listen to the knight's questions.

But there is hope and light at the end of this dark tunnel. However, one must listen closely to what Death says and observe the play actors to find that hope and light. While Antonius searches desperately for answers to the meaning of existence, the answers are right before him.

Antonius has perhaps been crusading and searching too long. He is tired, has grown indifferent to people, and wants to die, but not without first gaining knowledge. He knows instinctively that God exists, but wants outer proof.

He asks: "Is it so hard to perceive God with one's senses? Why must He hide in a mist of vague promises and invisible miracles? How are we to believe the believers, when we don't believe ourselves? What will become of us who want to believe but cannot? And what of those who neither will nor *can* believe? Why can I not kill God within me? . . . I want to tear him out of my heart, but He remains a mocking reality which I cannot get rid of."

Many believing faithful have such questions, usually unvoiced.

The knight's mistake is that he keeps asking Death for answers. He's asking the wrong person or idea. Death, in fact, professes to know nothing, but Antonius won't accept "nothing" for an answer. In Truth, Death does know nothing, because death is an idea that doesn't exist in God, but only in the mind of humankind. In an omnipotent, omnipresent God, life is eternal, and there *is* no death. When we cross the veil we call death, we discover that life continues.

Death says that most people do not think of death, or nothingness. This

193
✳

is true of most of the characters in the movie, including the smith and his wife, and the young housekeeper. The smith's philosophical take on life is "Isn't life . . . a dirty mess?"

The knight's squire, Jons, however, is the type of person who is convinced that there is no ultimate meaning. There is only emptiness beyond, he says, and he tells Antonius, "You are reflected in your own indifference."

His philosophy is to "feel, to the very end, the triumph of being alive." He is correct that life has more answers than death, but he doesn't see the answers, only the experiences. He doesn't connect experiences to get meaningful answers, and he doesn't see the continuity of life.

Antonius refuses to accept his squire's nihilistic thinking. He prays, at the hour of his death, "God, who are somewhere, who *must* be somewhere, have mercy on us!"

Where is the truth about life that Antonius seeks? It is there the whole time. Ironically and significantly, it is symbolized by the actors, Joseph and Mary, and their child Michael, who travel in a caravan. Joseph is an innocent, happy and loving. He also has visions of the Virgin Mary and Christ and angels. His visions are true, Joseph tells his wife, "not the reality you see, but another kind." It's the kind of reality Antonius seeks. Indeed, the knight is drawn to this family of holy allusions and says that he will treasure the time of peace with them. At a subconscious level, he may be attracted to them because of their love and joy in living, and he may sense that they possess life's meaning. He stalls the chess game so the family can escape Death. When Death has called the knight and his companions, Joseph sees them dancing "away toward the dark lands while the rain cleanses their cheeks from the salt of their bitter tears." The group is dancing, with its idea of death, toward the unknown. Joseph's expression, however, is not sad or frightened, and his allusion to rain cleansing tears from their cheeks suggests the peace and joy that he knows await after death.

YE VIEW

1. What do you think is the significance of having Death and the knight play chess? What abilities does chess require?
2. Choose one of the knight's questions, presented in Meta View, and discuss it. Try to provide a reasonable answer to the question.
3. What is the meaning of the movie's title? How does it relate to the knight's quest for meaning and to the events in the country?

IN THE SAME SPIRIT

Bergman's "faith" trilogy:
Through a Glass Darkly—A woman with schizophrenia and her family seek answers about God in the first in the director's complex "faith" trilogy. (1961, Swedish, 91 minutes, NR) Like *The Seventh Seal,* the dramatic trilogy, involving various unsettling and unsettled characters, explores deep, dark outreaches of faith. Next in the series are *Winter Light,* about a priest (1963, Swedish, 80 minutes, NR) and *The Silence,* concerning two sisters. (1963, Swedish, 95 minutes, NR)

195

❋

SIMON BIRCH

PREVIEW

A 12-year-old boy who is a dwarf, Simon Birch (Ian Michael Smith), awaits his God-given opportunity to be a hero, while his best friend, Joe Wenteworth (Joseph Mazzello), searches for the father he has never known in this film suggested by John Irving's novel *A Prayer for Owen Meany.* (1998, 110 minutes, PG, *)

God's on first

In the same summer that Mark McGwire hit 70 home runs, theaters premiered this movie about a boy who hits *one*—but Simon's hit is a foul ball, not a record homer, and it has far-reaching results that pose this question: Is there a divine plan for our lives?

As it does in *Simon Birch*, life at times may seem to be in divine disorder, but things must be in divine order in a universe with an omnipotent God, so things are actually in divine order when they appear to be in divine *dis*order. Sounds like an old Abbott and Costello routine about Simon's favorite sport: "Who's on first?" The answer is that God is always on first. The game of life *does* make sense; we just don't always know how all the innings are playing out.

Simon believes there is a divine plan for everyone, and he takes the action required of us to live from the perspective that all is in divine order. Here is our role in the game:

- "Seek first the kingdom of God and His righteousness" (Mt. 6:33 NKJV), which is having faith that God is the only power and presence, and that everything works together for the highest good of all and eventually comes together in the eternal energy of God.

Simon is clear that there is a God and that *he* is part of God's grand plan. "I'm God's instrument," he says. "There are no accidents. God has a plan for all of us."

He is convinced that God is going to make him a hero, but Joe asks him what proof he has. "I don't need proof," Simon responds. "I have faith."

The young Joe, however, thinks that believing in God is like believing in Santa Claus and the Easter Bunny, and tells Simon to stop trying to make sense of everything.

- Be aware of what a friend calls the wonderful "God stuff" happening in our lives, all around us, in order to connect events and better understand the Big Picture.

The adult Joe (Jim Carrey) asks in narration about unresolved and sorrowful events during his childhood, "How could we have known that everything was working together for a reason?"

It is often difficult to know, but we can with faith and with an awareness of our intuitive feelings and of the synchronicities in our lives. Simon intuitively knows when his moment to be a hero arrives.

- Have patience while the game is going on. Wait patiently and know that the kingdom of God is unfolding in divine order.

That's frequently easier said than done. With all of his faith and despite his young age, Simon still naturally gets impatient that God hasn't made him a hero yet. "I'm going to be a hero. I keep waiting for God to show me a sign. I have been patient, but I'm running out of time."

Along with impatience we often encounter feelings of doubt that all is in divine order, but impatience and doubt come to all at times. Simon asks Reverend Russell (David Strathairn) to assure him that God has a plan for all of us, and the minister says, "Simon, I can't."

- Even with occasional impatience and doubt, remain expectant and assume an attitude of excitement and anticipation that the will of God—which is always good—is unfolding in our lives. Simon has this sense of expectancy about him, and it befuddles his friends and those who come in contact with him.
- Give thanks that all is in divine order, no matter what the appearances may suggest. Simon knows that God has made him like he is for a reason, and he lives his thankfulness with a positive, hopeful, expectant attitude.

197

Joe learns from Simon's example. The adult Joe says that Simon is the reason he believes in God. "It is Simon who made me a believer."

YE VIEW

1. What personal strengths does Simon show as a hero?
2. What does Joe mean when he says that he has finally found his "real father"?
3. Discuss events and situations in your own life that seem to support or negate Simon's contention that there are no accidents and that there is a divine plan for everyone.

SLIDING DOORS

PREVIEW

Two possible but very different scenarios for the life of Helen (Gwyneth Paltrow) play out based on whether she catches or misses a London underground train. (1998, 105 minutes, PG-13)

META VIEW

Explore parallel lives and probable realities

When the doors in this movie slide, they reveal some challenging questions about the very nature of reality.

Sliding Doors poses these questions by engagingly, intelligently, and cleverly following Helen's two parallel lives. In one scenario, Helen gets on the train and comes home, to find her boyfriend having an affair with his mistress; she then goes to a bar and is befriended by a caring, personable guy named James (John Hannah). In the second scenario, Helen misses the train, as well as her boyfriend's rendezvous, but she later *suspects* that he is cheating on her. Writer and director Peter Howitt artfully juggles the two possible lives at once, and helps viewers keep the story lines straight by having Helen change her hairdo in one plot. As strictly an entertainment experience, the first scenario is the most enjoyable, because a pleasing romantic attachment develops between Helen and James.

However, the movie isn't just about romance. It's ultimately more concerned with questions that arise from varying reverberations which ripple through people's lives by events they encounter and decisions they make. It's always intriguing (and sometimes slightly maddening) to think about what has happened and what *might* have happened in our lives (for example, what if I *had* taken that bureaucratic job in Washington, D.C., fresh out of college?), so it's rather fun to have Howitt give us a case history to follow. Questions about the characters' different actions and reactions start haunting us as the movie progresses, and we muse whether or not one scenario is more "real" (whatever *that* is) than the other. Somewhere along the way, one may even wonder: What if Helen's parallel lives play differently but end up the same way? What would that say about parallel lives and fate?

Further, *Sliding Doors* opens up issues that are dear to the minds and hearts of readers of the "energy personality essence" named Seth and other proponents of probable realities and probable selves.

If our thoughts are prayers and lead to actions, where do multiple, conflicting thoughts and actions lead? Might we, without consciously knowing it, be experiencing multiple probable realities with probable selves, each roaming around having its own individual field day with life? In *Seth Speaks: The Eternal Validity of the Soul* by Jane Roberts, we read, "The soul can be described for that matter, as a multidimensional, infinite act, each minute probability being brought somewhere into actuality and existence; an infinite creative act that creates for itself infinite dimensions in which fulfillment is possible."[6]

YE VIEW

1. What do you think influences what happens and doesn't happen in our lives?
2. Share an important situation in your own life about which you have wondered, "What if *another* scenario had happened?"
3. In *The Quest*, Richard and Mary-Alice Jafolla state, "We all live at Possibility Junction. Each 'now' moment is another junction, the chance to make another decision. In each now moment, we decide what we want out of life."[7] How might this statement apply to Helen's scenarios?

THEME MATES

Traveling through realities:

Back to the Future—"Doc, are you telling me that you built a time machine . . . out of a DeLorean?" an incredulous Marty McFly (Michael J. Fox) asks Dr. Brown (Christopher Lloyd). Doc's time machine has enough plutonium to get Marty back to 1955, where he must help his parents meet or he won't exist in 1985. (1985, 116 minutes, PG) This popular comedy and its sequels, *Back to the Future Part II* (1989, 107 minutes, PG) and *Back to the Future Part III* (1990, 118 minutes, PG), actually offer intriguing possibilities about multiple realities. Marty and Doc use a time machine to access other realities, where they influence events in multiple realities, but perhaps they are only doing what our souls are already doing at levels that we are not aware of.

2001: A SPACE ODYSSEY

PREVIEW

A large black monolith of unexplainable origin puzzles apelike hominids and, four million years later, their astronaut descendants who journey toward Jupiter to solve the mystery in this visionary, visual masterpiece. (1968, British, 139 minutes, G)

META VIEW

My, how time flies!

The future is now and then and will be again. Time, like the whirling space station of *2001*, goes around and around to celestial waltzes, and yet somehow remains in place. Apelike hominids one minute and astronauts the next, the energy of life continually rotates and projects. We take monolithic strides that return us to the beginning.

Since its own creation in the imagination and intellect of author Arthur C. Clarke and director-author Stanley Kubrick, *2001* has intrigued and mystified with its seeming comprehension of life and infinity. What exactly does this big picture say about the Big Picture? What is *your* reaction to it? That's the odyssey it presents; that's the Big Picture. Surely its creators wanted the meaning of the movie to be open-ended. One view of Truth is as absolute as the next, but paradoxically Truth itself never changes.

From one perspective, *2001* may be viewed as a breathtaking, visually exciting glimpse of the all-encompassing, ever-revealing energy of God, Spirit, or Universal Mind—or whatever you call All That Is.

As it seems to in life, the nature or substance of God-energy remains unfathomable and mysterious in the movie. Through special effects and artful photography and editing, we see and sense that the Presence is powerful and

201

vast and that it is dazzling light and profound quiet, even though we're not certain exactly what It is.

The movie shows something of humankind's relationship with the Infinite, which can be symbolized by the black monolith. In the initial Dawn of Man section, our apelike ancestors reveal reactions that have always characterized humankind's response to its Source: they are inquisitive, puzzled, fearful, and awed. In encounters with the monolith several million years later, humankind displays the same reactions. Throughout the ages, we have felt compelled to be near the Infinite, to touch It in whatever way we can, and to understand Its wonders. Like the apelike creatures before us, we continue to circle around the Infinite and reach out to It.

This exploration, this odyssey, of ours seems part of the cosmic dance of God-energy. When we are closest in conscious recognition of creative God-energy, we make quantum leaps as a species. After reaching out to the monolith, the hominids discover weapons (bones that can be used in defense or in food gathering). After finding the monolith on the moon, later humans chase after the monolith's signal source and come face-to-face with the mystery of birth itself and the cycle of life.

Along the way, the human mind is free to apply its discoveries and inventions in ways that may be labeled "good" or "bad," but that nevertheless just "are," and these ways are learning experiences. Hominids, for example, are shown using their weapons apparently for the sheer experience or fun of hurting others (it has been ever thus). Modern humans in the movie deal with problems arising from their own use of Universal Energy with the invention of the supposedly perfect HAL 9000 computer. In the person of the commander of the *Discovery* mission (Keir Dullea), humankind is shown rising to new challenges with admirable calmness and assurance.

Throughout the expanse of time and space, monoliths appear, new dawns arise, and humankind continues its odyssey to know and understand the Infinite.

YE VIEW

1. Do you think that aliens placed the monolith on the Earth and the moon? If so, for what purpose?
2. HAL says, "I am putting myself to the fullest possible use, which is all, I think, that any conscious entity can ever hope to do." Comment on the statement, specifically in light of what happens to HAL, and generally in terms of human achievements.
3. What is your own understanding of the ending of the movie? What does it say about life, birth, and God-energy?

IN THE SAME SPIRIT

If you want an "official" meaning and ending:
2010—Americans and Soviets join forces to find out what happened on the Jupiter mission. (1984, 114 minutes, PG)

The Really Big Picture: The Mahabharata

Just how serious are you about wanting to grasp life's Big Picture?

If you're *really* serious, you could read the *Mahabharata,* India's great spiritual epic. Allow some time, though. There are 100,000 verses, which add up to seven times the combined length of the Greek epics the *Iliad* and the *Odyssey.*

Life's too busy to take that much time to read about life? Consider instead the movie *The Mahabharata.* Watching the movie will take less time than reading the eighteen books and appendix of the epic, but you'll still have to allow more than five hours.

Director Peter Brook's 1989 film is a three-video, 318-minute adaptation of the Jean-Claude Carriere stage production.

The viewing is an incredible experience, though, that sends the mind and the heart reeling into human and cosmic dramas. "If you listen carefully, at the end you will be somebody else," says the epic's storyteller, Vyasa (Robert Langdon Lloyd).

The Mahabharata is a complex, mythical, symbolical story of two feuding families, the Pandavas and the Kauravas. It is, Vyasa says, "the poetical history of mankind," but it is also the story of good versus evil, of wars and relationships, of kings and kingdoms, of Hindu gods and spiritual lore.

Particularly powerful is the section, in Part Two of the movie, known as the Bhagavad Gita. Here Krishna (Bruce Myers), an incarnation of the god Vishnu, preserver of the world, instructs the Pandavas hero Arjuna (Vittorio Mezzogiorno) about life:

- "Don't withdraw into solitude. Renunciation is not enough. You must act. Yet action mustn't dominate you. In the heart of action, you must remain free from all attachment."

204
✳

- "There's another intelligence beyond the mind."
- "I am all that you think, all that you say. Everything hangs on me. . . .
  I am appearance and disappearance. . . . I am the radiance of all that
  shines. I am time grown old. All beings fall into the night, and all beings are pulled back to the daylight. I have already defeated all these
  warriors. To you who thinks he can kill and he who thinks he can be
  killed (both mistaken): No weapon can pierce the life that informs
  you; no fire can burn it; no water can drench it; no wind can make it
  dry. Have no fear and rise up, because I love you."

Completing his lesson, Krishna tells Arjuna: "Now you can dominate
your mysterious and incomprehensible spirit. You can see its other side. Act
as you *must* act."

Arjuna responds: "My illusion is dissolved, my error destroyed. By your
grace, now I am firm; my doubts are dispersed."

May your five hours of viewing be so rewarding.

205

Rosalind Russell in *Auntie Mame*, Warner Bros.
Photo: The Museum of Modern Art Film Stills Archive

Chapter 5

Affirmin' in the Rain

O utlook is everything. How we view life and what we think about life form our experiences. As the song says, "Our thoughts are prayers, and we are always praying." We always have a choice how to react to whatever raindrops or challenges are pelting us. Like Gene Kelly, we can sing in the rain—(that is, affirm that we see the sunshine in the midst of the rain)—or we can mope about the rain—(that is, wallow in negative and limiting appearances). The movies in this chapter focus on positive, imaginative, life-affirming characters—both real, such as Jaime Escalante in *Stand and Deliver*, and fictional, such as Melanie in *Gone With the Wind*—who choose to see and proclaim the *good* and the potential for even *better* in their conditions and in others.

ANNIE

PREVIEW

"Leapin' lizards," Little Orphan Annie (Aileen Quinn) is as optimistic as ever as she comes to the screen via the stage and the comic strip, runs from orphanage director Miss Hannigan (Carol Burnett) and imposter parents, and wins the heart of billionaire Oliver Warbucks (Albert Finney). (1982, 128 minutes, PG, *)

META VIEW

The sun is out now too!

208

❋

Annie's anthem of positive thinking is the popular song "Tomorrow." She tells President Franklin D. Roosevelt, "Just thinking about tomorrow clears away the cobwebs and the sorrow." Annie sings that on grey, lonely days, she sticks out her chin, grins, tells herself that "the sun will come out tomorrow," and knows that she must "hang on" until then.

On the surface, that sounds quite uplifting, with the clear implication that good times and happy circumstances are ahead. However, the question before the metaphysical house is: How do thinking about tomorrow and holding the vision that the future will be better square with the spiritual directive to live in the now and practice the presence of God?

The answer is that it all depends on how one approaches tomorrow.

The "Tomorrow" philosophy isn't compatible with the living-in-the-now stance, if thinking about tomorrow means not putting value in the present moment, ignoring what it has to offer, and putting all of one's mental, emotional, and spiritual energy into hopes and dreams about the future. Such activity is totally bypassing the living, creating energy of God in the present. People who divorce themselves from earthly concerns and pin all their hopes on a "promised land" or heaven in the future are missing the kingdom of God at hand.

However, the "Tomorrow" philosophy works with living in the now, if thinking about tomorrow means letting go of any concerns and fears about the future and being able to concentrate on present situations and relationships. It is wise to entrust the future, like the present, to the will of God and to know that God's will for us is always good.

The truth is that the sun is always shining, today as well as tomorrow. Just as the sun is always beaming above the clouds in our atmosphere, the sunshine is always present in our lives, despite the apparent troubles. The problem is that we aren't always seeing the sunshine in our lives. Our perception is frequently only of the clouds. When we rise above our day-to-day concerns and have faith that divine order is outplaying, despite whatever appearances to the contrary, then we can appreciate our lives in the now. We can also rest assured that our present awareness of God's presence is creating a continued awareness of God's presence "tomorrow."

Annie lives from the latter "Tomorrow" philosophy. She has an enthusiasm for life, even in the orphanage, and uses her energy to bring about a better tomorrow by taking advantage of opportunities in the present, such as by describing *herself* when Warbucks' private secretary Grace Farrell (Ann Reinking) is specifying an orphan to adopt for a week. She also finds things to enjoy in the present, such as her dog Sandy or Daddy Warbucks' mansion. Just as she does for herself, Annie shows other people how to feel better in the present by thinking positive thoughts about the future.

Not only does Annie show that she is tuned in to the present, but she also helps other people become more observant of present surroundings and opportunities. Annie tells Daddy Warbucks, "I know it's none of my business, but you never notice anything." Her comment starts him thinking. He becomes more observant of Grace and of Annie, and gradually his capitalistic heart softens. "Making money was all I ever gave a damn about, up 'til now," he tells Annie, adding that he knows his money is worthless unless he shares it.

YE VIEW

1. What effect does Annie have on the other orphans? On Warbucks' staff, especially Grace? Why do you think she has such an effect?
2. What extrasensory powers does Warbucks' bodyguard Punjab (Geoffrey Holder) exhibit? How does he use those powers?
3. "You're Never Fully Dressed Without a Smile" the orphans sing. How does this idea relate to getting the most out of life in the present?

AUNTIE MAME

PREVIEW

The exuberant and wealthy Mame Dennis (Rosalind Russell) takes orphaned nephew Patrick Dennis under her flamboyant wing in 1928 and shows him how to fly through life with love and joy. (1958, 143 minutes, NR)

META VIEW

"Life is a banquet"—help yourself!

"'Z,'" according to Deepak Chopra in *The A-to-Z Steps to a Richer Life*, stands for "zest for life." That means "to appreciate life in all its vitality and exuberance. . . .

"As Don Juan once said to Carlos Castaneda, 'It does not matter what our specific fate is, as long as we face it with ultimate abandon.' This is carefreeness. This is joy. This is freedom. This is zest for life."[1]

Zeal, the attitude of excitement and enthusiasm that is one of humankind's twelve spiritual powers as enumerated by Unity's Charles Fillmore, is another word for *zest*. "To be without zeal is to be without the zest of living," Fillmore says.[2]

As a star of stage and screen, Mame burst out of Patrick Dennis' memories of his colorful relative in the novel *Auntie Mame*. Mame's appeal, in whatever media, is based in large measure on her particularly zestful approach to life. Her oft-quoted philosophy is:

"Life is a banquet, and most poor suckers are starving to death."

Live! Live! Live! is the title of her memoirs, and it is her personal motto.

To Mame, truly living at the banquet of life means two things: (1) being open to experiences and (2) loving.

When Patrick comes to live with her, Mame tells him: "Your Auntie Mame is going to open doors for you, Patrick, doors you never even dreamed existed. Oh, what times we're going to have!"

Through proverbial good times and bad, Mame keeps her promise. Patrick sees his aunt throwing her whole self into whatever life offers. Riding in a fox hunt for the first time, Mame does so well that the Southern plantation matron yells, "Mother of Jefferson Davis, she's passing the fox!" Mame "passes the fox" in overcoming any obstacles, even if she does so by the literal seat of her pants (as in the fox hunt).

Similarly, Mame gives wholeheartedly of herself in compassion and love—to Patrick, to others close to her, and to *anyone* in need. With love as a motivating force, Mame is in tune with Spirit.

"You're a loving woman, ma'am," says one of her household staff. "Oh, you're odd, but you're loving."

Patrick is raised realizing not that one has to be eccentric to enjoy life, but that one must retain a "zest for life," whatever happens. Sometimes that's

211

not easy, as when Mame and Patrick are in the doldrums during the Depression. Their zestful solution is to celebrate Christmas early, because "we need it now."

In her zest, Mame has a sense of humor and a sense of the absurd about the human condition. She really enjoys life, although she doesn't take the human too seriously. But in life's banquet, she definitely prefers caviar to tuna fish.

YE VIEW

1. What are some exciting doors that Mame opens for Patrick?
2. Why does Mame say that Patrick has become a snob? What do you think of her solution to bring Patrick back to life's banquet?
3. Discuss people you know who exhibit a "zest for life." Are they like Mame in any way?

IN THE SAME SPIRIT

Other movies about characters who feast at life's banquet, even in the appearance of famine:

Cabaret—In Berlin before World War II, Sally Bowles (Liza Minnelli) approaches events with the rousing outlook that "life is a cabaret." (1972, 128 minutes, PG)

Thoroughly Modern Millie—Muzzy (Carol Channing) is a wealthy "jazz baby" who loves exploring life and "good fun and good friends," and who is an exuberant mentor to Millie (Julie Andrews), seeking to be a modern 1920s girl and to find her true love. "Follow your heart—no raspberries!" Muzzy tells Millie. (1967, 138 minutes, NR)

The Unsinkable Molly Brown—The determined Molly (Debbie Reynolds) learns to "belly up to the bar" and climb the social ladders, and nothing keeps her down, not even the Titanic, in this truth-inspired musical story. (1964, 128 minutes, NR)

BAGDAD CAFE

PREVIEW

After angrily parting from her husband in the Arizona desert during their vacation, a resourceful German woman named Jasmin (Marianne Sagebrecht) walks to a roadside motel-gas station-cafe in Bagdad, takes up residence, and brings magic and inspiration to the business, its bossy owner, Brenda (CCH Pounder), and other colorful locals and passersby. (1988, West Germany, 108 minutes, PG)

META VIEW

Make lemonade in your desert

213

When life hands you a lemon, make lemonade is a traditional adage designed to spur people on in the face of adversity. It's the make-the-best-out-of-a-bad-situation philosophy. Jasmin does just that and becomes an ethereal paragon of quiet determination in this charming story.

Being stranded after a fight with her husband is the lemon Jasmin is handed. What's more, she receives this lemon in a desert in a foreign country; symbolically, she is wandering in an emotional wilderness. However, she seems not at all perturbed by her predicament. She seems, in fact, to have a marvelous outlook and mental recipe for making lemonade out of the lemon.

First, she stirs in an inner calmness that enables her to cope with whatever happens; as a result, she appears serene to observers. For example, when Jasmin discovers that she has her husband's suitcase instead of her own, she quietly makes do with his clothes and toiletries, and makes good use of the magic set she finds in the suitcase. Brenda, however, is suspicious, and calls the sheriff. "It don't make no sense," she says. In-control people *often* mystify others.

The song "Calling You," hauntingly sung by Jevetta Steele at the beginning and end of the movie, perhaps suggests Jasmin's connection with a higher power. "I am calling you . . . I know you hear me," the song states. Jasmin often seems to be listening to and following the directions for her lemonade from an unseen Great Chef.

Second, Jasmin mixes in a large portion of compassion and love. She sees what others need and what will make them happy, and she tries to help. When she notices Brenda's dirty office, for instance, Jasmin gives it a thorough cleaning. Again, Brenda is suspicious and upset. "I thought you would *like* it," Jasmin says simply. To her obvious admirer, painter Rudi Cox (Jack Palance), Jasmin extends a warm friendship. By becoming intimately involved in the lives of those around her, Jasmin opens new avenues of love for herself and others.

Third, Jasmin turns her life into a satisfying, delicious, and exotic drink by adding her own special brand of creativity. She uses the magic set and her own imagination, and draws out others' special talents to free herself and others from mental and spiritual wildernesses. One trucker even sings, "Don't start shovin', 'cause life's just a lovin' situation."

Jasmin proves that life's lemons can be used to good advantage.

Ye View

1. Cite some specific examples of Jasmin's reaching out to others and helping them.
2. What kind of visions does Jasmin have? What do they indicate about her personality?
3. Discuss the movie's "show time" number. How has Brenda changed? Do you think Jasmin has made a good lemonade? Why or why not?

IN THE SAME SPIRIT

Another quirky tale of changes:
> *Cold Comfort Farm*—A young orphaned woman stirs up life at her eccentric relatives' farm. (1995, British, 95 minutes, PG)

CINDERELLA

PREVIEW

A cruel stepmother and two foolish stepsisters can't stop Cinderella from going to the ball, meeting Prince Charming, and living happily ever after in this celebrated animated Disney treasure, one of Walt Disney's personal favorite films. (1950, 76 minutes, G, *)

215

META VIEW

Dreams can come true!

"A Dream Is a Wish Your Heart Makes" Cinderella sings at the beginning of this movie based on the Charles Perrault version of a fairy tale that has been told throughout the world for centuries.

"Have faith in your dreams and someday your rainbow will come smiling through," the song goes. "No matter how your heart is grieving, if you keep on believing, the dream that you wish will come true."

Therein lies the reason for the story's appeal from generation to generation. Even though the tale may ostensibly be set "once upon a time in a faraway land," we know that the time and land are here and now, and that dreams do come true today and forever.

How? Cinderella provides a four-step method.

First, she has a vision. At the beginning of the movie, the narrator explains how Cinderella has become a servant girl in her own house, but says, "With each dawn she found new hope that someday her dreams of happiness would come true."

Second, Cinderella is *herself* loving and giving. The narrator also says that "through it all, Cinderella remained ever gentle and kind." She befriends and helps the mice (the delightful Gus and Jaq), and they, in turn, care for her. Cinderella proves the axioms that if you want to receive, you first need to give, and that you receive what you give.

Third, Cinderella has faith. Oh, sure, sometimes that faith would seem to be exhausted, but it is never completely diminished. When it looks as if her dreams of going to the ball are shattered, Cinderella sobs, "There's nothing left to believe in, nothing." Just then, however, her Fairy Godmother appears, and says: "Nonsense, child. If you'd lost all of your faith, I couldn't be here, and here I am." The Fairy Godmother is the symbol of Cinderella's faith, and that faith creates "Bibbidi-Bobbidi-Boo" magic.

Fourth, Cinderella always gives thanks for the goodness and kindness in her life. She thanks her mouse friends and she thanks her Fairy Godmother. Like giving, being thankful is an attitude and an action that multiply the good in one's own life and in *all* life.

Ye View

1. When Cinderella falls in love at the ball, she doesn't know that she has fallen for the prince. What does this tell you about Cinderella's character?
2. Using the four-step method (vision, giving, faith, thankfulness) for making dreams come true, analyze why the dreams of the stepmother and stepsisters don't come true?
3. What dreams would *you* like to come true? How can the four-step method help?

COOL RUNNINGS

PREVIEW

People laugh at the idea of a Jamaican bobsled team in the Olympics, but it's no laughing matter to four young Jamaican men and their American coach, Irv (John Candy), in this film based on a true story from the 1988 Olympiad. (1993, 97 minutes, PG, *)

META VIEW

Hey, mon, go for the gold!

While practicing for the Olympic qualifying competition, Jamaican team member Sanka (Doug E. Doug) quips, "Nobody's had that much fun in a sled since Santa Claus." Watching (and listening to) the Jamaicans practice and compete is fun, and thrilling, but it is also inspiring.

This Disney venture teaches having strength, determination, and integrity to accomplish dreams and goals; being true to one's self; and supporting one another as we go for the gold in life.

Jamaican Derice Bannock (Leon), set back in his attempts to run in the Olympics, latches on to the idea of a former Olympic competitor, Irv, to use Jamaican sprinters to push bobsleds. Irv doesn't want to become involved, but Derice persists.

"Do the words *give up* mean anything to you?" Irv asks.

"Not a thing," Derice replies.

That's the affirmative spirit needed to succeed in our goals. Derice is convinced he was born to compete in the Olympics, and he holds that vision. The difficulties and odds—such as an obvious lack of ice in Jamaica and just three months to choose a team and practice—don't faze Derice at all. He proves that even a so-called crazy idea can be achieved with belief, a positive attitude, and hard work.

Derice also shows how important it is to see beyond the obvious, beyond appearances, and beyond the negative comments and outlooks of others. When the team receives a broken-down old bobsled to use in the Olympics, Derice studies it lovingly and says, "She's beautiful." He sees the bobsled's future rather than its past, its potential rather than its wear.

Irv teaches the team members about bobsledding, but he also teaches them about getting in touch with their own goals and identities and having integrity.

"Now, if we're even going to *think* about qualifying, we're each going to have to sit down and take a nice, deep look inside," Irv tells them. He knows that inner strength determines outer show in any competition.

Irv, who cheated during the 1972 games and was stripped of his gold, tells Derice that there is more to life than merely winning, though.

"A gold medal is a wonderful thing, but if you're not enough without it, you'll never be enough *with* it," Irv says.

Irv and the team members are good support systems for one another, and exemplify the value of real teamwork to accomplish individual and group goals.

For example, when team member Yul Brenner (Malik Yoba) is made fun of for dreaming of living in a palace, teammate Junior (Rawle D. Lewis) defends him and says, "All he has to do is know what he wants and work hard for it, and if he wants it bad enough, he'll get it." Yul helps Junior have the gumption to stand up to his rich father and tell him, in effect, what he has been rehearsing for some time: "A man has got to do what a man has got to do."

Ye View

1. How do other Olympic competitors react to the Jamaican team? Why? Discuss their reactions in relation to Yul's statement: "We're different. People are always afraid of what's different."
2. How do the Jamaican team members, Irv, other competitors, and people in Jamaica react to the team's finish at the Olympics?
3. Derice names the team's bobsled *Cool Runnings* and says the name means "peace be the journey." Why do you think he chooses this name? What does the concept mean to you?

DEAD POETS SOCIETY

219

Preview

Unorthodox teacher John Keating (Robin Williams), who has a love of poetry and a talent for motivating students to live fully and think for themselves, inspires a group of boys to follow their passions at a New England prep school in 1959. (1989, 128 minutes, PG)

Meta View

"Carpe diem—seize the day!"

Special teachers still pop out of the jumbled classrooms in my memories. Don't they for you? A few are recalled simply for unusual traits: the algebra teacher who wiggled his ears and ate peanuts while explaining unilateral triangles, or the government teacher who constantly adjusted her bra strap while talking about the legislature. Most of us have teachers like that we can't forget.

A very few teachers are always in my mind, decades after their classes ended, because they cared enough to guide and push me into experiencing life and identifying and achieving my dreams: the journalism teacher who, screaming, chased me out of the building more than once for some "clever" remark, or the drama teacher who called up one dull summer day and invited me to a play. Such teachers change our lives, and we give them high marks of gratitude.

John Keating is one of those superspecial teachers. He is certainly a gale of academic fresh air at Welton Academy. The typical teachers there are of the boring, impersonal, unrealistically demanding variety who bring no life or joy of knowledge to the classroom. In contrast, Keating captures the attentions of his students with theatrical, playful stunts and exercises, while all the time affirming their self-worth and urging them to get the most out of life while they can.

Keating shows the boys a picture of Academy students from long ago. All the students are dead now, Keating points out. Their legacy, he says, is the Latin phrase *carpe diem.*

"Carpe diem—seize the day, boys! Make your lives extraordinary!" Keating urges, suggesting that students "gather ye rosebuds while ye may."

He tells them, "The human race is filled with passion . . . poetry, beauty, romance, love—these are what we stay alive for."

Keating encourages his students to think for themselves and to be true to their beliefs, no matter how unpopular those beliefs are. He also asks them to look at life from different perspectives (this he bids while standing on his desk), to find their own voices, and to contribute their own distinctive and original verses to the play of life.

"Thoreau said most men 'lead lives of quiet desperation.' Don't be resigned to that. Break out. . . . Dare to strike out and find new ground."

The movie focuses primarily on two troubled boys: Neil Perry (Robert Sean Leonard), who desperately wants to be an actor—against his stern father's insistence that he become a medical doctor, and Todd Anderson (Ethan

Hawke), who is afraid of public speaking and living up to his older brother's reputation. Neil, especially, takes Keating's "carpe diem" philosophy to heart and spearheads a revival of a secret society of poetry lovers.

It is painful to see the light and life go out of Neil's whole being when his father refuses to relate to Neil as a person with hopes and dreams of his own. Keating has ignited the natural spark to create and express within Neil, but Neil's situation shows how people's lights can be put out by the insensitivity of others.

Seizing the day and striving to live in ways that satisfy the soul's highest longing can be difficult in a world of conflicting consciousnesses. But is it wrong to take full advantage of every now moment to make extraordinary experiences for ourselves, when doing so may lead to hurt and trouble? For the answer, look at Neil's joy and pride after the play. To adapt the words of an old song, they can't take that away from him.

221

Ye View

1. How do Mr. Keating and the "carpe diem" philosophy influence the boys *other* than Neil and Todd?
2. Is Mr. Keating responsible for Neil's decision about his life? Why or why not?
3. Discuss a special teacher or teachers in your own life who inspired or motivated you. Were they in any way like Mr. Keating?

In the Same Spirit

Mr. Holland's Opus—A high school music teacher (Richard Dreyfuss) helps students hit the right notes in their lives. (1995, 142 minutes, PG)

GOING MY WAY

PREVIEW

Father O'Malley (Bing Crosby) has his own unique way of helping people and solving the financial difficulties of New York's Church of Saint Dominic, much to the initial chagrin of the church's longtime priest, Father Fitzgibbon (Barry Fitzgerald). (1944, 126 minutes, NR)

META VIEW

"You could be swinging on a star"

While you probably would expect a priest to be rather optimistic, you might not expect him to be quite the crooner and golf enthusiast that Father O'Malley is, but then Father O'Malley has a lot of Bing Crosby in him. Passions for singing and sporting are just in their natures, and are ways that Father O'Malley uses to get people to affirm and enjoy life.

Father O'Malley says he derives "great happiness" out of helping people realize that religion doesn't have to be solemn and funless. "It can be bright and bring you close to happiness."

He not only shares his own happiness in song, but also uses his musical knowledge and abilities to help a young girl who has run away from home, to transform a rowdy gang of boys into a peaceful church choir, and to raise money to save the church.

There is definite instructional method in the seeming madness of the song "Swinging on a Star," which he and the choir sing:

"Oh, would you like to swing on a star, carry moonbeams home in a jar, and be better off than you are? Or would you rather be a pig? . . .

"All the monkeys aren't in the zoo. Every day you meet quite a few. So you see, it's all up to you. You can be better than you are. You could be swinging on a star."

With a catchy tune and playful lyrics, Father O'Malley gives the boys (and viewers) a painless but memorable lesson in the importance of initiative and personal choice. He's saying that it is up to each person to make the most out of life through individual choices.

Father O'Malley also connects with young and old through his interests in sports. He takes the boys to a baseball game and gets Father Fitzgibbon on the golf course for the first time. In both cases, Father O'Malley is proving his laudable knack of knowing what other people truly need to bring more happiness and contentment into their lives—to make them better than they are.

"He was always thinking of others," Father Fitzgibbon says of Father O'Malley.

Ye View

1. What are some other examples of ways in which Father O'Malley is "always thinking of others"? What is his big surprise for Father Fitzgibbon?
2. Who are some people changed by Father O'Malley's cheerful, hopeful attitude? In what ways are they changed?
3. If you could "swing on a star" right now, what would it be? In other words, what would you most like to do to make your life better? What are some steps you could take to accomplish that goal?

In the Same Spirit

Still going his way:

The Bells of St. Mary's—Father O'Malley teams up with Sister Benedict (Ingrid Bergman) at a needy parochial school in this sequel. (1945, 126 minutes, NR)

GONE WITH THE WIND

PREVIEW

Scarlett O'Hara (Vivien Leigh), feisty daughter of a Southern planta-tion owner, and Rhett Butler (Clark Gable), a dashing rogue, fight their own battles in this Civil War classic based on Margaret Mitchell's novel. (1939, 220 minutes, NR)

META VIEW

Frankly, my dear, it's Melanie

The venerable *GWTW* is here for basically one reason. Certainly not be-cause Scarlett is going to think about it tomorrow (how unmetaphysical not to live in the now). Nor because of Rhett, although he's actually a decent man, worthy of even Mammy's admiration. No way for the weak-willed Ashley (not to be judgmental, but then critics tend to be a bit like that). Frankly, it's Melanie, Scarlett's gentle, unselfish friend (beautifully, radiantly played by Olivia de Havilland). You won't find a more Christlike character in all of filmdom, outside of a movie about Jesus.

In Mitchell's acclaimed novel of the Old South and its equally lauded movie version, Melanie genuinely smells as sweet as a magnolia. No matter what Scarlett does or Rhett does or her husband Ashley does or doesn't do, Melanie beholds the Christ in them. Melanie doesn't forgive, in the sense that humans normally view forgiveness. She forgives as God does, which is to say that she doesn't; she realizes there is nothing *to* forgive, because all is perfect and whole from God's perspective and in God. She is an inspiration for all of us.

As Melanie, de Havilland is the perfect picture of purity, especially shin-ing when introducing Scarlett to the tongue waggers at husband Ashley's birthday party and in answering Mammy's call to help Captain Butler after his daughter's death. "I expect the angels fights on your side, Miss Melanie," Mammy (Hattie McDaniel) declares. Melanie, who is ill and has spent all of her energy comforting Captain Butler, promptly faints.

It is Rhett who most thoroughly understands and appreciates Melanie's character, and he doesn't mind pointing out Melanie's admirable traits to Scarlett:

- "There's too much honor in her to ever conceive of dishonor in anyone she loves."
- "She's never had anything but heart."
- Upon hearing of Melanie's death, "Well, God rest her. She was the only completely kind person I ever knew, a great lady, a very great lady."

The truth of Rhett's remarks finally sinks in to Scarlett, who says of Melanie, "She thought of everybody except herself."

Watch this Civil War epic for a multitude of reasons—for the historical sense, the soap-opera twists of Scarlett's life, the color and pageantry, the fine acting. But follow Captain Butler's lead, and pay special attention to the character of Melanie—the effects of such a soul are not gone with the wind.

YE VIEW

1. Recall a favorite scene that illustrates Melanie's goodness and love.
2. Do you think Scarlett has absorbed any of Melanie's character? Why or why not?
3. Discuss some "Melanies" that you have known.

HAPPY GILMORE

PREVIEW

To earn money quickly to save his grandmother's house, Happy Gilmore (Adam Sandler), an unpleasant, ill-mannered guy who wants to be a pro hockey player, enters golf tournaments when it is discovered that he has a phenomenal drive. (1996, 92 minutes, PG-13)

META VIEW

Go to your "happy place"

Happy Gilmore is a short fuse with a lot of misdirected energy. He fancies himself a hockey player, but he's not good at the game. He's the type who curses, belittles, and fights—with no regard for the feelings of others—and then insincerely apologizes for his behavior. Despite his name, he's not fun to be around.

But the Christ, the spark of divine love, is within him, as it is in everyone, so Happy is not without hope. Happy loves his grandmother, and that love is enough to start him on a journey which will teach him to more wisely use his God-given energy.

A golf pro, Gary Palmer (Kevin Nealon), says he sees Happy's strong, positive aura, and tells him, "You've got to harness in the good energy, block out the bad. . . . Feel the flow, Happy. . . . It's circular." The brief appearance of Palmer may seem like just a New Age gag to some, but he offers sound advice for dealing with all challenges in life.

Happy's coach, Chubbs (Carl Weathers), teaches Happy how to begin to harness his energy. "It's all in the head," Chubbs says and later advises, "You have to clear your mind of everything else and stay focused."

To his credit, Happy is intrigued with the concept and open to its possibilities. When Happy asks how to clear his mind, Chubbs replies, "Think of a place that's really perfect—your own happy place. Go there, and all of your anger will just disappear, and then putt."

Happy does so. He says he feels better, and he is able to make an amazing shot on a miniature golf course.

The advice of Chubbs is golf specific, but it has applications throughout Happy's life. Indeed, it's a method of affirmative meditation that can be applied with successful results by anyone, by all the frustrated Happys in the world. Going to the "happy place" in the mind is getting in touch with what brings us peace and love, and discovering the goodness at the center of being. Negative associations from our lives may at first appear in our meditation on the way to the "happy place" but will fade away, because there is no anger or dis-ease of any sort in the true "happy place." When we reach that place of contentment and spiritual strength within us, anything is possible for the highest good of all concerned.

227

❋

YE VIEW

1. During the golf tournaments, what are specific examples of Happy's going to his "happy place" and achieving success?
2. Under what conditions does Chubbs say, "We've only just begun to live"? What does the image of Chubbs and companions at the end of the movie suggest to you about an ultimate "happy place"?
3. What is your own "happy place"?

THEME MATES

Spreading happiness to patients:

Patch Adams—A medical student in the early 1970s, Hunter "Patch" Adams (Robin Williams), pains the medical establishment when he begins using humor therapy for patients. Laughter, the future doctor affirms and shows in this movie based on a true story, can indeed be a powerful medicine. (1998, 110 minutes, PG-13)

HAROLD AND MAUDE

PREVIEW

Seventy-nine-year-old Maude (Ruth Gordon) teaches Harold (Bud Cort), a young man with a death fixation, how to live and love in this cult-movie favorite, a black comedy written by Colin Higgins. (1972, 90 minutes, PG)

META VIEW

"Go and love some more!"

Every Harold—that is, every alienated, neglected, directionless young person—should have a Maude, someone to transmit passion for life! Such a desire has made this film popular with youths ever since the early '70s. True, the relationship of Harold and Maude is not exactly the norm, but the contrast makes their story all the more memorable and inspirational.

Harold is the son of a wealthy socialite (Vivian Pickles). In futile efforts to get his mother's attention, Harold fakes suicides (some of the film's most amusing moments). He drives a remodeled hearse and goes to funerals for fun, and it is at funerals that Harold first starts seeing Maude.

Maude, played with zest and warmth by Gordon, is an eccentric woman who also loves to attend funerals ("They're such fun!"), because she sees them as links in "the great circle of life." Maude has a rich past that is only suggested in the movie; she apparently is Austrian and had been in a Jewish concentration camp. Now living in a railroad car among various memorabilia, Maude says she is "always looking for the new experience."

"Try something new each day," she urges Harold, who is fascinated with the lively Maude. "After all, we're given life to find it out. It doesn't last forever." (Maude herself plans to get on with life in another realm, come her eightieth birthday.)

Maude teaches Harold to value life and enjoy its opportunities, to be observant, to appreciate growth and change, to take chances, and to act for worthy causes. She gives him a banjo and teaches him a new song of life (a Cat Stevens original): "If you want to sing out, sing out. If you want to be free, be free. . . . There's a million things to be; you know that there are. . . . There's a million things to do; you know that there are. . . . You can do what you want. . . . and if you find a new way, you can do it today. . . . You can make it all true."

Harold realizes, "I haven't lived." Harold tells Maude how he began faking suicides because he liked being dead.

Maude responds, "A lot of people enjoy being dead, but they're *not* dead, really. They're just backing away from life." She tells Harold to "reach out, take a chance (get hurt even), play as well as you can!"

When the distraught Harold tells the dying Maude that he loves her, Maude says: "Oh, Harold, that is wonderful! Go and love some more!" Maude knows that she has taught Harold well.

229

✳

Ye View

1. What do Harold's actions at the end of the movie indicate about his outlook and his future?
2. Maude says that she prays by communicating with life. Do you consider her method to be prayer? Explain.
3. Maude fights for big issues in her "small, individual way." Name at least one way in which you could do the same.

In the Same Spirit

The Grass Harp—Dolly Talbo (Piper Laurie) gives her nephew Collin Fenwick a spirited view of life, even from the perspective of a tree house in the woods, in this story based on Truman Capote's memoirs of growing up in the South during the 1940s. (1996, 107 minutes, PG)

JONATHAN LIVINGSTON SEAGULL

PREVIEW

A seagull who dares to fly high and fast and believes there's more to life than fighting over fish heads to eat is cast out of his flock, but discovers a world of wonders and meaning on his own. (1973, 120 minutes, G)

META VIEW

Even birds know "I Am"

Existential seems to be the word most associated with the seagull of Richard Bach's popular novel, and the movie loosely based on Bach's story follows a free-thinking bird who affirms existence. The movie is dedicated "To the real Jonathan Livingston Seagull, who lives within us all."

When watching this rather strange movie, remember the dedication and keep in mind that the film is a parable about the human situation. It probably isn't wise to examine too closely the basic premise that seagulls want to fly more often and higher than they do (but we can apply the idea to humans). Know, too, that this is a movie to be heard more than seen. The photography is nice, but the "action" consists mainly of seagulls flying in the air over the ocean. The birds aren't endearing and they are way too talky, but their main messages are rich.

To begin with, Jonathan voices that restless longing within so many to rise above traditions and really experience life. He refuses to accept excuses: his mother dismisses his longings by saying that everyone dreams of better things when they are young; his father tries to convince him that it's best to be content with the status quo. The flock's elders send him away for not conforming. Jonathan adamantly declares, "I will know all there is to know of this life."

Jonathan sees many beautiful sights, such as waterfalls and majestic, snowy mountains, before he joins a new flock taking him "home" to a "higher place." A new friend tells Jonathan, "One school is finished, and it is time for another to begin."

A pure white bird asks him: "Do you have any idea how many lives we must have gone through before we even got the first idea that there is more to life than eating or fighting or powering the flock? Many lives, Jonathan, and then other lives to learn there is such a thing as perfection, and others again to finally get the idea that our purpose for living is to find that perfection and show it forth. But you, Jonathan, you learned so much at one time that you didn't have to go through a hundred lives to reach this one."

When Jonathan mentions heaven, the elder Chiang tells him: "Heaven isn't a place. Heaven is perfection. . . . We don't go there as much as we express it." Chiang, too, touches upon reincarnation by emphasizing that learning continues over various lifetimes.

Further, Chiang takes Jonathan—and thinking viewers—into some deep spiritual waters. Chiang tells Jonathan that perfect speed is not about moving fast but about "being there," and suggests that space and time are not quite real.

"To fly as fast as thought to anywhere that is now, or has been or ever will be, you begin by knowing that you've already arrived." Chiang is expressing here the importance of visualizing desires and concentrating on their realization in the now.

Jonathan quickly grasps the idea and recites a list of affirmative statements that begin with the powerful words "I am," which mystically mean God and God's being within us:

"I am already there on that highest peak.
I am not limited by anybody.
I am not limited by space.
I am not limited by time.
I am a perfect expression of freedom here and now."

Jonathan concentrates more, and it dawns upon him: "Real is real. I really *am* a perfect idea." He has discovered the power of thought and mind action.

Once he understands his identity as an "I Am" being, Jonathan is ready to begin what Chiang calls the most difficult and powerful journey of all: "to fly up and know the meaning of kindness and love."

Love, Jonathan comes to realize, is seeing the good in everyone and helping everyone see it in themselves.

Jonathan, Chiang says, was born to be a teacher and "to give the truth to anyone struggling to break out of his limits." Chiang adds, "It is important to give what you have found as a gift to whomever will accept it."

YE VIEW

1. What is the gift that Jonathan gives? How does Jonathan choose to give what he has found?
2. Where does Jonathan tell Fletcher to look for his understanding?
3. What is meant by the flock's allusion to "the Son of the Great Gull"? What is Jonathan's reaction to the comparison?

THE MUSIC MAN

PREVIEW

A traveling con artist of a salesman, Professor Harold Hill (Robert Preston), convinces citizens of an Iowa town that they need a boys' band so he can sell instruments and uniforms, but along the way he loses his heart to Marian the librarian (Shirley Jones) in this rousing Meredith Willson musical. (1962, 151 minutes, NR)

META VIEW

Strike up the band for "the think system"

Yes, they've got trouble, right there in River City, but where does it come from? Trouble starts with *t*, which rhymes with *p*, and that stands for *pool*—and that's where the trouble originates, to hear Harold Hill sing about it. Hill then proposes to "keep the youngsters moral after school" by creating a boys' band.

But where does the trouble *really* come from? Hill is a smooth, fast talker, but more important he's a smooth, fast thinker. The trouble is invented in the working-all-angles mind of Hill himself. There is no trouble until Hill thinks of it and convinces the whole town to think of it too. Such is the power of the mind; such is Hill's adeptness at manipulating the thoughts of others, and humankind's ability literally to think up situations and experiences for themselves.

How trouble comes to River City is, in fact, a mind-over-people version of Hill's "the think system."

Hill explains how he intends to teach a band, even though he can't read music: "I now have a revolutionary new method called 'the think system' where you don't bother with the notes. My boy, someday reading music is going to be absolutely obsolete." Hill is proposing that people can accomplish their desires simply by thinking them into actuality.

Instructing the boys, Hill says, "And remember, men, if you want to play the Minuet in G, think 'the Minuet in G.' It's a simple meeting of two minds—yours and Beethoven's."

Hill declares that his "think system" is as simple as whistling, which no one had to think up.

Marian, supporting Hill's ideas, actually declares the basic principle of the system: "One can do anything, if one puts one's mind to it."

Hill transforms the whole town by convincing its citizens to think in certain ways. Through the power of their thoughts, people discover and display previously hidden abilities and talents.

Of course, Hill is also setting up scenarios in which people can learn to believe in themselves and their abilities. Young Winthrop (Ronny Howard), for example, overcomes his shyness and lisping (results of emotional trauma over his father's death) after Hill begins spending time with him and filling him with thoughts of self-worth.

Perhaps it has something to do with the transitory nature of his life and work, but Hill is a big proponent of using thoughts in the *now*, rather than giving thoughts over to the past or the future.

"Never allow the demands of tomorrow to interfere with the pleasures and excitement of today," he says.

Also, to Marian: "You pile up enough tomorrows and you'll find you've collected nothing but a lot of empty yesterdays. I don't know about you, but I'd like to make today worth remembering."

Think about those ideas—now!

Ye View

1. What are some examples of ways in which people are transformed by Hill's encouragements and "think system"? For starters, consider the mayor and his family, and Marian and her mother.
2. How does Hill use "the think system" himself at the end of the movie?
3. Have you used some variation of Hill's "think system"? Discuss your experiences in creating your own reality.

POLLYANNA

PREVIEW

An orphan girl (Hayley Mills) comes to live with her wealthy and auto-cratic Aunt Polly (Jane Wyman) and soon transforms the New England town with her "glad game" in this truly heartwarming Disney production. (1960, 134 minutes, NR, *)

META VIEW

Play the "glad game" and win!

We've taken Pollyanna's name in vain. It's a lovely sounding word and stands for an admirable concept. The word *Pollyanna*, meaning a person who tends to look for the good in everything, is in our vocabulary from "the glad girl" of Eleanor Porter's 1913 novel *Pollyanna*, as well as from the movies based on that novel.

The problem is the connotation that has been given the definition. "Oh, don't be such a Pollyanna," people will say to someone they feel has come across as a bit too optimistic about a situation. Or people apologize for themselves, saying, "I don't mean to be Pollyannaish," if they fear their re-marks will be construed as putting too good a spin on a situation. Being a Pollyanna is not usually considered an admirable trait in our culture, and that fact is an alarming comment on the outlook of the times. Many people are uncomfortable around someone who constantly looks on the bright side and can find good in any situation or person.

Playing the "glad game," though, can be life-affirming and life-enhancing by getting one in the habit of viewing the goodness, joy, and beauty that can be found, somewhere, in every so-called bad, gloomy, or ugly situation. It's

235

✳

a very practical, useful concept to raise one's sights, mental and physical, beyond difficulties and unhappiness.

Pollyanna says her father, a minister and missionary, taught her the game, which "helps sometimes, when things aren't going so well."

When Aunt Polly's household staff questions Pollyanna about her game, she gives them an example. The servants aren't glad about Sundays because of the preacher's "hellfire and damnation" sermons. But Pollyanna says that they *can* be glad, because "it will be six whole days before Sunday comes around again."

Perhaps people associate the Pollyanna attitude of finding good in things as being a form of denial, a "head in the sands" approach to the problems and realities of life. A rather dour maid complains to Pollyanna: "Glad this. Glad that. Do you have to be glad about everything? What's the matter with you, anyway?"

There's nothing the matter with Pollyanna. She isn't denying challenging situations. She knows what Sundays are like; she's heard the preacher. Her optimistic approach is a deliberate attempt not to let the unpleasant details of life get in her way of enjoying life. Rather than denying, she is replacing. Rather than dwelling on that old negative, she is finding some positive to accentuate. There are times in life, of course, when it seems impossible to play the "glad game," as Pollyanna herself discovers, but those are the times it is needed the most.

The beauty of the "glad game" is that life becomes richer for oneself and for others when the game is played, and the more often it is played and the more people by whom it is played, the more everyone is a winner. Examples of this can be found in the lives and situations that Pollyanna's outlook influences. The effects of Pollyanna's "glad game" are seen dramatically in the lives of Aunt Polly, Mrs. Snow (Agnes Moorehead), Mr. Pendergast (Adolphe Menjou), and Reverend Ford (Karl Malden).

In addition to the "glad game," Pollyanna tries to live from the premise

236
✳

of a quotation from Abraham Lincoln that helped to transform her father's life: "When you look for the bad in mankind expecting to find it, you surely will." Pollyanna tells Reverend Ford that after discovering the quotation, her father made up his mind to look for the good in people. He also counted the "glad passages" in the Bible, and concluded, "If God took the trouble to tell us 800 times to be glad and rejoice, He must have wanted us to do it."

YE VIEW

1. What are some specific things and situations that Pollyanna finds to be glad about?
2. How do Pollyanna's "glad game" and positive outlook change Aunt Polly, Mrs. Snow, Mr. Pendergast, and Reverend Ford? What is the overall effect of the game on the town of Harrington?
3. Think about a challenging situation in your own life and play the "glad game." What is there in the situation that you could be glad about?

IN THE SAME SPIRIT

Glad all over:

Anne of Green Gables—The Anne Shirley of L. M. Montgomery's beloved novel set on Canada's Prince Edward Island delights in finding what she calls "kindred spirits." The upbeat Anne (played by an actress who took her character's name) would certainly find Pollyanna a soul mate. (1934, 79 minutes, NR, *)

Pollyanna—Here's a silent "glad game" with Mary Pickford charming in the title role. (1920, 60 minutes, NR)

SINGIN' IN THE RAIN

PREVIEW

This acclaimed musical has fun with the challenges of changing from the sound to the talking eras in Hollywood during the 1920s through the story of silent-screen romantic duo Don Lockwood (Gene Kelly) and Lina Lamont (Jean Hagen). (1952, 102 minutes, NR)

META VIEW

Find creative joy in change

Change is a certainty in life, and dealing with change is a problem for many people. Why? Because we frequently aren't looking at change with the right perspective. Most people probably think of themselves as resisting change, in whatever form it crops up (such as a different job, a new relationship, or even a death). People usually think of change as unpleasant, negative, and unwanted. But how many people think of themselves as resisting creation? People generally view creation as something positive, purposeful, fulfilling, and even exciting.

What we need to do, then, is view change as creation. That's what change is—the eternal energy or substance of God constantly creating and renewing itself. Our task is to realize that change is divine creation and is therefore always in divine order. We may label change or creation "good" or "bad," but the Truth is that it just *is,* and is just as we see it. As creative expressions of God, we are always creating and can learn to use creative energy in joyous ways.

Singin' in the Rain is a singing-and-dancing testimonial to the creative joy that can be found in change. When confronted with the prospects of converting films to sound, the executives and thespians of Monumental

Pictures are at first grim and frightened—natural reactions. But they don't give in to those emotions. Their creative juices start flowing—and the rest mirrors Hollywood history.

The attitude of happiness and excitement in recognizing the creative potential during a time of change is perfectly captured in Kelly's classic musical number "Singin' in the Rain" and in the words: "Let the stormy clouds chase everyone from the place. Come on with the rain, I've a smile on my face. I'll walk down the lane with a happy refrain, just singin', singin' in the rain." And Donald O'Connor is a delight clownin' out of the rain.

YE VIEW

1. What other musical numbers portray an uplifting view of life in times of change or seeming difficulty?
2. How is the change from silent to talking pictures a boon for Kathy Selden (Debbie Reynolds)? Other than the obvious reason, why is Lina Lamont not able to take advantage of the change?
3. Think about a change in your own life recently or currently. What aspects of this situation can you find to "sing" about with a "happy refrain"?

239

THEME MATES

Creatively changing:

Houseboat—A widower with three children (Cary Grant) and his Italian houseboatkeeper (Sophia Loren) fall in love. Spiritually memorable are the dad's talks with his children about change—that everything changes in life, but life itself never ends but merely alters forms. He masterfully illustrates life's changing with a pitcher of water. (1958, 110 minutes, NR, *)

A Star Is Born—On her climb to Hollywood fame, a singer (Judy Garland) is helped and loved by a leading actor (James Mason).

Being open to life's changes and changing opportunities is brilliantly captured in Garland's "Born in a Trunk" number. (1954, 170 minutes, NR)

STAND AND DELIVER

PREVIEW

Jaime Escalante (Edward James Olmos), a teacher at an East Los Angeles *barrio* high school, strives to improve the lives of his students by preparing them to take an Advanced Placement Calculus Test in this film based on actual events. (1987, 105 minutes, PG)

META VIEW

Keep those expectations high!

Escalante leads his Garfield High School students in regular motivational drills:

"You're the best. You guys are the best."

"This is going to be a piece of cake—upside down."

"Step by step."

Escalante has unflinching faith in his students. He is convinced that his affirmative drills and challenging, humorous, and personal teaching style can give them the impetus they need to break away from stereotypes and dead-end jobs.

Some of Escalante's fellow teachers are skeptical, but he answers them that "students will rise to the level of expectations."

That's the heart of this involving story of perseverance and courage—on the part of both teacher and students—and is one key to our spiritual, emotional, mental, and physical growth. If we demand high expectations of ourselves, we can reach them with diligence and faith. If we hold high expectations of others, they will sense those expectations and most likely rise to meet or exceed them. It's so much easier being the proverbial little engine that thought it could, if others think we can too.

Escalante looks beyond the students' socioeconomic conditions and the defensive postures that many of them have adopted in order to survive, and thus invites them to follow his example. Escalante inspires with practicality and teaches students to desire better conditions and futures for themselves.

He tells the students that they already have two strikes against them: "There are some people in this world who will assume that you know *less* than you do, because of your name and your complexion." What Escalante tells the students in various ways is, "Don't accept that for yourselves!"

Escalante does say to them quite clearly, "You are the true dreamers, and dreams accomplish wonderful things."

He delivers hope, and the students stand for it. He stands firm in his expectations, and they do their best to deliver. They stand—and dream—and deliver together.

YE VIEW

1. Identify and discuss some individual challenges faced by the students.
2. What do the statistics at the conclusion of the movie indicate about Escalante's outlook and teaching methods? About possible changes in the school and community?
3. What are some affirmations that have helped you get through tests or other trying circumstances?

THEME MATES

My Left Foot—With the loving support of his mother (Brenda Fricker), Irishman Christy Brown (Daniel Day-Lewis), born with cerebral palsy in 1932, uses the toes on his left foot to become a successful painter and writer in this true story based on Brown's book. During times when Christy gives up on himself, his mother remains steadfast and affirmative enough for both of them. "If *you've* given up, *I* haven't," she tells him. Touching her heart, she tells Christy, "It's in *here* battles are won." (1989, Irish, 103 minutes, R)

STARMAN

PREVIEW

In this sci-fi romance, a stranded alien (Jeff Bridges) assumes the body of the husband of a lovely and lonely widow, Jenny Hayden (Karen Allen), and forces her to take him across country so he can meet his mother ship and return home. (1984, 115 minutes, PG)

META VIEW

Redeemed by Dutch apple pie, for starters

The opening irony of *Starman* is impossible to miss. We humans invited him to Earth. He has listened to the recording that was sent into space with the Voyager probe. That disk includes greetings in fifty-four Earth languages.

So when Starman's observation craft is in trouble, it is logical that he would assume he could come to this friendly planet and receive help. Instead, he is met with fear, stupidity, and outright hostility—and all of that is before the United States military arrives.

As he and Jenny rush against time and troops from Wisconsin to Arizona, Starman observes that humans constitute a "primitive species" which ranks among the many "intelligent but strange" species in the universe. He doesn't understand, for example, why humans would kill a deer for food and strap it to the top of a car, when deer don't eat people and people don't eat people. In fact, Starman is so moved by the deer's plight that he brings the deer back to life, which of course results in a fight with the hunters.

But just as Starman holds up a mirror to what he terms the primitive leanings of our species, so he shows us our admirable, civilized side. Just as people tend to recall the good and not the bad in later years, one suspects that Starman's memories will affirm humankind's positive qualities.

For starters, Starman discovers at a roadside cafe that he is crazy about Dutch apple pie. "It's terrific!" he exclaims with his mouth full.

Jenny replies, "For a primitive species, we have our points."

He also learns about earthly love as his affections grow for Jenny, and Jenny learns to fall in love all over again—same body, different creature. (Starman has cloned the body of Jenny's late husband by using hair saved in a photo album.)

Along with love and Dutch apple pie, sensual pleasures and beauty are new to Starman, who is a quick and observant student of earthly life. (He first learns about kissing by watching television.) As rich as those desserts are, though, Starman is most impressed with one important human trait:

"Shall I tell you what I find beautiful about you?" he asks a sympathetic SETI (Search for Extraterrestrial Intelligence) worker (Charles Martin Smith). "You are at your very best when things are worst."

With his gentle but amazing power of discernment, Starman is able to see into the human psyche and identify a trait that people sometimes overlook. His observation reminds us that we aren't as bad as the 6 o'clock news makes us appear. As a species, we *do* blossom when conditions worsen; we *do* gather strength in adversity. Usually these times are those that call for people to respond in big ways to the needs of others—and time and again we're up to the task. Think of the loving, caring, giving support that pours out to people in times of natural or man-made disasters.

243

✳

Thank you, Starman, for helping us realize our inner strengths. Pass the Dutch apple pie, please.

Ye View

1. What are some scenes that show Starman's reverence for life?
2. What evidence have you seen or heard about to support Starman's contention that humankind is at its "best when things are worst"?
3. Discuss whether or not the ending of *Starman* is hopeful.

STUART SAVES HIS FAMILY

Preview

Despite good intentions and all sorts of positive reinforcements, Stuart Smalley (Al Franken) goes into an emotional tailspin when his *Daily Affirmation With Stuart Smalley* TV program is canceled, his nurturing aunt dies, and he must return home to deal with an alcoholic father, a negative and co-dependent mother, an overweight and single-parent sister, and an unemployed, pot-smoking brother. (1995, 97 minutes, PG-13)

Meta View

Affirmations are tools for laboring humans

The plot may not sound like a comedy, but it is, although a serious one. That's life. Stuart Smalley is a modern Everyman. Like many people, Stuart has a lot with which to cope, and he often feels overwhelmed. In this time of great soul-searching, Stuart, again like many, tries various trendy ways to get his life in order. He's a member of several twelve-step programs, including Dull Children of Alcoholics and Debtors Anonymous. He listens to self-help tapes, walks/jogs to uplifting songs, and decorates his home with crystals and framed motivational sayings. He journals. Stuart knows all the right jargon of inspiration and improvement: he apologizes "I owe you an amends," he "owns" his emotions, he "lets go and lets God," he doesn't "should" himself, he has an "attitude of gratitude," and he gets in touch with the "inner child." Above all, Stuart uses affirmations, and in fact makes his living helping others use affirmations as a tool to self-empowerment.

Why then is Stuart's life a mess? Because he's a spiritual being still going through a human experience. Why aren't all the help and affirmations bringing him total peace and joy? Because he's a work in progress, and he's still learning. When he reaches the stage where he doesn't need affirmations or coping assistance of any kind, chances are he will be either a saint or an ascended master. In the meantime, affirmations are for Stuart what they are for thousands of other people: focusing tools for still-laboring humans. The tools work only to the extent they are *worked* or seriously used.

On his TV show in the movie (a spinoff from Franken's actual *Saturday Night Live* skits), Stuart recites such affirmations as *I deserve good things, I am an attractive person*, and *I am fun to be with.* His signature affirmation is, *I'm good enough, I'm smart enough, and doggone it, people* like *me.*"

Many viewers write to Stuart and tell him how much he has helped them. Others, of course, don't identify with his message at all. One viewer calls it "touchy-feely New Age drool." His family certainly doesn't understand Stuart and his approach to life. Not even Stuart is successful at using his focusing tools all the time. During a crisis, he tends to lock himself in his room and eat cookies, and say things like "No one will ever love me; I could kill myself" and "When anything good ever happens, I'm always waiting for the other shoe to drop." Sound familiar?

There are reasons Stuart is like he is, though, as viewers discover the more they get to know Stuart's family. While both Stuart and his family are somewhat exaggerated stereotypes, they do represent the dysfunctional dynamics within many modern families. As Stuart says after his aunt dies: "Death is something we Smalleys can pretty much deal with. It's life that seems to be the problem." Stuart himself is an affable guy, with a genuine desire to help people, his family, and himself.

Stuart and all members of his family are exactly those who are most in need of affirmations. In her landmark book *Lessons in Truth*, metaphysician H. Emilie Cady writes: "Affirmations should be used by the timid and by those who have a feeling of their own inefficiency, those who stand in fear of other minds, those who 'give in' easily, those who are subject to anxiety or doubt, and those who are in positions of responsibility. People who are in any way negative or passive need to use affirmations more."

Dr. Cady says that people in the early stages of spiritual growth need both to deny the "reality and power of apparent evil" and to affirm the desired good already in their lives; eventually, "rote repetitions" are not needed. She succinctly explains the fundamental reason for using affirmations: "In reality, God is forever in process of movement within us, that He may manifest Himself (All-Good) more fully through us. Our affirming, backed by faith, is the link that connects our conscious human need with His power and supply."[3]

YE VIEW

1. How does Stuart's friend Julia (Laura San Giacomo) help him overcome his "shame spiral"?
2. Do you feel hopeful about the members of Stuart's family at the end of the movie? Discuss their changes in consciousness, if any.
3. Are affirmations valuable in your own spiritual focusing? Why or why not?

:::: **FEATURE PRESENTATION**

With a Song in Your Heart

"Make a joyful noise to the Lord," says the Psalmist. Direct tuneful energies to your concept of Universal Spirit and to yourself as a part of that Spirit.

Singing is a powerful, enjoyable way to lift up your spirits to the Spirit within, to bring your natural bliss to the surface—in short, to make you feel good! It's difficult not to be happy and positive when singing or hearing songs that are happy and positive.

Movies are great sources for inspirational songs. The next time you need to march or sing to a different, more upbeat drummer, many movie songs are available for your inner pleasure.

Songs can be affirmations set to music. They can convey conviction, direction, exciting expectation, emotional and spiritual strength, happiness, hope, and faith. And, like all good affirmations, they are direct in doing so. For example, "The Bare Necessities" instructs you to "forget about your worries and your strife." "Little Drops of Rain" insists that you "never let a minute lie there on the shelf, for there may be in it all of life itself."

On the next page are two lists of marvelously affirmative songs to make your spirits sing. The first set includes songs closely identified with Hollywood movies; the second includes songs brought to the screen from classic Broadway plays.

Test your knowledge of movie musicals. Match the numbered song title on the left with the lettered movie title on the right. The answers are printed upside down following the lists.

HOLLYWOOD HITS

1. "Ac-cent-u-ate the Positive"
2. "Happy Days Are Here Again"
3. "High Hopes"
4. "Look for the Silver Lining"
5. "The Bare Necessities"
6. "Little Drops of Rain"

7. "When You Wish Upon a Star"
8. "I'll Build a Stairway to Paradise"
9. "Whistle While You Work"
10. "Movin' Right Along"

a. *An American in Paris* (1951)
b. *The Jungle Book* (1967)
c. *The Muppet Movie* (1979)
d. *A Hole in the Head* (1959)
e. *Beau James* (1957)
f. *Snow White and the Seven Dwarfs* (1937)
g. *Gay Purr-ee* (1962)
h. *Here Come the Waves* (1944)
i. *Till the Clouds Roll By* (1946)
j. *Pinocchio* (1940)

BROADWAY SOUNDS

1. "Tomorrow"
2. "Oh, What a Beautiful Mornin'"
3. "Open a New Window"
4. "Something's Coming"
5. "Climb Ev'ry Mountain"
6. "I Whistle a Happy Tune"
7. "Don't Rain on My Parade"
8. "Happy Talk"
9. "You'll Never Walk Alone"
10. "Everything's Coming Up Roses"

a. *The King and I* (1956)
b. *Gypsy* (1962)
c. *Funny Girl* (1968)
d. *South Pacific* (1958)
e. *Carousel* (1956)
f. *Oklahoma!* (1955)
g. *West Side Story* (1961)
h. *Mame* (1974)
i. *The Sound of Music* (1965)
j. *Annie* (1982)

(Answers: Hollywood Hits—1-h, 2-e, 3-d, 4-i, 5-b, 6-g, 7-j, 8-a, 9-f, 10-c; Broadway Sounds—1-j, 2-f, 3-h, 4-g, 5-i, 6-a, 7-c, 8-d, 9-e, 10-b)

Patricia Neal and Michael Rennie with robot in *The Day the Earth Stood Still*,
20th Century Fox
Photo: The Museum of Modern Art Film Stills Archive

Chapter 6

Lights, Camera—
Unity and Peace

The spotlight now focuses on what the hit song from *The Lion King* refers to as the "circle of life." We're all on this Spaceship Earth together, and what's more, we're all on this Space Station Universe together. All life connects in a cosmic circle, because all life is part of Infinite Mind. This chapter concerns movies that remind people to live in unity and harmony with each other; to recognize how intricately our lives are woven together; to be aware of and appreciate our similarities rather than annihilate each other because of perceived differences; to understand how challenges can unite rather than divide; to consider a world without weapons, intolerance, and suspicion; and to be open to loving contact with all life in the universe, in all the rooms or realms of the heavenly mansion, however alien to our current level of knowledge.

THE ABYSS

PREVIEW

Oil-rig workers including Bud Brigman (Ed Harris) and his estranged wife Lindsay (Mary Elizabeth Mastrantonio) encounter a variety of hazards and unexpected company in the ocean depths when they embark on a mission to find and examine a sunken American nuclear submarine. (1989, 145 minutes, PG-13)

META VIEW

"You have to look with better eyes"

"We all see what we want to see," Lindsay says of a zealous, aggressive soldier who thinks mysterious creatures are Russians. "He sees hate and fear. You have to look with better eyes than that."

It takes "better eyes" looking for different kinds of abysses to get to the bottom of this movie, directed and written by James Cameron. Multiple abysses are to be found.

On the most obvious level, there is the abyss of the deep ocean, and the action-packed plot that takes place there (and the mostly mundane and earthy dialogue which accompanies the action).

On closer inspection, viewers find the abyss of the human mind—the intellect and consciousness—that is resistant to and reluctant to recognize and accept the goodness and immensity of life.

A few characters in the movie reject the peacefulness of both alien and human life forms; others (Bud, for one) are at first skeptical of the possibility of aliens and their intentions, but change their minds through experience and observation.

Lindsay is on the same wavelength as the aliens, described by one oil-rig worker as UFOs, or "underwater flying objects."

"Something really important is happening here," Lindsay says.

"There is something down there," she tells fellow workers after a lone encounter with a gliding machine or entity that emits purple light. "It was the most beautiful thing I've ever seen . . . . It was a machine, but it was alive. It was like a dance of light."

Lindsay's face grows happy and bright when she is around the objects, and she's convinced that they mean no harm.

The military complex, as depicted in many other films about aliens (such as *Starman*), tends to suspect the worst, and responds with hasty directives to fight.

As Lindsay says, "You have to look with better eyes than that."

A third type of abyss is the endless pit in early theories about the universe's origin. In suggesting this pit with its title, the movie underscores the fact that modern theories about life and the origin of life would certainly be challenged if there existed intelligent life forms, like those in the movie, from other planets or realms.

Another abyss in the film is that perceived gulf between Bud and Lindsay. How they come to demonstrate their true love for each other is an exercise in looking "with better eyes." And the aliens seem to be looking at the couple with similar eyes.

Ye View

1. Describe the aliens and their abilities. Do they remind you of angels? Of E.T.?
2. Why do you think the aliens are attracted to Lindsay? Why, in your opinion, do they respond as they do to Bud's situation?
3. Which character best exemplifies how *you* would respond to an alien encounter? Why?

AMAZING GRACE AND CHUCK

PREVIEW

Twelve-year-old Chuck Murdock (Joshua Zuehlke) gives up playing baseball in protest of nuclear weapons, and his efforts have far-reaching effects when he is joined by basketball superstar "Amazing Grace" Smith (Alex English) and other athletes around the world. (1987, 115 minutes, PG)

META VIEW

"But wouldn't it be nice . . . ?"

When a story begins with "once upon a time," as this one does, we know it's a fairy tale. Some fairy tales we'd like to come true, and others we wouldn't. Here's one that we would—a tale of total nuclear disarmament. The possibility seems as improbable as many events in this movie, but you never know with fairy tales.

The spirit of peace is contagious in *Amazing Grace and Chuck*, beginning with Chuck's simple but monumental decision after a class tour of a missile silo. The boy follows his principles and decides to give up his "best thing" to make a statement.

After reading a newspaper story about Chuck's actions, Amazing Grace announces to the press, "I am giving up basketball until there are no more nuclear weapons." It's a noble shot that's heard around this sporting world of ours. When Amazing Grace is told that there will *always* be nuclear weapons, he responds, "But wouldn't it be nice if there weren't?"

Idealism also is infectious in the plot, as Chuck, Amazing Grace, and sports stars from near and far never back down in their protest, founded on the firm belief that nuclear weapons are dangerous to life and unnecessary, and should be eliminated entirely.

While Chuck's movement gains momentum, many people oppose the concept, including neighbors in his Montana town, behind-the-scenes world power brokers who seek to control the public, and even the President of the United States (Gregory Peck), who claims the campaign jeopardizes disarmament negotiations rather than helps them. Some people view the antinuclear stance as un-American and yell at Chuck's family to "get out of America."

The President tells Chuck that the First Amendment does not give anyone the right to rush into a theater and yell "Fire!"

"But, sir, what if there *is* a fire?" Chuck asks.

Having once participated in an antiwar march that drew demonstrators who felt threatened by peace lovers, I know that the warring mentality dies hard. The ego mind projects hatred, distrust, and even destruction in efforts to extend itself and perpetuate beliefs in separation.

In the face of such resistance, people of peaceful principles hold the vision of unity for all. Doing so can be difficult, and that's what makes Amazing Grace, Chuck, and all their supporters truly amazing.

255

YE VIEW

1. What effect does the movement begun by Chuck have on the world? On nuclear disarmament?
2. Of nuclear weapons, Chuck says, "Aren't you scared, just knowing they're there?" Discuss your response to the question.
3. If you gave up your "best thing" for a cause such as nuclear disarmament, what would it be? What cause might you support in such a way?

THEME MATES

A completely different amazing tale of unity:

The Dark Crystal—Jen, a gentle Gelfling, is charged with finding and returning a shard to the Dark Crystal so the cruel Skeksis do not gain control of the land. This fantasy directed by Jim Henson and Frank Oz and starring Muppet creations is more than a tale of good versus evil. It ultimately is a glorious statement that "we are all a part of each other," and that the perceived separation which resulted from "our arrogance and delusion" long ago can be reversed. (1983, British, 94 minutes, PG, *)

The true story of a peace worker:

Born on the Fourth of July—Traumatized Vietnam vet Ron Kovic (Tom Cruise) becomes an antiwar activist in this powerful film directed by Oliver Stone. (1989, 144 minutes, R)

BABE

PREVIEW

Babe, the new little pig on the Hoggett Farm, is cared for by Fly, the sheepdog, and soon displays a sheepdog's keen herding abilities, which gives Farmer Hoggett (James Cromwell) the idea to enter him in the National Sheepdog Championships. (1995, 92 minutes, G, *)

META VIEW

This little piggy cries acceptance, understanding, and love

In his famous satirical novel *Animal Farm*, George Orwell wrote years ago, "All animals are equal, but some animals are more equal than others."[1] It is still thus in the highly original and enjoyable movie *Babe*, in which the animals talk quite freely. Both *Animal Farm* and *Babe* are, of course, parables with human parallels.

The animals down on the Hoggett Farm in Australia may be equal in the eyes of Universal and mortal law, in theory, but in actuality they don't consider themselves equal. The farm animals think that pigs are stupid. The sheepdogs consider the sheep inferior creatures. The sheep call the sheep-dogs "wolves" and "brutal savages." Both the sheepdogs and the sheep think it's "a cold fact of nature" that the others are stupid. Pigs and ducks aren't allowed inside the house, but dogs and cats are. The haughty house cat says that ducks and pigs "don't have a purpose," except to be eaten.

Into this farmyard of discrimination comes Babe, an unlikely champion of acceptance, understanding, and love. Babe is an orphan with a kind heart ("a heart of gold," says Maa, the elderly ewe) and a stout soul. He inno-cently believes in the equality and goodness of each animal, and boldly de-clares that he is not stupid.

While Babe doesn't like "the way things are" on the farm, he is not judgmental. However, the facts require him to call upon amazing reserves of inner strength from so small a pig. For example, when confronted with other animals' hostilities toward each other, Babe is saddened and under-standing. He loves both the sheep and the sheepdogs, and at first is upset and doesn't know what to believe when he hears them calling each other names. But then Babe makes a commitment to himself that he will "never think bad of any creature again." When he finds out that people eat pigs, he is resigned but disappointed that even his beloved Farmer Hoggett would do such a thing.

At the beginning of the film, the narrator says, "This is a tale about an unprejudiced heart and how it changed our valley forever." Babe's goodness and kindness do indeed bring new perspectives to the animals and a new understanding between the sheepdogs and the sheep.

This thoroughly charming film is itself a tribute to imagination, but the character of Farmer Hoggett embodies the imaginative, creative spirit. When

257
✳

Farmer Hoggett gets the idea to enter Babe in the sheepdog trials, he exhibits complete faith in his idea and in Babe, despite family and public opinion. The narrator says, "Farmer Hoggett knew that little ideas that tickled and nagged and refused to go away should never be ignored, for in them lie the seeds of destiny."

YE VIEW

1. The narrator says that Babe "changed our valley forever." Describe how you imagine animal life on the farm after the championships.
2. Some people have become vegetarians after seeing *Babe*. What scenes do you think might most strongly prompt a viewer to that choice?
3. Have you ever found yourself in a group of prejudiced people? How did you react? How could you have made the situation better? Discuss.

258

IN THE SAME SPIRIT

How to keep them down on the farm:

Babe: Pig in the City—In an effort to save the family farm, Babe and Mrs. Hoggett (Magda Szubanski) travel to the city to enter a contest, but instead become entangled in extremely fanciful and imaginative escapades with strange animals and humans (sections of the movie are labeled "Chaos Theory"). This is a burlesque but rather dark-toned parable about the perils of city life. "This place can really take it out of you," Babe says. The around-the-world, theme park-like cityscape is inventive; the apes are most expressive; and Babe is once again a hero with "a kind and steady heart." (1998, 96 minutes, G, *)

BAMBI

PREVIEW

A new prince of the forest, the fawn Bambi, is born and comes of age in Disney's beloved animated adaptation of Felix Salten's novel. (1942, 69 minutes, NR, *)

META VIEW

Beware of dangerous animal: man

"Oh, no!" a friend said when asked if she owns a copy of Disney's *Bambi*. "It's too sad."

She was thinking of the death of Bambi's mother.

The villain also makes *Bambi* a sad film. Some people say that many Disney animated movies, though they are aimed at children, aren't appropriate for children because they contain terribly frightening villains such as the witch in *Snow White and the Seven Dwarfs*. But *Bambi*, in many ways one of the gentlest of Disney films, presents a particularly fearsome villain, one who sends all the forest creatures running for cover: man.

The film certainly portrays humanity in a less than favorable light. Into the idyllic, innocent, beautiful world of the forest—where birds sing about love and delightful animals such as Thumper, the rabbit, and Flower, the skunk, frolic—humans bring weapons of death and ravaging fire.

The very mention of "man" sends shivers up and down the animals' spines.

When Bambi asks his mother why they suddenly had to run away, his mother says simply but chillingly, "Man was in the forest."

The Great Prince of the Forest has a similar explanation later when the animals must go deep into the forest: "It is man. He is here again. There are many this time."

259

That humanity should be portrayed as such a villain is cause for sadness. The movie makes a strong case for humankind's needing to "get a life," as they say, and respect life by not harming other animals and by protecting their habitats. Modern man, take note!

Hunters have traditionally joked about *Bambi* and the sentiment of anti-hunting that it represents. While there have been and probably still are some people whose lives depend on hunting food, most hunting today is for sport rather than by necessity. From the standpoint that all life is God-energy and interconnected, the sport of hunting frankly does not seem like a spiritual pursuit. But enough. As Thumper's father taught him, "If you can't say something nice, don't say nothin' at all."

Ye View

1. Discuss *Bambi* as an early Disney treatment of the "circle of life" theme developed in *The Lion King* and *Pocahontas*. How is the cycle of seasons shown? What is the significance of the final scene of Bambi with the Great Prince of the Forest?
2. Is fear a natural or a learned response? Support your opinion with illustrations from the movie.
3. In your own environment, why might animals fear humanity's presence? What could be done to lessen their fears?

COLD FEVER

Preview

A young, successful Tokyo businessman, Hirata (Masatoshi Nagase), journeys to a river in Iceland to perform memorial rites for his parents, who died there seven years earlier. (1995, English-Icelandic, 82 minutes, NR)

META VIEW

Invisible ties bind

Hirata is busy with work and also with planning a vacation to leave cold Japan and play golf in warm Hawaii. Therefore, he initially strongly resists his grandfather's insistence that he go to Iceland to put the souls of his parents to rest. "Why should I go to the North Pole to chant by some river?" Hirata asks.

However, Hirata finds that he cannot resist ancestral traditions and family responsibility; these invisible ties won't let him rest until he performs the sacred rites for his parents. Once he is committed to the journey, the formerly reluctant Hirata lets nothing deter him from his purpose; it's almost as if he is under an ancestral spell.

As soon as he arrives in Iceland, Hirata begins to discover there are even more ties that bind him. He finds himself on a mystical journey that reveals strong ties to a variety of unusual characters who all help him in strange ways to reach his destination. For example, there's the woman who suddenly appears and offers him a car. "There is a strong psychic connection between us. Can't you feel it?" she asks.

An other-worldly mystique envelops the Iceland that Hirata experiences. People tell him of ghosts and spirits. A helpful man says, "Just the stupid people only believes things they can see and touch."

One suspects that on the way to put his parents' souls to rest, Hirata is also putting his own to rest and finding peace for himself through the associations, connections, and ties with the past and present he encounters. With an admirable single-minded fever or fervor, he pushes beyond cold exteriors to the warmth of inner peace. He says of his experiences, "I learned that sometimes a journey can take you to a place that is not on any map."

261

YE VIEW

1. What does the photographer Laura have to say about funerals and rituals? Do you think she influences Hirata's thinking? Why or why not?
2. To what place "not on any map" has Hirata's journey brought him?
3. Do you think Hirata will remain in Iceland? Why or why not?

THEME MATES

Other journeys beyond traditional maps:

Map of the Human Heart—Avik (Jason Scott Lee), an Inuit taken as a youth from his Arctic home to Montreal by a mapmaker in the 1930s, discovers life to be a glorious, mystical journey of love and adventure, in this film from New Zealand director Vincent Ward. (1933, British-Australian-French-Canadian, 126 minutes, R) Ward also directed *The Navigator: A Medieval Odyssesy,* in which villagers escape the plague by tunneling through time to a modern city. (1988, New Zealand, 92 minutes, PG)

CONTACT

PREVIEW

A brilliant astronomer, Dr. Eleanor "Ellie" Arroway (Jodie Foster), takes the ride of a lifetime when she fulfills a dream to make contact with extra-terrestrials in this intellectual, gripping story based on a Carl Sagan novel. (1997, 150 minutes, PG)

META VIEW

Religion and science make contact

Baby boomers grew up on UFOs—well, not literally, in most cases. Our psyches teethed on reports of the Roswell incident. We learned the lyrics to "The Purple People Eater" and watched situation comedies about our favorite Martian. We and later generations became Trekkies. We seem, the lot of us born after World War II, to be particularly open to the possibility of what Ellie sarcastically calls "little green men," and in general we probably hold her view that making official connection with extraterrestrials "could potentially be the most important discovery of the human race." In short, we're ready for contact, and *Contact,* the movie, doesn't seem at all far-fetched or alien.

Our search for meaning in life doesn't ignore the cosmos. Ellie's argument in trying to receive business backing for her search for intelligent life out in space sounds rational: "All I'm asking is for you just to have the tiniest bit of vision, you know, to step back for one minute and look at the big picture, to take a chance on something that just might end up being the most profoundly impactful moment for humanity, for the history of history."

Ellie receives her money, and the powerful machines operated by her group in the New Mexico desert pick up radio and TV transmissions from life on the star Vega, twenty-six light years away. The alien message consists of engineering plans to build a machine, apparently for the purpose of transporting a human passenger to another planet or dimension. Ellie is logically destined to take that ride.

It really comes as no surprise in *Contact* that contact is made with aliens. It also is no surprise that the public has widely different reactions to the contact, from the denouncements by religious zealots to the carnival antics of fun worshipers. Nor do the United States government's general antagonism and political maneuvering for best advantage of the situation seem out of

263

place or unexpected. The movie promises and delivers lots of action and intrigue along these lines.

What is pleasantly surprising perhaps is the movie's unmistakable marriage of two long-battling partners: religion and science. The movie, directed by Robert Zemeckis, is a skillful weaving and coming together of the two traditionally opposing positions.

Religion/spirituality is represented by the character of Palmer Joss (Matthew McConaughey), a noted theologian, author, and political advisor nicknamed "God's diplomat." Early in the movie, Palmer and Ellie, who represents science, develop a relationship. Both, it turns out, are searching for meaning in life.

Palmer tells Ellie about the profound experience that led to his faith. He says that he had the feeling of not being alone or scared, even of death. "It was God," he says. Ellie counters that he perhaps made up the experience out of his own needs. No, Palmer insists, "My intellect—it couldn't even touch this."

Later Ellie, the skeptical voice of science, says she wants proof of God's existence, and wonders if people didn't create God "so that we wouldn't have to feel so small and alone."

"I couldn't imagine living in a world where God didn't exist," Palmer says. "Who would want to?"

To make his point that God exists, Palmer then asks Ellie to prove that she loves her father. She can't "prove" what she feels and knows at the core of her being.

Ellie's science and technology, however, take her on a journey in "a tunnel through the fabric of space-time," and she has her own profound experience that echoes Palmer's experience of God. Ellie says, "I was given something wonderful, something that changed me forever—a vision of the universe that tells us undeniably how tiny and insignificant and how rare and precious we all are, a vision that tells us that we belong to something that is greater than ourselves, that we are not, that none of us are alone." The experience, she indicates, must be accepted on faith, and she would like to be able to communicate the awe, humility, and hope that she experienced to everyone.

Science and religion have taken different approaches to Truth, but they eventually make contact. Palmer acknowledges as much when he tells reporters that he and Ellie share one goal—"the pursuit of truth."

The alien that Ellie encounters in the form of her father says that Ellie's journey is only the first step of contact and that there will be more.

Just as Ellie and Palmer point to the ultimate oneness of science and religion, the alien also shows the need for unity and interaction: "You're an interesting species, an interesting mix. You are capable of such beautiful dreams and such horrible nightmares. You feel so lost, so cut off, so alone, only you're not. You see, in all of our searching, the only thing we've found that makes the emptiness bearable is each other."

265

The movie opens with gorgeous views of space, and more are seen during Ellie's journey. The scientist in her feels absolutely inadequate to describe what she sees. Such beauty, she suggests, is the province of the arts, not science. "They should have sent a poet," she says. But it was her time to behold the proof, for of course Truth, like beauty, is in the eyes of the beholder.

YE VIEW

1. Discuss your reaction to the movie's recurring refrain about the possibility of life on other planets: "If it's just us, it seems like an awful waste of space."
2. Answer Palmer's question, "Is the world fundamentally a better place because of science and technology?" Defend your position.
3. Would you have ridden the alien-designed spacecraft? Why or why not?

IN THE SAME SPIRIT

An earlier contact:

Close Encounters of the Third Kind—A telephone lineman in Indiana (Richard Dreyfuss) is among those who are linked in efforts to make contact with alien beings and who head to Devils Tower in Wyoming to do just that in this exciting science fiction story written and directed by Steven Spielberg. (1977, 135 minutes, PG)

DANCES WITH WOLVES

PREVIEW

After the Civil War, Lieutenant John Dunbar (Kevin Costner) requests assignment to a remote post so that he can see the frontier before it is gone, and there he makes friends with a Sioux tribe and falls in love with Stands With a Fist (Mary McDonnell) in this sweeping epic filmed in South Dakota. (1990, 181 minutes, PG-13)

META VIEW

Let us all dance in harmony

From the film's beginning when he becomes an unlikely hero, Lieutenant Dunbar clearly is not your run-of-the-mill soldier. He is a thoughtful, introspective, sensitive man who recognizes that "the strangeness of this life cannot be measured." He has the vision to know what is coming for the American frontier, as well as for the American Indian, and he is saddened.

Experiencing the frontier, Dunbar writes in his journal, "It seems every day ends with a miracle here, and whatever God may be, I thank God for this day."

Through Dunbar's appreciative eyes, we see the beautiful expanse of land and its animals (he is befriended by a wolf that he names Two Socks, and takes part in an incredibly filmed buffalo hunt), and we come to know the Indian people and their way of life.

Dunbar is surprised by the quality of life and family that he finds among the Sioux.

"Nothing I have been told about these people is correct," he says. "They are not beggars and thieves. They are not the boogeymen they have been made out to be. On the contrary, they are polite guests and have a familiar humor I enjoy."

He also comments, "I had never known a people so eager to laugh, so devoted to family, so dedicated to each other, and the only word that came to mind was *harmony*."

Seeing as Dunbar sees, the movie viewer is as distressed and disheartened as Dunbar by the reaction of United States soldiers to the Indians and their land. The soldiers have only a stereotypical view of the Indians and regard them with blind hatred and ignorant disrespect.

Of course, it should be noted that the Sioux have similar notions about all whites, until they get to know Dunbar. The Sioux holy man Kicking Bird (Graham Greene) comments before meeting Dunbar, "The whites are a poor race and hard to understand." He later acknowledges that Dunbar has a good heart.

The profound theme of *Dances With Wolves* is that people need to learn to dance in harmony with all life—with the land, with the animals, and with people of all races and cultures. We need to discover our common bonds and appreciate our essential similarities rather than focus on and fight over our differences. Lieutenant Dunbar is a great role model for people truly interested in honoring diversity.

YE VIEW

1. Why is it that Dunbar feels a pride he never felt before in battle when he joins the Sioux against the Pawnee? What is different about the purpose of the Indian fight?
2. Kicking Bird says Dunbar is on the "trail of a human being," which is the trail that matters most in life. What do you think he means?
3. In your opinion, what are the main causes for disharmony and distrust between the Indians and the white soldiers and settlers?

THEME MATES

Others discovering that the "savages" have their own cultures and beliefs: *Black Robe*—Father LaForgue (Lothaire Bluteau) leads an expedition to convert the Hurons in Canada in the 1600s, but his faith is severely tested in this violent and graphic but beautifully filmed story. LaForgue says: "What can we say to people who think their dreams are the real world; this one is an illusion? Perhaps they're right." (1991, Canadian-Australian, 101 minutes, R) *The Emerald Forest*—A father searches for his son, who has been kidnapped by an Amazon tribe in Brazil. (1985, 113 minutes, R) *Walkabout*—An Aborigine boy (David Gulpilil) rescues a brother and sister wandering in the Australian outback. (1971, Australian, 95 minutes, PG)

THE DAY THE EARTH STOOD STILL

PREVIEW

In this classic science fiction film from director Robert Wise, Klaatu (Michael Rennie), a visitor from a neighboring planet 250 million miles away, lands his spaceship in Washington, D.C., and serves Earthlings an ultimatum: Be peaceful or be destroyed. (1951, 92 minutes, NR)

META VIEW

Peace? Let's answer "Yes!"

Watching the movie as another war erupts in the Middle East and a peace pact once again disintegrates, I am struck by just how relevant this film still is and how much the world still needs its message. Wars and rumors of wars abound; it was ever thus.

Klaatu's visit emphasizes both the petty foolishness of human fighting and the detrimental consequences our fighting may have for the welfare of the planet and the whole universe.

When Klaatu announces that he wants to meet with representatives of all Earth's nations and speak to them about an important matter that concerns all the people on the planet, a presidential assistant tells him: "Our world at the moment is full of tensions and suspicions. In the present international situation, such a meeting would be quite impossible."

A presidential assistant might say the same thing today as he would have fifty years ago—and an actual alien envoy for peace might meet with the same suspicion, fear, and aggressiveness as does Klaatu.

Klaatu remains focused and implacable. "My mission here is not to solve your petty squabbles," he says. "It concerns the existence of every last creature on Earth." He does admit, however, to being "impatient with stupidity" (his people have learned to live without it) and to being fearful "when I see people substituting fear for reason." Klaatu is politely implying that humankind is being stupid and fearful in its use of and reliance on weapons of mass destruction.

Klaatu informs the Earth in no uncertain terms that we are not alone here in the cosmos—and our neighbors are watching and are most con-

269

cerned about our increasing capabilities to destroy each other and the planet, and perhaps upset an interplanetary balance. Humankind's preoccupation with atomic weapons is a clear threat and danger to other planets, and will not be tolerated, Klaatu warns.

Other planets, Klaatu says, have organized to protect all planets and to eliminate aggression. He invites Earth to join the group. "Your choice is simple—join us and live in peace or pursue your present course and face obliteration," he says.

Klaatu is still waiting for an answer, and he's not the only one.

YE VIEW

1. How do the American government, armed forces, newspapers, and people generally respond to Klaatu's arrival and presence? Be specific. Discuss whether or not people would really react in these ways to such a visit.
2. What happens on "the day the Earth stood still"? What do you think would be the effect of such a demonstration today?
3. Give your views of the method Klaatu explains that his and other planets have devised to preserve peace among the planets. Would people on Earth be inclined to support such a plan today? Why or why not?

DESTRY RIDES AGAIN

PREVIEW

Tom Destry (James Stewart), the son of a famous gun-slinging lawman, encounters unbelief and laughter when he becomes the deputy sheriff of the

Wild West town of Bottleneck and announces that he will keep the peace without using guns. (1939, 94 minutes, NR)

META VIEW

The ideal is a loaded one

Destry's father carried six-shooters and was shot in the back and killed. When asked why he doesn't use guns as weapons, Destry drily replies, "I don't believe in them."

"What *do* you believe in?" asks Wash (Charles Winninger), formerly the town drunk but recently appointed sheriff by the corrupt saloon establishment.

"Law and order—without them [guns]," Destry replies. He explains that shoot-outs can make criminals look like heroes. Instead, he says, "Put them behind bars and they'll look little and cheap, the way they *ought* to look."

"My pa did it the old way, and I'm going to do it a new way."

Destry's peace-loving way, other than not toting guns, includes telling parables to help people see the value of nonviolence, having a hobby to work off rage (his is carving wood), encouraging people to understand each other, and using his intelligence to outsmart the enemy, which here is saloon owner Kent (Brian Donlevy) and his gang. All of these alternatives to bloodshed are most admirable.

From the accounts of most westerns, anyway, Destry's way certainly went against the norm during the country's frontier days. In fact, it seems to go against the accepted way of fighting during *every* age, including our own.

Giving up weapons and using peaceful methods to defeat opponents is a noble ideal—and certainly a very spiritual one supported by most scriptures and sages—but unfortunately it has not been widely successful. The old saying is true that people who live by the sword die by the sword, but it

271

✳

is also true that a lot of people who live by peace have died by the "sword," including Jesus; Gandhi, whose nonviolent noncooperation movement in India was known at the time the movie was made; and Martin Luther King, Jr. These three men remained true to their principles and died.

Destry does not remain true to his principles, and therefore presents a moral dilemma. When the going gets particularly rough, Destry chooses to strap on his guns—and use them. Does he do the "right" thing? Chances are he will be killed if he does not defend himself. It can be argued that he must resort to using weapons once to remain alive in order to help his ideals take root and to save others from needless bloodshed. It also can be argued that, in going against his beliefs, he sacrifices himself for others. Regardless what one thinks about his decision to use guns, Destry's ideals do live on. Such ideals, even when compromised, can still offer inspiration in a world of conflict.

272

Ye View

1. Cite some examples of Destry's using his intelligence to outsmart the enemy.
2. In your opinion, is saloon singer Frenchie (Marlene Dietrich) an enemy or a friend to Destry? Explain your answer.
3. Give your response to the moral dilemma posed by Destry's going against his belief and using firearms.

Theme Mates

Other western heros with pacifist leanings:

High Noon—Retiring marshal Will Kane (Gary Cooper), who has just married a Quaker woman (Grace Kelly), faces a vengeful gunman. (1952, 84 minutes, NR)

Shane—A former gunfighter (Alan Ladd) helps homesteaders. (1953, 118 minutes, NR)

E.T. THE EXTRA-TERRESTRIAL

PREVIEW

A little space creature, frightened and confused after being accidentally stranded on Earth, is befriended and "adopted" by a 10-year-old boy, Elliott (Henry Thomas). (1982, 115 minutes, PG, *)

META VIEW

E.T. also stands for "Empathy Teaches"

The animated conversation of two red-haired teenage girls on a public bus in Edinburgh, Scotland, caught my attention. The girls were talking about their families and boyfriends and school—the same subjects occupying their peers across the Atlantic, and all over the world. Their talk really pointed to the fact that people everywhere are actually concerned about the same things, even though they may live in different countries and different cultures.

Or on different planets. We don't know much about the background of the creature affectionately tagged E.T., but we do have a definite sense that he values home. Not since Dorothy in *The Wizard of Oz* has a movie character been so concerned about getting home—and understandably so. Because we know what "home" generally means to us, we can project that "home" to E.T. means family, friends, security, familiar possessions, comfort, and love. We can identify with his desire: "E.T. phone home."

Being able to feel a common bond with another, to empathize with another—whether it is a young girl in Scotland or a creature from another planet—increases our understanding of the truth that somehow all life is a part of one big family.

E.T. successfully enables the viewer to have empathy for the creature

273

✲

and feel his wonder, confusion, and fear. We understand, for example, when E.T. and Elliott first encounter each other and scream in surprise and fear, because that's a common reaction to a surprise meeting with an unknown entity.

Elliott literally comes to share E.T.'s feelings to the extent that his body responds to what E.T. is doing and feeling. After being briefly startled at their first meeting, Elliott is able to place himself in E.T.'s position and feel what he is going through, and thus he desperately wants only what is right and good for E.T. Elliott is the epitome of empathy.

Ye View

1. What are some universal situations and concerns within Elliott's family?
2. Who, other than Elliott, seems to have an empathy for E.T.? How do you know?
3. What indications are there that E.T. has a concern for the feelings of others and for an appreciation of life itself? Consider especially E.T. and Elliott's parting.

THE LION KING

Preview

Simba the cub flees a Serengeti paradise after his father Mufasa, the lion king, is murdered by Mufasa's jealous brother Scar, but returns as an adult to confront his uncle and heal a wasted land. (1994, 88 minutes, G, *)

META VIEW

We're all in the "circle of life"

Artistic images of various animals zoom across the gorgeous African scenery as we hear the words to "Circle of Life"—"It's the circle of life, and it moves us all, through despair and hope, through faith and love." The song assures us that we are all moving together through life's conflicting emotions and situations, and that we all have a place in the great "circle of life." The animated scenes and the song by Elton John and Tim Rice are perfect openers for this extremely popular and superbly animated Disney film. They set the tone and offer the first glimpse of the film's core teaching: We're all in this circle together.

Now, make no mistake about it, *The Lion King* draws the circle as it is. Life can be full of beauty and laughter and love, and there is plenty of all of these. The wisecracking little sidekicks that have become a Disney trademark are cleverly represented by Pumbaa, the warthog; Timon, the meerkat; and Zazu, the bird. Simba and Nala provide the lion's share of the romance.

But life can also be a *vicious* circle, and can include sadness, stupidity, crassness, selfishness, and treachery, and these too are amply represented. As you perhaps noted from the Preview summary, *The Lion King* is basically an adaptation of Shakespeare's tragedy *Hamlet*. Disney does not leave it to the imagination that Scar purposely kills Mufasa and then lies to Simba and fills the young cub with guilt. These are heavy issues for an animated movie designed for children. It is indeed a tale, as described in *Hamlet*, "whose lightest word would harrow up thy soul, freeze thy young blood, make thy two eyes, like stars, start from their spheres."[2] Something is certainly rotten in the Serengeti. Why animate such a tale? Parents and educators can debate at what age children should be exposed to life's darker side, but they can't deny that a darker side is a part of the "circle of life."

275

Much to the Disney team's credit, however, the movie doesn't just present the dual nature of the circle; it also gives instruction about how to live in that circle. *The Lion King* teaches that the "circle of life," even with its seeming imperfections, requires both respect and responsibility, and what an important lesson for thousands of young viewers to receive!

Mufasa is a worthy teacher for all our young, as represented by Simba. The lion king tells his son: "Everything you see exists together in a delicate balance. As king, you need to understand that balance and respect all the creatures, from the crawling ant to the leaping antelope."

Simba points out that lions eat antelopes, and Mufasa responds with a lesson about nature's food chain, "When we die, our bodies become the grass, and the antelope eat the grass, and so we are all connected in the great circle of life."

The circle is properly maintained when everyone accepts responsibility, and that includes the responsibility to make conditions better. Those who choose to ignore responsibility are humorously characterized in the song "Hakuna Matata," the title of which means "no worries." While a "problem-free philosophy" with "no worries for the rest of your days" may sound appealing, as it does to Simba in exile, such a philosophy isn't helping those in need in the "circle of life." In a way, it's like stepping outside the circle.

Simba comes to realize that. Nala tells him that he has a responsibility to the lions. Rafiki, the mystic baboon who practices yoga and martial arts, helps Simba see his rightful place. And the spirit of Mufasa in the stars says to him: "Look inside yourself, Simba. You are more than what you have become. You must take your place in the circle of life."

Ye View

1. What does Rafiki do to teach Simba a lesson about the past? What is that lesson?
2. Discuss how the film's ending reflects the "circle of life."

3. How can you take more responsibility for your own "circle of life"?

IN THE SAME SPIRIT

Circling on:

Pocahontas—Disney's animated feature about the brave American Indian girl who fell for English Captain John Smith includes another memorable "circle of life" song—"Colors of the Wind," which contains the lyrics "We are all connected to each other in a circle, in a hoop that never ends." (1995, 82 minutes, G *)

THEME MATES

Completing the circle:

The Trip to Bountiful—A widow (Geraldine Page) determined to go home to Bountiful, Texas, reminds us that we all have an innate desire, whether realized or not, to return to our bountiful spiritual home. The return is one of consciousness, for we are always, in fact, one with Spirit. (1985, 106 minutes, PG)

PLACES IN THE HEART

PREVIEW

When her husband, the sheriff of Waxahachie, Texas, is shot and killed by a drunk black man during the Depression, Edna Spalding (Sally Field) keeps her home and children together by accepting the help of a black panhandler, Moses (Danny Glover), who teaches her about cotton farming, and by taking in a blind boarder, Will (John Malkovich). (1984, 102 minutes, PG)

277

✵

META VIEW

Conflicts unite us

The characters down on this Southern farm plow through conflicts with a right admirable spiritual determination, even though their pain and heartaches are many. They dramatically face three of humankind's major areas of conflict—person versus him/herself, person versus person, and person versus nature.

In dealing with each conflict, they not only illustrate the calm courage that Ernest Hemingway described as "grace under pressure,"[3] but they also show that conflicts can be a powerful and beautiful catalyst for uniting diverse people in human bonds.

Edna and Moses especially, as well as several other characters in the story, go through enormous soul-searching and discover "the stuff" of which they are truly made. Edna, who cared for the children and house when her husband was alive but never paid bills or worked outside the home, is resolute in the face of threats of losing her home and children. She finds the inner resources to meet whatever difficulty comes along. "I'm not going to give up," she says. Moses talks to God and thinks there must be some mistake that he has become involved in a white family's problems, but he opens his heart and practical know-how to the family's plight.

The movie effectively presents some of the many person-versus-person, or relationship, problems that can plague society, but then suggests those problems can be overcome through hearts of love. For example, the tragic accidental death of Edna's husband is a further cause of racial divisiveness within the community (the KKK is quite active), but Edna is not vindictive toward blacks. In the midst of her grief, she readily prepares meals for Moses and then takes him in. She later builds up Moses' self-esteem by telling him: "Colored or white, you're the one who brought in the first bale of cotton this year. Don't you ever forget that."

Other relationship problems include those of Edna's sister and brother-in-law, who have marital difficulties to work out, and of Will, whose loss of sight in war has left him unsociable and in need of learning to connect with others.

A ferocious storm serves to reveal hidden emotions and bring people together. For example, during the storm Will rescues Edna's daughter, Moses rescues her son, and all the extended family huddle in a storm shelter. It's a time to reflect upon the seemingly strange twists of fate that unite people.

YE VIEW

1. Discuss the role of prayers and hymns in the movie. What do you think is the significance of showing black and white families praying? What is the theme of Mr. Spalding's prayer? What hymn is sung at the beginning?
2. What are some other specific incidents that show the courage and integrity of individuals dealing with conflicts?
3. The church scene at the end of the movie is a dynamic statement about our unity with God. Discuss the scene, its participants, and why it is a memorable and moving closing. (Consider "Peace of God.")

IN THE SAME SPIRIT

Representing the strength of the whole human family:

Friendly Persuasion—A Quaker family copes during the Civil War in this screen version of Jessamyn West's novel. (1956, 140 minutes, NR)

The Grapes of Wrath—The Joads leave the Oklahoma dust bowl and travel to California during the Depression in director John Ford's exquisite telling of John Steinbeck's classic novel. (1940, 129 minutes, NR)

SIX DEGREES OF SEPARATION

PREVIEW

Manhattan art dealers Ouisa and Flan Kittredge (Stockard Channing and Donald Sutherland) take in—and are taken in by—a young man (Will Smith) who calls himself Paul and claims to be the son of famed actor Sidney Poitier. (1993, 112 minutes, R)

META VIEW

We're all connected

There's much to ponder in this film of John Guare's thought-provoking, and in many ways unsettling, play—perhaps the most intriguing being the concept for which the work is named. Her unexpected and astounding relationship with Paul prompts Ouisa to discuss the idea of "six degrees of separation."

"I read somewhere that everybody on this planet is separated by only six other people—six degrees of separation between us and everyone else on this planet," Ouisa says.

The idea is comforting "that we're so close," Ouisa says, adding that everyone is a door opening into other worlds. "It's a profound thought."

The theory is based on whom you know and whom the person you know knows and whom the person you know knows knows, and so on. By tracing the "who knows who" connection to the sixth-degree persons, a vast network of interconnections is established. An Internet service and a board game based on "six degrees of separation" are now part of our culture.

The concept applies equally to all people of all walks of life, but is perhaps most dramatically illustrated with an example involving famous names. To use a personal example, I know television actress Lauren Lane (first degree), who has met actress Susan Sarandon (second degree), who knows actress Julia Roberts (third degree), who knows Richard Gere (fourth degree), who knows the Dalai Lama (fifth degree), who has met Pope John Paul II (sixth degree). When one considers all the people each of these people knows, the relationship web expands tremendously. "Six degrees of separation" really means six degrees of unity.

The "six degrees of separation" concept touches that innate longing within humans to recall their oneness with God and all of God's creation. In an age that retains a mental picture of our planet as Spaceship Earth, the concept accents the interconnectedness of human life on the spaceship.

The concept of the "six degrees of separation" intrigues Ouisa, prompts her to seriously examine her own connections and interconnections, and to realize that the people who touch our lives matter as individuals. Ouisa sees that she and Flan have been telling Paul's story over and over at social occasions with their friends and business associates, as if the story itself and not the person was most important. She is appalled at herself.

"How do we keep what happens to us? How do we fit it into life without turning it into an anecdote?" she wonders.

"Have we become these human jukeboxes spilling out these anecdotes?" she asks. "But it was an experience [the encounter with Paul]. How do we keep the experience?"

"Six degrees of separation," then, implies a responsibility to acknowledge the connections by recognizing that people are *people,* with lives touching others' lives, and are not just numbers and statistics or anecdotes.

YE VIEW

1. Paul talks a lot about the importance of imagination. How does Paul use his imagination to get what he wants? What are your opinions of his methods?
2. What changes come about in Ouisa's life because of her

281

association with Paul? Consider her dreams and her relationship with Flan.

3. Develop a "six degrees of separation" chart for yourself or explore the possibilities at www.sixdegrees.com.

THEME MATES

Discovering their connections, sometimes painfully:

The Chosen—Two men of different Jewish backgrounds become friends. (1981, 108 minutes, PG)

Cry, the Beloved Country—Racial tensions in a divided South Africa are high when the path of an African minister (James Earl Jones) looking for his son crosses that of a white landowner (Richard Harris) whose son has been killed, in this adaptation of Alan Paton's novel. (1995, United States-British-South African, 120 minutes, PG-13) Also filmed as *Cry, the Beloved Country* (1951, British, 111 minutes, NR) and the musical *Lost in the Stars* (1974, 114 minutes, G).

Our Town—Thornton Wilder's play about a New England town, faithfully adapted to the screen, beautifully shows the connectedness of human communities, even beyond the grave. (1940, 90 minutes, NR)

Playing by Heart—Touching, sometimes painful, often humorous true-to-life stories of various couples show vividly just how intricately woven are the fabrics of our lives. The relationship between punk youths Joan (Angelina Jolie) and Keenan (Ryan Phillippe) is especially appealing. (1998, 120 minutes, R)

The Power of One—A white South African youth (Stephen Dorff) takes on apartheid in this tale with great scenery, a look at "the voices of Africa"—justice, hope, courage, and love; and a classic thought—"Changes can come from the power of many, but only when the many come together to form that which is invincible . . . the power of one." (1992, 111 minutes, PG-13)

To Kill a Mockingbird—In an Alabama town in the 1930s, the lives of attorney Atticus Finch (Gregory Peck), a black man he is defending (Brock Peters), Finch's daughter Scout (Mary Badham), and the retarded neighbor Boo Radley (Robert Duvall) are intertwined in this sharp telling of Harper Lee's novel. (1962, 129 minutes, NR)

STAR TREK IV: THE VOYAGE HOME

PREVIEW

When Earth in the twenty-third century is threatened by a mysterious alien probe, Admiral Kirk (William Shatner), Mr. Spock (Leonard Nimoy), and the rest of the *Enterprise* crew travel back to the late twentieth century to obtain what is needed to save the planet—humpback whales. (1986, 119 minutes, PG)

META VIEW

It's a whale of a cautionary tale

So what's the big deal if humankind hunts a species to extinction? Is the world going to end because of it? Our shortsightedness could indeed have such a devastating effect in a later century. That's the premise of this space odyssey for the age of endangered species.

The film postulates that people should give more thought to the importance, capabilities, intelligence, and interconnectedness of all creatures.

An alien power is transmitting strange sounds that are causing the evaporation of Earth's oceans and wide-scale power blackouts. Spock, the logical half-Vulcan, half-Earthling, thinks that the unknown intelligent energy form is apparently unaware its transmissions are destructive. While the humans may characteristically jump to conclusions of evil intents, Spock says, "I find it illogical that its intentions should be hostile."

But the sounds don't make any sense, Dr. McCoy (DeForest Kelley) replies.

"There are other forms of intelligence on Earth," Spock says. "Only human arrogance would assume the message must be meant for man." Humans, of course, *do* usually assume that the universe revolves around their activities and interests. Spock's point is downright revolutionary—even several centuries hence, unfortunately.

Spock determines that the probe's sounds are like the songs of humpback whales under water. Humpbacks, which were on Earth ten million years before humans, were heavily hunted by humans and have been extinct since the twenty-first century, Spock says.

"It is possible that an alien intelligence sent the probe to determine why they lost contact."

How fascinating and ironic to speculate that right now, as UFOlogists all over the world are searching for and debating about the possibilities of alien contact, humpback whales and aliens could be on a first-song basis.

The *Enterprise* gang decides to return to the time of the whales and bring a few into the twenty-third century so that they can sing to the probe and stop its deadening sounds. When two perfect specimens are found, Spock communicates to them and, not surprisingly, discovers that the whales are unhappy about the way their species has been treated by humans.

Dr. Gillian Taylor (Catherine Hicks), the assistant director of the Cetacean Institute where the whales are kept, becomes enraged when a coworker suggests the fate of the whales doesn't matter, because it has not been determined that whales are intelligent. "My compassion for someone is not limited to my estimate of their intelligence," she says.

Here's another valuable message for humans, who tend to judge and classify most animals, other than pets, by intelligent standards, without considering them as fellow beings, with emotions and consciousness.

Hearing Gillian talk about the number of extinct animals, Spock says, "Two hundred species to extinction is not logical."

Gillian replies, "Who ever said the human race was logical?"

Perhaps it can learn to be.

YE VIEW

1. "There are other forms of intelligence on Earth" besides humans, Spock says. Discuss the validity of this comment.
2. Kirk calls the 1980s world of humans "an extremely primitive and paranoid culture." What examples of these attributes are seen in the movie?
3. What are your views about whaling and the hunting of endangered species? Have your views been influenced at all by the movie? If so, how?

IN THE SAME SPIRIT

Cautionary tale two:

Silent Running—After nuclear destruction on Earth, a botanist on a space station strives to preserve remnants of Earth's last plant life. (1971, 89 minutes, G)

285
✳

::: **FEATURE PRESENTATION**

Woe Stoppers: <u>The</u> <u>Thin</u> <u>Red</u> <u>Line</u> and Beyond

Perhaps one motion picture about war is worth a thousand words. The following fourteen movies clearly show the physical and mental suffering of war, and suggest the profound absurdities of war. These movies are recommended to help any viewer combat idealistic images of war and to develop a consciousness of peace and brotherly love. Some of them were made with the explicit purpose to help prevent future wars and the woes of war.

Warning: Some scenes are inhumane, horrible, frightening, and gory—but that's war, and that's the point.

1. **ALL QUIET ON THE WESTERN FRONT**—The brutalities of war are seen from the perspective of German boys in World War I trenches in this acclaimed antiwar movie based on the Erich Maria Remarque novel. (1930, 105 minutes, NR)

2. **APOCALYPSE NOW**—A manhunt through Cambodia, based on Joseph Conrad's *Heart of Darkness*, exposes the Vietnam War. (1979, 150 minutes, R)

3. **DAS BOOT (THE BOAT)**—A German U-boat is on a fatal course during World War II. (1981, German, 145 minutes, R)

4. **FORBIDDEN GAMES**—WWII becomes grim, poignant child's play in this antiwar tale of a little girl whose parents are killed. (1951, French, 87 minutes, NR)

5. **GALLIPOLI**—Youthful idealism shatters during especially senseless WWI battle. (1981, Australian, 110 minutes, PG)

6. **GLORY**—Black soldiers march through the bloody battlefields of the Civil War in this story based on fact. (1989, 122 minutes, R)

7. **JACOB'S LADDER**—A Vietnam vet discovers it's difficult to wake up from the nightmares of war. (1990; 115 minutes, R)

8. **JOHNNY GOT HIS GUN**—And his body was blown away in this dramatization of Dalton Trumbo's devastating look at the effects of WWI. (1971, 111 minutes, PG)

9. **A MIDNIGHT CLEAR**—Young soldiers search the Ardennes Forest for enemies during Christmas of 1944 in this antiwar stunner based on William Wharton's novel. (1992, 107 minutes, R)

10. **PLATOON**—Oliver Stone's personal and all-too-realistic memories of the Vietnam War. (1986, 120 minutes, R)

11. **SAVING PRIVATE RYAN**—Steven Spielberg's long opening depicting the landing on Omaha Beach during WWII sets a chilling stage for a rescue mission. (1998, 170 minutes, R)

12. **THE STEEL HELMET**—The fighting vividly continues in the Korean War. (1951, 84 minutes, NR)

13. **THE THIN RED LINE**—This film, surely the most metaphysical war movie ever made, leads viewers to consider the spiritual implications of war in the natural world while focusing on the WWII battle of Guadalcanal. Private Witt (Jim Caviezel) ponders the broad questions of life, such as the origins of evil and war and love, and speculates about the "one big self" of humankind that somehow became disconnected from its "glory." "How did we lose the good that was given us?" he asks. "What's keeping us from reaching out and touching the glory?" With the backdrop of a beautiful natural world that transcends suffering and confrontation, Witt seeks and sees the glory in everything. (1999, 170 minutes, R)

14. **WAR AND PEACE**—The first part of the title—Napoleon's invasion of Russia in 1812—upstages the second in this grand presentation of Leo Tolstoy's novel. (1968, Russian, 373 minutes, NR)

287
✳

Leslie Caron and Mel Ferrer with puppet friends in *Lili*, MGM,
Turner Entertainment
Photo: The Museum of Modern Art Film Stills Archive

Chapter 7

Loving One Another

· ·

The movies reflect the myriad dimensions and, yes, passions of human love. They can also help us realize that human love in whatever form—for example, romantic, brotherly, parent-child—is but a glimpse of divine love. All loving is an exercise in spreading God-energy. What we are ultimately longing for is to know our oneness with God, to know God's love. To do so, we must take responsibility and get very specific. Jesus said the Great Commandment is this: "You shall love the Lord your God with all your heart, and with all your soul, and with all your mind," and the second commandment is this: "You shall love your neighbor as yourself." He put loving God squarely on human territory. The movies in this chapter teach us to express the unconditional love of God in all relationships—regardless of race, creed, religious beliefs, sexual preferences, and physical appearances.

AS GOOD AS IT GETS

PREVIEW

A rude, inconsiderate, reclusive, obsessive-compulsive novelist, Melvin Udall (Jack Nicholson), becomes involved in the lives of his favorite waitress, Carol (Helen Hunt), and his gay neighbor, Simon (Greg Kinnear), with heartwarming results. (1997, 139 minutes, PG-13)

META VIEW

Love and make it better

The title comes from the desperately confused Melvin's unscheduled visit to his psychiatrist. Melvin asks the patients in the waiting room, "What if this is as good as it gets?"

It's a question asked frequently by people muddling through life but vaguely aware of a deep discontent and emptiness. The question may not be voiced or even thought, but nonetheless lingers in the subconscious.

What is the answer? When and how does it get as good as it gets?

Obviously, when the question is asked at any level of consciousness, the answer is not being seen in the present circumstances. When Melvin asks the question, he doesn't find hope in what he sees. In fact, his worldview in many ways is indicative of as *bad* as it gets when we don't relate to others, when we don't give of ourselves to others, when we have trouble giving and receiving love, when we're lonely, when we're worried about loved ones, and when we're hurt, abused, or betrayed.

Then when does it get as *good* as it gets?

When we know love for ourselves and others and appreciation for the differences and similarities among people.

On this earthly plane, as good as it gets is being aware of and loving the

Christ—the God essence, the divinity, spiritual being, or God-power and potential, within each person. It is to experience God as love and to join our hearts and souls with that universal Christ love at the core of all of His creations. A wonderful saying is, "The Christ in me beholds the Christ in you." That's as good as it gets.

As circumstances push Melvin out of his shell, he learns to love the Christ within others (and thus within himself)—although, of course, he doesn't call it by that name. Melvin's awareness of his capacity to love and his awareness of the love within those around him comes gradually—first with love for Simon's dog Verdell, then for Carol, and then for Simon. Carol and Simon expand their horizons of love too.

With Melvin's character, the movie shows that the seed of love is within, even though it may have a difficult time coming out. Melvin is clearly a tough, extreme case. Simon initially considers Melvin an "absolute horror of a human being."

But Simon also says, in explaining how he observes people for his artwork, "You look at someone long enough, you discover their humanity."

The technique even works on someone like Melvin, if one is willing to look long and deep enough. There are clues that Melvin has a loving center, though. He is at first observant and kind for selfish reasons, but at least we know that he has it in him to *be* observant and kind. Melvin eventually realizes how good it feels within himself to see the goodness within another.

Seeing the goodness within others doesn't mean that we see only perfection. It is often necessary to combine love with the realization that people are doing the best they can at any given time. It behooves us to be realistic as we learn together to open ourselves to more love.

"Why can't I just have a normal boyfriend . . . who doesn't go nuts on me?" Carol cries.

Her mother responds: "Everybody wants that, dear. It doesn't exist."

We learn to love people where they are and *as* they are.

Living a contented, satisfying life that is as good as it gets also involves

291

realizing divine order—that God is always good and that all is unfolding toward the ultimate good of all concerned, even though appearances may suggest otherwise.

The concept is twice introduced to Melvin, and twice he shoots it down.

Nora, the housekeeper, tells him to open Simon's curtains "so he can see God's beautiful work, and he'll know that even things like this (Simon's beating) happen for the best."

Melvin replies: "Sell 'crazy' someplace else. We're all stocked up here."

Later Carol tells Simon, "When it comes to your parents or your kids, something will always be off for you unless you set it straight, and maybe this thing happened to you just to give you a chance to do that."

Melvin's response is "Nonsense."

Events in this insightful movie written by director James L. Brooks and Mark Andrus, however, suggest otherwise.

Ye View

1. What are your feelings about Melvin by the end of the movie? How do they change during the course of the story?
2. What do you know about Melvin's childhood? About Simon's? How might their childhoods have influenced their adult personalities?
3. Write a description of your life, envisioning as good as it could get for you. What would you have to do to make this picture appear?

BEAUTY AND THE BEAST

PREVIEW

A selfish, mean prince who has been turned into a beast, and the beautiful woman who can break his spell if she loves him are joined by an entertaining cast of singing and dancing castle objects in this animated wonder from Disney. (1991, 85 minutes, G, *)

META VIEW

"Tale as old as time": love can transform

In matters of love, what does it mean to be a beauty, and what does it mean to be a beast?

To begin with, being a beauty is knowing that looks aren't everything. In the spiritual scheme of things, in fact, they're nothing. Being a beast is taking people literally at face value. That's what the handsome but selfish and unkind prince does when he refuses to give a woman shelter because she is haggard. The old woman is an enchantress who detected no love in the prince's heart. The narrator says, "She warned him not to be deceived by appearances, for beauty is found within."

Going past appearances, being a beauty is looking for an individual's real personality. Being a beast is remaining attached to stereotypes, preconceived notions, or prejudices about a person. Belle's would-be husband Gaston, for example, is a beast, even though he is a physical standout, because he doesn't see past Belle's outward beauty. He doesn't care about her inner beauty or recognize her love of books, her intelligence, or her sense of adventure. The Beast is actually a beauty when he gives Belle his library, because he shows insight into her particular interests.

Being a beauty is giving people the benefit of a doubt and a chance to

293

✳

change if need be. It's also giving *oneself* permission to change. Being a beast is being closed-minded. Belle is open to the possibility of change within the Beast. With a little coaxing from his household staff, the Beast is willing to work at changing himself. Mrs. Potts sings of the results for the two: "Tale as old as time, true as it can be,/Barely even friends, then somebody bends unexpectedly . . ./ Bittersweet and strange, finding you can change, learning you were wrong."

A beauty is one who demonstrates unselfish love and compassion. A beast is one who does not. Belle shows unselfish love when she volunteers to take her father's place as prisoner in the Beast's castle. She demonstrates compassion when she twice helps the wounded Beast. The Beast shows unselfish love and compassion when he frees Belle to care for her father, even though he knows it means the spell probably won't be broken. He has compassion, too, when he spares Gaston's life.

Belle is beautiful, but the Beast does not love her for her looks. It is her compassion and caring that he comes to love, and he is changed by recognizing and responding to her goodness. "I've never felt this way about anyone," he says, and soon declares his love for her. Belle learns to love the Beast, in spite of his appearance, when he begins being transformed by her love. "I know he looks vicious, but he's really kind and gentle."

Being a beauty, then, is opening to the transformative power of love built on compassion and respect. Being a beast is remaining closed to unselfish, unconditional love. Now you know why Beauty is truly beautiful and how the Beast turns into a real beauty himself.

In his book *Play of Consciousness*, Swami Muktananda speaks about the spiritual dimension of transforming love such as seen in *Beauty and the Beast*: "Love turns man into an ocean of happiness, an image of peace, a temple of wisdom. Love is man's very Self, his true beauty, and the glory of his human existence."[1]

YE VIEW

1. What specific advice for self-improvement do his servants give the Beast?
2. Do you think the Beast would have fallen in love with Belle if she were not beautiful? Why or why not?
3. How might you apply the love lessons in *Beauty and the Beast* to your own life?

IN THE SAME SPIRIT

Seeing and loving beyond appearances with other Disney animation:
The Hunchback of Notre Dame—Within that misshapen body, Quasimodo has a heart worth its weight in golden gargoyles. (1996, 85 minutes, G, *)
Lady and the Tramp—He may be a dog, but the Tramp also knows about love and "Bella Notte." (1955, 75 minutes, NR, *)

THEME MATES

Two real-life beauties:
Mask—Love helps smooth the way for a boy with a disfigured face, Rocky Dennis (Eric Stoltz), and his mother, Rusty (Cher). (1985, 120 minutes, PG-13)
Really overcoming physical differences:
Splash—A mermaid (Daryl Hannah) and a man (Tom Hanks) take the plunge in this delightful comedy-romance. (1984, 111 minutes, PG)

CITY LIGHTS

PREVIEW

The Little Tramp (Charlie Chaplin) falls in love with a blind girl who sells flowers (Virginia Cherrill) in this silent "comedy romance in pantomime" written and directed by Chaplin. (1931, 86 minutes, NR)

META VIEW

To give love is to receive more love

You can't give from an empty bucket, the saying goes, and that's especially true with love. When one gives from a heart full of love, more and more love returns to always keep the heart full and overflowing.

In *City Lights*, which Chaplin considered his best work, both the Little Tramp and the blind girl he loves give from full hearts. The results are beautiful to behold. Surely, never have such genuine lovesick looks been captured on film as those the tramp directs to the blind girl!

With the Tramp, it's practically love at first sight. Giving from his reservoir of love, he is considerate and respectful, and even charming and gallant. He spends time with the girl, brings her food and joy, goes to work in an effort to pay her back rent, and even accepts a prison rap so that she may have money to go to a doctor to be cured of blindness.

With the blind girl, it's not love at first encounter, but it *is* appreciation of the Tramp's kindness that grows into love. On their first meeting, the girl dips into the fullness of her love and gives the Tramp, whom she assumes to be a rich man, a flower. The girl's grandmother comments that the mysterious suitor (the Tramp) must be wealthy, to which the girl replies, "Yes, but he's more than that." The girl's loving response when she discovers the truth about her benefactor leaves no question about the contents of her heart.

An important point about this mutually giving relationship is that both parties are naturally filled with love, which gives them optimism when appearances would suggest they have not much else. Both are poor and disadvantaged in the eyes of the world; both are private persons who, no doubt, have come to value their freedom and independence, while perhaps longing, too, for companionship. When they give freely of their love, however, their love multiplies and wondrous things happen in their lives.

YE VIEW

1. The Little Tramp tells the suicidal millionaire: "Tomorrow the birds will sing. Be brave! Face life!" Discuss whether or not the Tramp follows his own advice.
2. Do you think the Tramp is justified in taking the money from the millionaire? Why or why not?
3. What kind of future do you imagine the Tramp and his love will have?

297

THEME MATES

Giving and receiving love:

Dominick and Eugene—Eugene (Ray Liotta), a busy intern, has his hands and heart full watching out for his brother Dominick (Tom Hulce), who is mentally slow and idolizes him, in this very involving story of true brotherly love. (1988, 111 minutes, PG-13)

Fried Green Tomatoes—Based on Fannie Flagg's novel *Fried Green Tomatoes at the Whistle Stop Cafe,* this Southern tale of female assertiveness and liberation offers great tastes of love, caring, and friendship. Plus, it affirms divine order in the midst of seeming chaos. God "never makes mistakes" says Buddy Threadgoode (Chris O'Donnell). And Ninny Threadgoode (Jessica Tandy) states what we often come to realize with patience, "Life has a funny way of working things out." (1991, 130 minutes, PG-13)

CYRANO de BERGERAC

PREVIEW

Cyrano de Bergerac (Gerard Depardieu), a notorious soldier in seventeenth-century France who is as famous for his long nose as for his rhymes and duels, is afraid that his young cousin Roxane (Anne Brochet) will laugh at him if he declares his love for her in this lavish telling of Edmond Rostand's classic play of 1897. (1990, French, 138 minutes, PG)

META VIEW

It's unconditional love, by a nose!

Cyrano's heart is bigger than his famed nose, and his story has several major themes concerning love.

Two of these themes are quite obvious:

1. We need to see beyond appearances to another's true personality. Roxane gives her love to the handsome Christian (Vincent Perez) and never considers Cyrano.

2. We need to overcome fears about making our feelings known. Doing so may avoid a lot of heartache. Who knows what may happen if Cyrano could tell Roxane how he truly feels?

Beyond these themes, however, is another that goes to the depth of Cyrano's personality: Unselfish, unconditional love is God in action. In his own case at least, Cyrano may be right when he says, "A great nose may be an index of a great soul." Greater an index than his nose, however, is his unselfish, unconditional love for Roxane.

With his lack of self-esteem ("I can never be loved, even by the ugliest; my nose precedes me by 15 minutes") and his loneliness, Cyrano is a pathetic character. But his actions on behalf of Roxane's welfare bespeak a most generous, loving soul that truly reflects the unconditional nature of divine love. When Roxane devastates him by stating her love for Christian, Cyrano immediately recovers and offers to protect her beloved. When he finds out that Christian isn't the intelligent, romantic wit that Roxane expects, Cyrano willingly offers to write Christian's letters and words of love. After Christian is injured in battle, Cyrano respects Roxane's opinion of her love. Even though he may be aching himself, Cyrano thinks only of what will make Roxane happy; he becomes resigned to his own unhappiness but finds solace in contributing to her love for Christian.

Cyrano senses, too, that he and Roxane are soul mates, and *have* been since childhood, even if they aren't romantic mates. Cyrano even thanks Roxane for being a "female friend" and providing him some measure of love and warmth, denied apparently by his own mother and other women.

They aren't a couple in the worldly sense, but they are soul mates expressing as friends. In his book *Soul Mates*, Thomas Moore writes, "Friendship is not essentially a union of personalities, it is an attraction and magnetism of souls. . . . It is as though souls recognize the hidden treasure in each other and forge the alliance, while the conscious mind goes on with its intentions, hopes, and expectations."[2]

The "conscious minds" of Cyrano and Roxane carry out what hopes and expectations they can imagine for themselves in the world, but their souls resonate on a deeper level. In giving his unselfish, unconditional love to Roxane, Cyrano honors their soul connection. As Cyrano writes to Roxane, "I am and will be in the next world the one who loved you with all his soul."

YE VIEW

1. What do Cyrano's letters to Roxane, supposedly from Christian, reveal about his own personality and his ideas about love?
2. Do you think Christian acts honorably concerning Cyrano's

299

affections for Roxane? Consider both the courtship and Christian's final words.

3. How would you describe Roxane's emotions at the end of the story? What is your reaction to her at this point?

IN THE SAME SPIRIT

Other Cyranos for our times:

Cyrano de Bergerac—Jose Ferrer leads with a large proboscis and much flair. (1950, 112 minutes, NR)

Roxanne—Cyrano is now a fire chief (Steve Martin) at a ski resort, but he's still in love with Roxanne (Daryl Hannah) in this pleasing modernization by Martin. (1987, 107 minutes, PG)

THE ENCHANTED COTTAGE

PREVIEW

A disfigured Army flyer, Oliver Bradford (Robert Young), and a homely maid, Laura Pennington (Dorothy McGuire), discover the miracle of love in a bewitching New England cottage in this movie gem from the Arthur Pinero play. (1945, 92 minutes, NR)

META VIEW

The heart sees more than the eyes

Busybodies of love know that it is often difficult for others to understand why one person is attracted to another—one or both may be deemed less than desirable in some way. Questions arise such as "Why ever does she

stay with him?" or "What does he see in her?" People start with the "so's"—
he or she is so plain, so overweight, so critical, so tall, so short, so old, so . . .

Surely even the busybodies eventually reach some level of understanding that the human heart sees more than the eyes see. Have you heard the
old song "My Heart Has a Mind of Its Own"? The heart does, and love is
in charge.

Both Oliver and Laura elicit sympathy from people because of their appearances, but they sense a soul connection immediately. Oliver appreciates
Laura's kindness, thoughtfulness, gentleness, and common sense. Laura appreciates Oliver's charm, wit, and kindness. They see with the heart, and
not with the eyes; such vision transforms their world.

"You love each other," Mrs. Minnett, the widow who owns the cottage
tells them. "You've fallen in love, and a man and woman in love have a gift
of sight that isn't granted to other people." She tells the couple to keep their
love burning and they'll "never be anything to one another but fair and
handsome."

Major John Hillgrove (Herbert Marshall), the blind pianist who is a
friend of the couple's, tells Oliver how he learned to cope after being blinded
during a war. The advice helps pave the way for Oliver's experiences. Major
Hillgrove says that he learned to cultivate other senses: "It opens new worlds
for you. . . . In place of these two eyes that are gone, I have a hundred invisible ones that see things as they really are . . . . There comes a heighten-
ing of perception, a sort of sensitivity to all living things."

He tells Oliver to have faith in himself and to remember that he is, despite his injuries, "a complete individual."

YE VIEW

1. When watching the film, what were your own reactions to the
   situations of Oliver and Laura and to the response of Oliver's
   mother?

2. Major Hillgrove tells Oliver and Laura they have experienced a miracle and have been "touched by a power that is beyond this world." What is his meaning? What is the power?
3. What is the secret of "the enchanted cottage"? In what way is personal responsibility a part of the secret?

IN THE SAME SPIRIT

Marty—A butcher from the Bronx (Ernest Borgnine) who is considered homely and dull falls in love with a woman of the same description. (1955, 91 minutes, NR)

GUESS WHO'S COMING TO DINNER

PREVIEW

Joey Drayton (Katharine Houghton) puts the beliefs and principles of her white, affluent, liberal parents (Katharine Hepburn and Spencer Tracy) to the test when she brings home her black fiancé (Sidney Poitier). (1967, 108 minutes, NR)

META VIEW

Love sees no color

One of my favorite T-shirts is one that I bought years ago at an African store in Hot Springs, Arkansas. The T-shirt, tattered from frequent wear, is black with colorful lettering on the front that proclaims "Love sees no color."

The shirt has attracted much attention. Once while I was listening to Ecuadorian musicians at an outdoor plaza in Albuquerque, New Mexico, a biracial couple proudly pushing their baby's stroller did a double take at my shirt and flashed me large grins of appreciation.

A stranger once saw my shirt and yelled from her second-story balcony, "Love sees *every* color."

"Yes," I called back, "but it doesn't see a difference, so therefore sees *no* color."

The pure, unconditional love of God sees no color, and when we are truly loving as perfect reflections of God, neither do we.

Joey in *Guess Who's Coming to Dinner* is a beautiful, inspiring example of someone living the unconditional love of God. Doing so, she almost seems like too good a person to be true—an unfortunate statement.

But she absolutely sees no color. Joey's fiancé, Dr. John Prentice, says of her, "It's not just that our color difference doesn't matter to her; it's that she doesn't seem to think there *is* any difference."

Joey doesn't think that her parents will be shocked, because her father, a newspaperman, has spent a career fighting against discrimination and prejudice, and both parents raised her to believe that it was wrong to consider one race superior to another.

Her mother Chris, who recovers from the surprise quickly, says to her more troubled husband Matt: "People who thought that way [racially prejudiced] were wrong to think that way—sometimes hateful, usually stupid, but always, always wrong. That's what we said, and when we said it, we did not add, 'But don't ever fall in love with a colored man.'"

Matt, however, though he sees the couple's love and confidence, focuses on the problems his daughter and John will have in society as a biracial couple during the 1960s. John's father, who comes to dinner along with his wife, points out that if the couple marry, they will be breaking the law in more than a dozen states.

A friend of Joey's family, Monsignor Ryan (Cecil Kellaway), delights in the planned wedding. He says that biracial marriages usually work out well, perhaps because they require "some special quality of effort, more consideration and compassion than most marriages seem to generate."

303

The monsignor says that the couple will help change society's prejudices. "You two make me feel quite extraordinarily happy," he tells Joey and John.

For her part, Joey never falters in her unconditional love for John and for her parents, and she keeps her faith in her parents. She knows and sees only love.

I can imagine Joey as a child singing the Sunday school song about Jesus loving all the children of the world—"Red and yellow, black and white, they are precious in his sight"—and believing it. The civil rights dreams of Dr. Martin Luther King, Jr., would be closer to reality if more people were like Joey and radiated the unconditional love of God.

YE VIEW

1. What is the reaction of the housekeeper, Tillie, to Joey's marriage? Discuss the possible reasons for Tillie's feelings.
2. John tells his father, "You think of yourself as a colored man; *I* think of myself as a man." Discuss the difference in the two outlooks.
3. What is your opinion of Matt's final decision about the marriage? Do you think his words are prophetic? How do you see the future for Joey and John?

THEME MATES

Raising consciousness:

The Long Walk Home—The challenges involved in overcoming society's prejudices are vividly seen in this film that focuses on the relationship between a white woman (Sissy Spacek) and her black housekeeper (Whoopi Goldberg) in the segregated South of the 1950s. (1990, 97 minutes, PG)

LES MISERABLES

PREVIEW

Jean Valjean (Fredric March), after serving ten years of forced labor for stealing a loaf of bread, lives a respectable life of giving to others, but is relentlessly pursued by police inspector Javert (Charles Laughton) in a masterful telling of Victor Hugo's classic French novel. (1935, 108 minutes, NR)

META VIEW

Not loving, not forgiving are the real crimes

Hugo's epic story, which has spawned a number of films and a musical play with an exciting life (and groupies) of its own, contains grand truths about the freeing and transformative qualitites of love and forgiveness. These are internal states of consciousness that manifest in words and actions. *Les Miserables*, in all its incarnations, vividly shows what happens when people live with and without love and forgiveness.

Jean Valjean is inherently a man of great love: his sentence was for stealing a loaf of bread to feed his hungry family in nineteenth-century France. Valjean becomes hardened and embittered in the galleys, however, and after his release steals from a kind bishop (Sir Cedric Hardwicke), who sees every person a "brother" in God. The bishop, however, doesn't press charges, but teaches Valjean a life-altering lesson: "Life is to give and not to take." The bishop further says, "The right way, Jean, is always open to you."

Immediately the Truth of the bishop's statements transforms Valjean, and from that moment on he lives in order to give to others. He is the epitome of the biblical injunction "Be transformed by the renewing of your mind, that you may prove what *is* that good and acceptable and perfect will of God" (Rom. 12:2 NKJV). Time and again—in running his own factory, in serving as mayor of a town, in befriending an unfortunate factory worker and accepting responsibility for her young child, in rescuing injured people, in refusing to let an innocent man be falsely accused—Valjean gives out of love and compassion for others.

No matter how much the odds seem to be stacked against him, Valjean, though he sometimes momentarily falters, never loses his focus on love, the eternal love of God that sees beyond appearances. "God is just, but men sometimes are unjust," he declares. He tells adopted daughter Cosette (Rochelle Hudson) and her love Marius (John Beal), a member of a student group protesting inhumane prison sentences: "Remember to love each other always. There's scarcely anything else in life but that." And Valjean cannot find it in himself to condemn or harm even his nemesis, Javert.

Inspector Javert, however, is not a man of love or forgiveness but of law, and not just law, but law "to the letter." It was Paul who wrote in 2 Corinthians concerning a new covenant with God, "not of letter but of spirit; for the letter kills, but the Spirit gives life." Javert represents the letter; Valjean the Spirit. Javert pursues Valjean for years because he thinks of him only as a thief and a former convict; he doesn't see all the good that Valjean has done. Based on very little knowledge, Javert has incorrectly labeled Valjean for life. He doesn't realize that people can change and rise above their earlier circumstances and outlooks, and he doesn't make allowances for human needs beyond the law. Yet Valjean knows, "Whatever is wrong will be put right, law or no law"—referring to Spirit, or the will of God, which transcends human laws.

The movie is extremely faithful to Hugo's writing and is careful to establish the rationale for people's actions—even Javert's. Some segments are a bit melodramatic (such as the scene in which the reformed Valjean kisses the statue of the Madonna and Child while a sheep walks in the background and a chorus sings "Ave Maria"), but that was the style of the times and suits the black-and-white film.

YE VIEW

1. What in Javert's background may account for his rigid adherence to the law? Do you think he changes? Why or why not?
2. Discuss whether the story is still relevant in light of the following quotation from Victor Hugo at the beginning of the movie: "So long as there exists in this world that we call civilized, a system whereby men and women, even after they have paid the penalty of the law, and expiated their offenses in full, are hounded and persecuted wherever they go—this story will not have been told in vain."
3. Are there people in your own life whom you may have incorrectly accused or labeled? What can you do to remedy the situation?

IN THE SAME SPIRIT

Among other *Les Mis* films, same title but different results:
Les Miserables—Directed by Claude Lelouch, this is a powerful adaptation and updating of Hugo's story to World War II, where a man (Jean-Paul Belmondo) with Jean Valjean's spirit (figuratively) assists a Jewish family to escape the Nazis. (1995, French, 178 minutes, R)
Les Miserables—Liam Neeson is a sympathetic Valjean and Geoffrey Rush is a properly despicable Javert in a version that *looks* good, but lacks spark and also omits crucial motivational details. (1998, 129 minutes, PG-13)

THEME MATES

To forgive or not when the clock strikes:
Midnight in the Garden of Good and Evil—Wealthy Savannah, Georgia, antiques dealer Jim Williams (Kevin Spacey) makes a

choice between forgiveness and unforgiveness that determines his fate in this moralistic, spellbinding adaptation of the John Berendt best-seller. (1997, 113 minutes, R)

LIFE IS BEAUTIFUL

PREVIEW

In this unusual comedy-romance-drama set in Italy during the Holocaust, the zany Guido (Roberto Benigni) courts the repressed Dora (Nicoletta Braschi); they marry and have a son, Joshua (Giorgio Cantarini); and are later among Jewish families taken to a concentration camp, where Guido turns the experience into a game to hide the truth from his son. (1998, 114 minutes, PG-13)

META VIEW

Life is also a game of love

"Most people consider life a battle, but it is not a battle, it is a game," declares Florence Scovel Shinn in her small but potent 1925 book *The Game of Life and How to Play It.*

A knowledge of spiritual law, Shinn says, is necessary to successfully play the game, which has three simple rules: "fearless faith, nonresistance and love." And in this game, she says, love "takes every trick."[3]

Life is beautiful for Guido because he plays "the game of life" so adeptly and gives ingenious vitality to the rule of love. Guido's madcap and completely captivating pursuit of Dora during the first part of the film is love at its most joyous and uninhibited. Guido is exuberantly in love and has wit enough to turn every situation into a gesture of devotion. He amazes Dora with the seeming ability to appeal to Mother Mary and have his desires instantly granted, when in truth he is artfully drawing upon preexisting knowledge.

With Joshua in the concentration camp, Guido must muster all of his skills of game playing and all his unselfish love to keep Joshua's spirits up. Guido pretends that everyone in the camp is participating in a game. "We're all players," Guido tells Joshua, and the object of the game is to accumulate points toward the grand prize of a real army tank (a prize that greatly interests the boy). Points are lost, Guido says, for crying, wanting to see Mommy, and being hungry. "Those mean guys who yell" (Nazi officers) can take away points, he says.

Guido's elaborate ruse is developed out of love for his son, to shield and protect him from the horrors of the Holocaust. In this game, Guido is willing to sacrifice himself, giving unconditionally and lovingly. Only a person who loves life and family as intensely as Guido does can be so completely nonresistant in the midst of such horror. Life is beautiful to Guido precisely because he loves and recognizes that life is a testament of love, whatever the circumstances and conditions. For those same reasons, life is also beautiful to Dora, who makes her own sacrifices for love. Guido and Dora show that love *does* take every trick (even those deemed the most horrendous); their story truly is, as the narrator says, "full of wonder and happiness."

309

✳

Ye View

1. What two inventive methods does Guido use to communicate his love to Dora while they are in the concentration camp? What does Dora's response indicate about her outlook?

2. When does Guido use the power of thought to influence outcomes in his favor?

3. Discuss your reactions to the conclusion of the movie. In what ways could life be considered beautiful at the end?

THEME MATES

Realizing the tradition of love:

Fiddler on the Roof—Tevye (Topol), a poor Jew with five daughters in Russia, discovers that the traditions surrounding love change, but the power of love is constant. He finds that love, the essence of God-energy, is the grandest tradition of all and makes a person rich, in this Norman Jewison film of the Joseph Stein musical. Truly practicing the presence of God, Tevye talks constantly to God. (1971, 181 minutes, G)

Also sacrificing for love:

A Tale of Two Cities—In Charles Dickens's great novel of the French Revolution, attorney Sydney Carton (Ronald Colman) demonstrates his complete love of Lucie. (1935, 128 minutes, NR)

Also looking for the good:

The Truce—A Jewish-Italian chemist, Primo Levi (John Turturro), who has been released from Auschwitz, makes his way back home to Italy. In this adaptation of part of his autobiographical trilogy, Levi is portrayed as curiously detached but compassionate and seeing the good in people and situations. The worst thing done to prisoners, he says, is crushing their souls and compassion and filling them with hatred, even of each other. A most interesting thought for discussion and debate is Levi's statement "God cannot exist if Auschwitz exists." (1998, Italian-French-German-Swiss, 117 minutes, R)

LILI

PREVIEW

A sixteen-year-old French orphan, Lili (Leslie Caron), falls in love with a magician, Marcus the Magnificent (Jean-Pierre Aumont), joins the carnival where he works, and soon becomes a sensation, naturally interacting with puppets. (1953, 81 minutes, NR, *)

META VIEW

See beyond the puppet faces

When a department store clerk was unpleasant years ago, my mother-in-law dismissed the crossness by explaining, "Maybe her feet hurt." The phrase is often used in our family when someone is rude. It literally puts us in the mind-set of "walking in the other person's shoes" and not being quick to judge and to criticize. So often we just have absolutely no idea what people are going through that makes them behave in certain ways. Unless we react compassionately, we deny ourselves opportunities to receive love and to give love.

Lili's story is a good example of this denial. Lili is quick to label Paul (Mel Ferrer), the boss of the puppet show, as "the angry man" because he always seems cross, cold, unfriendly, and uncaring. She is too immature to realize that there may be good reason for Paul's coming across to others as he does.

In fact, as she is eventually told, Paul was once a great dancer, but he was crippled during the war, and had to become a puppeteer instead of a dancer. Lili also does not realize that Paul is in love with her and jealous of Marcus.

While dismissing Paul as simply "the angry man" and mooning over Marcus, a married womanizer, Lili grows to love Carrot Top and the three other puppets with whom she talks and confides her feelings. The puppets seem to know her so well. When Lili can't name the one thing that she'd like in all the world, Carrot Top says, "I think you'd like some day to have the feeling that you're loved, that somebody cares about what happens to you."

With her blind, misplaced love in Marcus, Lili doesn't see that it is actually Paul talking to her—and loving her. Captivated by her innocence and sincerity, Paul describes Lili as "a little bell that gives off a pure sound, no matter how you strike it."

Through experiences, however, Lili changes. She says, "We don't learn; we just get older, and we know," which suggests that we already have all Truth within us and simply need to access it. Lili comes to know the value of seeing beyond appearances—perhaps most especially in matters of love— and seeing people beyond the puppet faces they often present, out of self-defense, to the world.

YE VIEW

1. What are some signs that Paul is more than just "the angry man" he seems to Lili? How does he first help Lili?
2. What aspects of Paul's personality are displayed by each of the puppets? How does Lili's final dream sequence show her relationship with each of Paul's puppet personalities?
3. What kind of life do you envision for Paul, Lili, and the puppets? Will their "song of love" be a sad or a happy one?

PORTRAIT OF JENNIE

PREVIEW

When struggling artist Eben Adams (Joseph Cotten) meets a mysterious girl named Jennie Appleton (Jennifer Jones) in New York City's Central Park, his fortunes—as well as his concepts of love, time, and reality—begin to change. (1948, 86 minutes, NR)

Meta View

Love crosses time barriers

"Out of the shadows of knowledge, and out of a painting that hung on a museum wall, comes our story, the truth of which lies not on our screen but in your heart," the narrator says at the beginning of *Portrait of Jennie.*

This masterpiece bravely and interestingly addresses some large issues about life and time, but ends up becoming somewhat befuddled within the "shadows of knowledge." The movie gets major points for broaching the ideas, however. Consider how the narrator starts:

"Since the beginning, man has looked into the awesome reaches of infinity and asked the eternal questions: What is time? What is space? What is life? What is death? Through a hundred civilizations, philosophers and scientists have come with answers, but the bewilderment remains, for each human soul must find the secret in its own faith. Science tells us that nothing ever dies but only changes, that time itself does not pass but curves around us, and that the past and the future are together at our side forever."

Jennie, as becomes immediately apparent, is curving around time and is from an earlier period (early 1900s). In crossing over into Eben's time period (1930s), Jennie is speeding up her aging process so that she and Eben can be romantically linked before she dies again. It's not clear why, if Jennie can come back from what we traditionally call death, she doesn't just come back at one age and stay there, rather than die again.

Where Jennie has come from is equally fuzzy. She sings of herself, "Where I come from, nobody knows. And where I am going, everything goes. The wind blows, the sea flows, nobody knows . . ."

Even though the movie, based on a book by Robert Nathan, does get

313
❀

(enjoyably) lost in time and heavenly space, it does successfully spin a haunting fable about the timelessness of love. It is a lovely testimonial to the truth that love is eternal, that love crosses all time barriers, and that love offers life-transforming inspiration.

In one of the movie's most memorable lines, Jennie tells Eben, "There is no life, my darling, until you love and have been loved. And then there is no death."

Eben tells Jennie that he wants their love to be forever. She replies: "It *will* be. Have faith." She explains that the strands of their lives are woven together and can't be torn apart. "We have all eternity together, Eben."

Before he meets Jennie, Eben's paintings are loveless and lifeless. When he begins painting Jennie and her spiritual beauty, Eben's paintings reflect the love that he feels for her.

Eben says, "I was caught by an enchantment beyond time and change. I knew at last that love is endless and today's little happiness only part of it."

The movie is a memorable portrait of eternal love.

Ye View

1. In what specific ways does Eben's life change as a result of his love for Jennie?
2. Discuss how other characters are touched and inspired by Eben's inspiration from Jennie.
3. Does the movie's love story move you? Why or why not?

In the Same Spirit

Another time-hopper for love:

Somewhere in Time—The portrait of an actress (Jane Seymour) lures a playwright (Christopher Reeve) back in time for another fling in this sentimental story filmed at the majestic Grand Hotel on Michigan's scenic Mackinac Island. (1980, 103 minutes, PG)

THE PRINCESS BRIDE

PREVIEW

In this fairy tale-adventure-comedy told to a young boy by his grandfather, Buttercup (Robin Wright) and her true love, Westley the farm boy (Cary Elwes), are separated, and she is forced to become engaged to the evil Prince Humperdinck (Chris Sarandon). (1987, 98 minutes, PG)

META VIEW

True love conquers all

Romantics, especially those in the fairy tale tradition, probably agree that true love is worth fighting and dying for, but many might find it difficult to define exactly what arouses such strong and serious emotions.

The Princess Bride may help define true love—or then again it may simply confound the marvelous mystery of true love.

As shown throughout the movie, true love is a feeling that conquers all—"all," in this case, being a crazy abduction; the Cliffs of Insanity; the Fire Swamp with its flames, quicksands, and Rodents of Unusual Size; the Pit of Despair; the ruthless and six-fingered Count Rugen (Christopher Guest); and, of course, Prince Humperdinck.

Come what may, and much *may* come, Princess Buttercup remains certain that "my Westley will save me." She tells the prince, "Westley and I are joined by the bonds of love."

True love, then, is a bond—a bond so deep that it conquers all and knows no doubts.

For his part, Westley says: "I told you I would always come for you. Death cannot stop true love. All it can do is delay it for a little while."

True love is an emotional bond that is eternal.

315

It is souls in perfect harmony, two beings instinctively drawn together (as Buttercup and Westley are, initially, on the farm and ever after) with a spoken or unspoken communication all their own. Westley, for example, repeatedly says to Buttercup, "As you wish," which in their language translates, "I love you."

YE VIEW

1. What other ideas about love do you think the young boy (Fred Savage) might learn from the story of *The Princess Bride*?
2. Revenge may be sweet, but it's not very spiritual. What are some more constructive ways that Inigo Montoya (Mandy Patinkin) could use to work out his grief for his father?
3. How would you define *true love*?

IN THE SAME SPIRIT

Another original fairy tale of true love and imagination:
Princess Caraboo—English aristocrats believe a young woman (Phoebe Cates) to be a foreign princess—but *is* she? As the story shows, imagination can be used to help us rise above circumstances and conditions. (1994, United States-British, 96 minutes, PG)

RESURRECTION

PREVIEW

After surviving a car crash and experiencing a near-death experience, Edna McCauley (Ellen Burstyn) has a healing power that blesses many and troubles some. (1980, 103 minutes, PG)

META VIEW

God is love

The Bible, for those who look to the Scriptures for guidance, clearly says, "God is love." If you're wondering what God is, there's the answer. What could be more direct?

To many, the answer seems too simple to accept, even though other sacred writings and spiritual teachers throughout the ages also associate God with love. We humans, however, often want to make things more complicated than they are, especially with the so-called big issues of life.

We're not told that God is loving or that God loves, but simply that "God is love." God is love itself, the power of love in expression. If God is all-encompassing and if we are creations of God, then we, too, are love, the power of love in expression.

This power of love, so pure that it heals the sick, is what comes through Edna as a result of her near-death experience.

When Edna's wise grandmother (Eva LeGallienne) tells Edna that the power is a gift from God, Edna says that she doesn't know anything about God. However, she says, "If love is God, I guess I could try it."

Edna says that the healing power she has is "the simple holiness of love," and she tells people that she offers the power to them "in the name of love." A person obviously *filled* with love herself, even before the accident, Edna sincerely helps people because of love for them.

While she is an instrument of healing, Edna expresses the power of love so strongly that she completely identifies with her patients: "I *become* them. . . . It's like I feel them."

Love is even at the core of those patients who do not respond to her healing touch (about 30 percent). Edna explains: "Some people need their sickness to get love and attention. Some people need it to give those things. It's not up to me to judge right and wrong."

As always, there are those in Edna's community who just can't accept a good thing; they see Edna's ability to heal as the work of the devil. Her boyfriend Cal (Sam Shepard), whose strict Bible upbringing comes back to haunt him, reads Revelation and accuses Ellen of being "the living Christ," which Edna denies.

(In New Thought understanding, however, Edna *is* "the living Christ," as is every person, because the Christ is the essence of God within the individual—and the essence of God is love.)

Edna's grandmother articulates the great need for the power of God's love to manifest: "If we could just love each other as much as we say we love Him, I suspect there wouldn't be the bother in the world there is."

An insight into God as love also comes to Edna through her brief sojourn to the afterlife during the time she is clinically dead. Of her near-death experience, she says, "You begin to feel like you understand everything, and you don't feel your body anymore."

Edna's near-death experience (NDE) includes some of the major characteristics of such experiences: a pervasive feeling of love and peace, beloved relatives and friends, lovely music, and a comforting light at the end of a tunnel. Accounts of NDEs have been recorded throughout the world for centuries, and in our own time have been extensively and famously documented by Dr. Raymond A. Moody, Jr., and Elisabeth Kubler-Ross.

Ye View

1. What are some of the physical healings that Edna performs? How is she able to help herself?
2. Discuss Edna's relationship with her father. What role does Edna's love play in that relationship?
3. Esco Brown (Richard Farnsworth) tells Edna, "If life don't hand you nothing but lemons, you just make you a bunch of lemonade." How does Edna do that? Have you done that yourself? Discuss.

SLEEPLESS IN SEATTLE

PREVIEW

Destiny rides the call-in radio waves when widowed father Sam Baldwin (Tom Hanks) in Seattle bares his heart and soul, and listener Annie Reed (Meg Ryan) in Baltimore responds. (1993, 105 minutes, PG)

META VIEW

Intuition plays matchmaker

There's a telling little scene in *Sleepless in Seattle* when Annie—who is having second thoughts about her fiancé and wedding plans, and has flown across the country to meet a lonely man she doesn't know but has heard on the radio—asks her friend, "Beck, is this crazy?"

"No," Beck says, "that's the weirdest part about it."

That's because Annie is following her heart and intuition. As intuitive counselor Patricia Einstein writes in her book *Intuition: The Path to Inner Wisdom*, "Intuition is an inner awareness and a sense of knowing that is outside the realm of logical thought. Yet it possesses a wonderful flowing logic all its own."[4]

Such a sense of intuitive, flowing logic propels this satisfying romantic comedy directed and coscripted by Nora Ephron. The movie is a testimonial to the power of intuition to lead people—specifically here in matters of love—to their true destiny. A person's destiny, the movie asserts, is obvious from signs all around.

Opposing arguments, the rational arguments against destiny and fate and signs, are heard. Annie herself tells her mother before she gets the intuitive feeling for Sam (to radio fans a.k.a. "Sleepless in Seattle"), "Destiny is something we've invented because we can't stand the fact that everything

319
✹

that happens is accidental." Annie's brother Dennis tells her, "What we think of as fate is just two neuroses knowing they're a perfect match."

These jaundiced arguments hold no weight, however, against the signs and wonders of true love that are like "magic." And it is the "magic" of love that Annie is seeking. Intuitively, Annie knows what is right for her; Sam's son Jonah (Ross Malinger), who called the radio station in the hopes of helping his sad and lonely father, knows his new mother; Sam recognizes his new soul mate ("It was like I *knew* her—a *deja vu* sort of thing."); Annie's friend Becky (Rosie O'Donnell) knows what needs to be done; even Annie's fiancé Walter (Bill Pullman), knows. Inner feelings and outer signs abound.

Jonah's young friend Jessica, wise beyond her Earth years, says that Sam and Annie were star-crossed lovers in another lifetime. Jonah tells his dad: "So your hearts are like puzzles with missing pieces, and when you get together the puzzle is complete. The reason I know this and you don't is because I'm younger and purer, so I'm more in touch with cosmic forces."

There's a lot of logic in the situation, but it's logic of the heart, not the head. *Sleepless in Seattle* is a story of what's meant to be and what manifests when we go with our "gut feelings," our "I just know it" sense of what our destiny is, regardless of existing conditions and relationships.

YE VIEW

1. How would you imagine the life of Sam and Annie in a sequel to *Sleepless in Seattle*?

2. Recall a situation in which you let intuition be your guide. What happened?

3. How would you define *destiny*? What role does free will play in destiny?

IN THE SAME SPIRIT

Other enjoyable romantic comedies about love and destiny:

The Butcher's Wife—A clairvoyant (Demi Moore) watches for signs and wonders about her true mate, her "split apart." The plot exemplifies the truism that we often do things for a particular reason, only to discover that the real reason, what we might call the "God purpose," is something entirely different—and better. (1991, 105 minutes, PG-13)

Much Ado About Nothing—In love and clever barbs, Benedick (Kenneth Branagh) and Beatrice (Emma Thompson) are well matched and meant for each other in this exhilarating Shakespearean romp, directed by Branagh. (1993, British-United States, 111 minutes, PG-13) To catch the Bard himself (Joseph Fiennes) enraptured (with Lady Viola, played by Gwyneth Paltrow), see *Shakespeare in Love.* (1998, 120 minutes, R)

Next Stop, Wonderland—The personal ads indirectly provide the vehicle for Erin (Hope Davis) to eventually connect with Mr. Right (Alan Gelfant) in this film that could have been titled *Sleepless in Boston.* (1998, 104 minutes, R)

Only You—A woman tellingly named Faith (Marisa Tomei) searches for her destined partner, who she thinks is a man named Damon Bradley, in this engaging romp through Italy. However, the fortune-teller tries to set her straight: "The truth is you make your own destiny. . . . Don't wait for it to come to you." As fate would have it, Peter (Robert Downey, Jr.) meets Faith and follows his intuition that the two are destined to be together. (1992, 108 minutes, PG)

The Parent Trap—Twins (Hayley Mills) know their parents (Maureen O'Hara and Brian Keith) belong together, so they scheme to reunite them in this Disney treasure. (1961, 124 minutes, NR, *)

Still Breathing—Fletcher (Brendan Fraser), an eccentric street performer in San Antonio, sees his true love/soul mate (Joanna Going) in a dream and sets out to find her. (1998, 109 minutes, PG-13)

You've Got Mail—In their workaday worlds, megabookstore owner Joe Fox (Tom Hanks) and children's bookstore owner Kathleen (Meg Ryan) don't like each other, but they don't know that they are developing an anonymous relationship over the Internet. (1998, 116 minutes, PG) The story was inspired by *The Shop Around the Corner* (1940, 97 minutes, NR), later made into the musical *In the Good Old Summertime.* (1949, 102 minutes, NR)

STRAWBERRY AND CHOCOLATE

PREVIEW

In Havana in 1979, opposites attract when David (Vladimir Cruz), a university student who is a Communist and a materialist, and is in the doldrums because his girlfriend has married someone else, becomes friends with Diego (Jorge Perugorria), who is gay and lives and breathes the arts and literature. (1994, Cuban, 104 minutes, R)

META VIEW

Flavors blend in love

There are people in this world whose confectionery orientation is toward chocolate. Then there are others who prefer strawberry. We know that. Does the preference of some people for chocolate threaten the existence of those who prefer strawberry? Don't people have the right to want strawberry rather than chocolate? Is it really necessary to examine why someone would rather have strawberry than chocolate? Should those who choose chocolate *fear* those who favor strawberry, and vice versa? Is it impossible to like someone who orders chocolate? Is it impossible to love someone who must have strawberry?

These may sound like silly questions, but the analogy in the movie, of course, concerns sexual orientation, and begs these very questions. There is no doubt that people do get into serious, even fatal arguments and fights about matters concerning sexual orientation.

Alas, people can get so caught up in what they consider the importance of perceived human differences that they lose sight of their shared essence as children of God. It is important to remember, however, that the sweetest ingredient in any relationship is love. You can count on true love—the love that reflects the unconditional and nonjudgmental nature of God—to cut through human concepts. Sexual orientation is a *human* distinction, not a spiritual one.

In the movie, David is at first wary of being around Diego. David relies on prejudices and stereotypes to form his first impression of Diego, and sees nothing in common with him. David tells a Communist friend about meeting Diego while both were eating ice cream. David says he knew at once that Diego was gay because, "There was chocolate; he took strawberry."

In spite of himself, David is continually drawn into a friendship with Diego that is not sexual. It's a new type of relationship for Diego, but he tells David, "I believe in friendship. I think we can be friends."

When the two get to know each other, they discover a spiritual and philosophical connection that revolves around human rights, personal freedoms, national pride, and an appreciation of beauty.

Before meeting Diego, David probably never would have said, "We all have the right to do what we want with our lives."

YE VIEW

1. Diego tells David, "Art makes you feel and think" and says that the only way we can fly is "on the wings of imagination." How is David affected by an appreciation of art and imagination?
2. In what ways is Diego changed by his friendship with David?
3. Discuss your own views concerning the movie's statements about friendships, relationships, and prejudices.

IN THE SAME SPIRIT

For a similar look at friendship and love:
> *The Object of My Affection*—George (Paul Rudd), a first-grade teacher who is gay, and Nina (Jennifer Aniston), a social worker, share an apartment and a search to understand true friendship and love. (1998, 111 minutes, R)

WHEN HARRY MET SALLY

PREVIEW

It certainly isn't love at first sight when Harry Burns (Billy Crystal) and Sally Albright (Meg Ryan) travel from Chicago to New York City together in 1977 to begin careers after college, but friendship at third sight has promise as the two become closer while coping with separate relationship challenges. (1989, 95 minutes, R)

META VIEW

Friendship is best foundation for love

The leading characters meet, argue, part, meet again five years later, disagree, part, and meet again, and, as we expect, eventually fall in love. *When Harry Met Sally* is a feel-good romantic movie that is fun to watch every now and then with someone you love. More important, however, *When Harry Met Sally* is a fine movie about developing friendship that is fun to watch occasionally with a friend who is also a significant other.

As many couples—successfully married and otherwise—will tell you, friendship is the best foundation for lasting romantic relationships. True friendship, based on common and shared interests and outlooks as well as mutual respect, is a connection at the soul level. As such it is an extension of unconditional love. When a friendship turns into a romantic love, the union is developed from the soul connection and not just from a sensual connection. The depth of friendship provides a spiritual, emotional, and mental anchor for a relationship when the unexpected storms of life in the body threaten romantic attachments.

325

Harry and Sally struggle with realizing that they can have a love relationship based on friendship, and their lesson is a valuable case study for us all. Harry suffers from the mistaken notion that women and men can't be friends, because their sexual desires get in the way. That does happen, but it doesn't have to, as the two prove, when each opens to appreciating and enjoying the other's personality.

Through friendship, the two can see beyond negative first impressions and off-putting stereotypes. Harry comes to know that while Sally may describe herself as basically a "happy person," she has dreams and fears which trouble her, and Sally comes to know that there is a warm, humorous aspect behind Harry's admitted "dark side."

Writer Nora Ephron's clever dialogue, interludes of older people telling stories of how they met, and 1940s music combine to create a satisfying and significant glimpse into the interrelated nature of friendship and love.

YE VIEW

1. What are some early indications that Harry and Sally are becoming friends? What are some early indications that their relationship is becoming romantic?
2. Why are Jess (Bruno Kirby) and Marie (Carrie Fisher) attracted to each other? Would you say that they are friends? If so, what is the basis of their friendship?
3. In what ways, in your opinion, can friendship strengthen a relationship between couples?

IN THE SAME SPIRIT

Other couples who go from disdain to friendship to love:

The African Queen—An unlikely pair, spinster Rosie (Katharine Hepburn) and skipper Charlie (Humphrey Bogart) initially try to tolerate each other as they go downriver during World War I. Rosie wants to reform Charlie from his natural, earthy inclinations: "Nature, Mr. Allnut, is what we are put in this world to rise above." They gradually learn to respect and love each other's differences. (1951, 105 minutes, NR)

It Happened One Night—The Walls of Jericho eventually come down when a reporter (Clark Gable) and an heiress (Claudette Colbert) stop squabbling in this superb romance. (1934, 105 minutes, NR)

:::: **FEATURE PRESENTATION**

All Creatures Loved and Sacred

"Praise to thee, my Lord, for all thy creatures"—St. Francis of Assisi[5]

The patron saint of animals must have blessed filmdom. Loving our fellow creatures has always been a popular movie theme.

On the screen, as well as off, animals have loved us and helped us, and we in turn have loved and helped them.

Animals' extrasensory perception and intuition can appear absolutely mystifying to humans. Watch *Lassie* (1994) or *Lassie Come Home* (1943) or *The Incredible Journey* (1963) and be amazed at the intuitive sense of cats and dogs. Perhaps the animals are reminding humans of senses that all-too-often lie dormant within us.

The love affair and feeling of connectedness between animals and humans isn't all one-sided, though. Animals can call forth within us our most loving and compassionate, most spiritual natures. We want to love the animals and care for them and save them.

These live-action movies showcase a menagerie of animals for which humans have gone to great and almost impossible lengths to respond lovingly to the call of the wild:

- A zoo's giant turtles concern two loners (Ben Kingsley and Glenda Jackson) in *Turtle Diary.* (1985, British, 97 minutes, PG)
- An elephant is treated well as soldiers attempt to transport it to a Vietnamese village in ***Operation Dumbo Drop.*** (1995, 107 minutes, PG)
- Geese needing to learn how to migrate receive assistance from a girl (Anna Paquin) and her father (Jeff Daniels) in ***Fly Away Home.*** (1996, 107 minutes, PG, *)
- The fate of Arctic wolves leads author Farley Mowat (Charles Martin

327

Smith) to an up-close and extremely personal study in *Never Cry Wolf.* (1983, 105 minutes, PG)

- An orca whale is liberated by a 12-year-old boy (Jason James Richter) in *Free Willy.* (1993, 112 minutes, PG, *)
- A feisty talking parrot (voiced by Jay Mohr) and a Russian immigrant (Tony Shalhoub) quest together in *Paulie.* (1998, 87 minutes, PG)
- A lion in Kenya is raised by two game wardens in *Born Free.* (1966, British, 96 minutes, NR)
- A panda cub threatened by poachers receives aid from an American boy and a Chinese girl in *The Amazing Panda Adventure.* (1995, U.S.-China, 85 minutes, PG, *)
- A horse involved in an accident becomes the patient of a man (Robert Redford) who helps emotionally troubled animals in *The Horse Whisperer.* (1998, 160 minutes, PG-13)
- Mountain gorillas of Africa are the domain of researcher Dian Fossey (Sigourney Weaver) in *Gorillas in the Mist.* (1988, 129 minutes, PG-13)

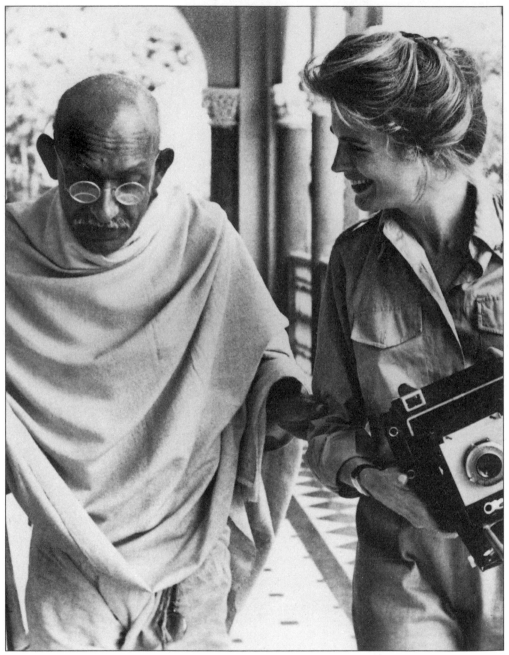

Ben Kingsley and Candice Bergen in *Gandhi*, Columbia Pictures
Photo: The Museum of Modern Art Film Stills Archive

Chapter 8

Meetings With Remarkable People

Prepare to meet some truly remarkable men and women whose lives and actions are monuments of inspiration. They are remarkable because of their faith and devotion, high principles, inner strength, service to humankind, and unceasing quest for meaning. "Meetings With Remarkable People" includes glimpses into the lives of a variety of respected personalities. Become acquainted with saints and sages such as Joan of Arc and Mohandas K. Gandhi and religious and spiritual leaders such as Brigham Young and Malcolm X, as well as others who walked more secular paths but accomplished extraordinary deeds, such as a teacher and pupil (Annie Sullivan and Helen Keller) and a businessman (Oskar Schindler). These are all inspiring people worth meeting on and off the screen.

BECKET

PREVIEW

The close friendship between King Henry II (Peter O'Toole), the great-grandson of William the Conqueror and ruler of England from 1154–89, and Thomas à Becket (Richard Burton) disintegrates when the king appoints Becket archbishop of Canterbury and Becket refuses to place the crown before God and the church. (1964, 148 minutes, NR)

META VIEW

True honor is godly

No one is more surprised than King Henry and Becket himself when Becket's life becomes a symbol of honor. Adapted from Jean Anouilh's play, this stunning, enthralling movie is one man's journey to understand honor.

At the beginning of the movie's action, just before he becomes chancellor of England, Becket is of the view that he has no honor. Where honor should be in him, he says, is "only a void." While he participates in amorous escapades and rowdy times with King Henry and delights in using his intellect to advise the king, Becket says that he hasn't found anything for which to care and can't stand the idea of being loved. But it is obvious that honor is a subject that interests and concerns Becket. He wonders about himself: "But what if one day he should meet his honor in truth, face to face? Where is Becket's honor?"

Another question is, "What does Becket mean by honor?" Becket seems to be seeking a sense of personal integrity, derived from moral and ethical values, that gives meaning and substance to his life, and something about which to care deeply. In fact, Becket is searching for something already within him to which he just hasn't put a name. He *does* have a natural concern for human rights and compassion for others (such as his treatment of a peasant girl), but he must exhibit these attributes secretly, so as not to go against the king's ways.

However, it is only when Becket is made archbishop (merely a cunning political move to the king) that he understands that the compassion within him is honor to God and service to God. Now he has identified something truly worthy of his love—God and the care of God's people (extending the compassion he already possessed).

Becket prays, "I've been without honor and feel unworthy. . . . I am a weak and shallow creature. . . . I gave my love, such as it was, elsewhere, putting service to my earthly king before my duty to You. Now . . . please, Lord, teach me now how to serve You with all my heart, to know at last what it really is to love, to adore, so that I may worthily administer Your kingdom here upon Earth and find my true honor in observing Your divine will."

His awakened devotion to God infuriates King Henry as much as it surprises Becket, who tells the king, "I have finally discovered a real honor to defend."

"*Whose* honor?" the king demands. "Whose honor is greater than the king's"

"The honor of God," Becket responds.

Becket attempts to use his office to work peacefully with argument and compromise to achieve the goal of making the honor of God and the honor of the king one.

At least Becket succeeds in getting King Henry to *think* about honor. After Becket's death, King Henry says: "The honor of God, gentlemen, is a very good thing, and all things considered, one gains by having it on one's side. Thomas Becket, our friend, always used to say so." At the king's request, the pope honored Becket with sainthood in 1173.

333

✵

YE VIEW

1. In your opinion, is the king's penitence sincere? Why or why not?
2. Becket says, "Honor is a private matter within . . . and every man has his own version of it." What do you think honor is to King Henry? To the bishop of London? To Brother John?
3. What does being honorable mean to you?

IN THE SAME SPIRIT

A later period but similar challenges:

A Man for All Seasons—Like Becket before him, Sir Thomas More (Paul Scofield) gets in royal hot water when he pits his honor, conscience, and religious principles against a king's wishes. In this story based on Robert Bolt's play, More's difficulties come after he becomes lord chancellor of England and refuses to support the efforts of King Henry VIII (Robert Shaw) to get a divorce. More tries to be diplomatic and supportive, up to the point of his own integrity. He says, "Whatever may be done by smiling, you may rely on me to do." More (1478–1535) was declared a saint by the Roman Catholic Church in 1935. (1966, British, 120 minutes, NR)

BOYS TOWN

PREVIEW

Father Flanagan (Spencer Tracy) strives to keep his Nebraska home for boys growing, while young, cocky Whitey Marsh (Mickey Rooney) strains the priest's conviction that "there's no such thing in the world as a bad boy." (1938, 96 minutes, NR, *)

META VIEW

Love creates good citizens

A convict about to be executed cries out, "One friend, one friend when I'm twelve years old, and I don't stand here like this." In the cell with the condemned man, who spent his formative years in a reformatory, is Father Flanagan, listening and thinking.

The man's plea inspires Father Flanagan to quit his refuge for men, whose lives are set, and concentrate on helping boys become good citizens.

With five boys from the slums and streets of Omaha, a rented house, and $100, Father Flanagan begins his home for boys in 1917. The home grows rapidly, moves to a farm in 1921, and becomes a thriving community.

In asking a friend for money, Father Flanagan gives a practical reason for his new home: "Every boy who becomes a good American citizen is worth $10,000 to the state. That's a fact."

Later, addressing money issues again, Father Flanagan offers broader justification for his efforts: "Hundreds of boys have gone through here, and they're out in the world now, with their heads up. They're making good, every last one of them. That's serving my Creator and my country."

Father Flanagan's techniques of child raising are so simple as to be revolutionary: he gives the boys love, and provides shelter, food, and schooling. He shows that he respects them and has faith in their innate goodness and their good conduct. He talks to the boys of God and honor. He admits that he cries, so that they can too. He takes time to know the boys as individuals, and is as comfortable joking with them as leading them. He encourages all to worship and pray as they desire. He is a stalwart, shining example for the boys.

He sticks to his beliefs despite dire financial predictions and threatening events. He knows that God is in charge, and tells a friend who asks what he

335

✲

is going to do about a money need, "Something I do very privately—say a prayer."

A newspaper owner tells Father Flanagan that he believes there are "some impossible young beasts" who should be locked up in reform schools. The man refers to an 11-year-old boy who has been convicted of second-degree murder. Father Flanagan explains that the boy saw his mother being beaten by a drunken father, so he took a gun and killed him.

Father Flanagan isn't trying to justify the boy's actions, but is emphasizing the point that, like so many boys, the 11-year-old needed a good home environment to prevent the situation from occurring in the first place. The real crime prevention, then and now, is to give children a loving, spiritual, morally upright, nourishing home life.

The film is dedicated to Father Edward J. Flanagan (1886–1948), a Roman Catholic priest, "and his splendid work for homeless, abandoned boys, regardless of race, creed, or color." Girls were admitted to Boys Town in 1979, and today the town's mission is "the care and treatment of troubled boys and girls, and families in crisis."

Ye View

1. What is Whitey like when Father Flanagan brings him to Boys Town? What is he like at the end of the movie?
2. Discuss the causes of Whitey's change. How much credit goes to Father Flanagan?
3. What does Father Flanagan mean when he says that there is no such thing as a bad boy? Do you agree with this philosophy about children? Why or why not?

IN THE SAME SPIRIT

For the rest of the story:

Men of Boys Town—Tracy, Rooney and many of the other boys
return for a sentimental sequel. (1941, 106 minutes, NR, *)

BRIGHAM YOUNG

PREVIEW

To escape religious persecution in 1846, in one of the greatest coloniz-
ing feats of the American West, Brigham Young (Dean Jagger) leads a wagon
train of Illinois Mormons across the Mississippi River and on to what became Utah. (1940, 114 minutes, NR)

META VIEW

"This isn't an easy religion"

His revelation for a better life on Earth came direct from God, says Mormon founder Joseph Smith (Vincent Price). The revelation occurred in a
land founded on religious freedom for all. Dubbed the United Order, Smith's
"brotherhood plan" calls for people to work and live together peacefully and
cooperatively, without caste distinctions, to share all labor and goods.

"It's up to us to work it out," Smith tells Brigham Young (1801–1877)
upon their first meeting. "This isn't an easy religion."

Indeed, the movie depicts quite powerfully that following a religion of
peace and brotherhood is not always easy, and forces us to deal with this
question: Why not?

While his home is being raided in Carthage, Illinois, a Mormon man is tied to a tree and whipped. He cries to his attackers: "Why are you doing this? We only want to live in peace with everyone." That scene occurs at the beginning of the movie, but remains in the mind throughout as Smith is tried for treason and then murdered by a mob, as the Mormons are chased out of their fourth state, and as families endure one hardship after another in journeying to their promised land.

Young, praised by Smith for his "courage, far-sightedness, and common sense," takes charge of the church following Smith's death. While he's not sure God speaks to him as directly as He spoke to Smith, Young is unbending in his determination to lead the people to safety. "Our only chance is to find some place that nobody else would even put foot on," he says.

The difficulties and dissensions along the way are mirrored in the family of Jonathan Kent (Tyrone Power), who falls in love with a non-Mormon, Zina Webb (Linda Darnell). Young's leadership abilities and the people's strength are tested again and again. Memorable scenes include the crossing of the frozen river, the plague of the crickets in the wheat fields, and the coming of the seagulls to devour the crickets.

Young knows the place intended for the Mormons when they come to it (the Great Salt Lake valley), and declares, "We're going to establish Joseph's idea of the United Order and build a mighty empire here based on labor and love and fellowship."

The Mormon church, formally the Church of Jesus Christ of Latter-day Saints, developed Utah. Young, who was born in Vermont, was a missionary and preacher for the Mormon church before he became the second president of the church.

YE VIEW

1. How does God seem to "talk" to Young? Cite some specific examples.

2. What do the seagulls represent to the Mormons?
3. Discuss the following quotation by Young in light of the experiences of the Mormons shown in the movie: "The whole point is, Brother Joseph Smith or any other American citizen has the right to worship God as he chooses."

THEME MATES

Also striking out on a new religious path:
Luther—The American Film Theatre re-creates John Osborne's play about Martin Luther (Stacy Keach), leader of the Reformation, the religious movement in Europe that birthed Protestantism. (1974, British, 112 minutes, NR)

339

FRANCESCO

PREVIEW

In medieval Italy, Francesco (Mickey Rourke), the son of a wealthy merchant, assumes a life of poverty, begins a mystical journey to know God, and leads a new religious movement, as dramatically explored in this life of St. Francis of Assisi. (1989, Italian-German, 105 minutes, PG-13)

META VIEW

St. Francis embodies the mystic's search

The gentleness which I've always associated with St. Francis, the patron saint of animals, birds, and ecology, and the peacefulness which I experienced while attending an early morning mass before his tomb beneath the imposing Basilica of St. Francis in Assisi, Italy, are in direct contrast to the driven and tormented title character in this movie.

As the modern-day but still brown-robed friars of the Franciscan order silently took their seats on wooden benches, I gazed with awe in the dimly lit, stone-arched room. The Franciscans recited the mass in Latin and sang chants of soothing blessings. While St. Francis' bones rested within this Umbrian shrine, the loving presence of St. Francis seemed to fill the room and all its inhabitants. From the mood there, one might think that St. Francis' life (1181?-1226) was one of utter calmness and bliss.

Actually, his life probably was more like that portrayed in *Francesco*—an often torturous journey to know God. As the movie so vividly shows, a mystic's life—despite the images that have come to us through the centuries and the peaceful feeling inside ancient churches today—was not always easy hundreds of years ago—and it's not always easy today either. An individual such as St. Francis who is called to experience God's presence intimately and intensely may reach the heights of earthly experience, but also the depths.

Francesco is the epitome of a person who quite strongly and completely is being transformed in mind as Paul beseeches in Romans, in order to prove the "good and acceptable, and perfect will of God."

To Francesco, the "good and acceptable and perfect" will of God is found in The Gospels. To prove that will, Francesco takes The Gospels quite literally as a rule and program by which to live. He reads from The Gospels: "If you would be perfect, go sell what you possess and give everything to the poor" and "He who would come with me must renounce himself and take up his cross and follow me."

Francesco says that he and his followers are "the brothers without anything . . . and therefore those without fear, free."

His example and sincerity in denouncing material possessions and ministering to the poor and sick soon attract many other followers, including those from his own privileged class. Francesco himself is a humble man who says quietly; "I know nothing. I have been only able to listen, listen, and finally I have succeeded in hearing these words: 'Blessed are the poor and blessed are those who weep, for they shall laugh.'" He echoes Jesus' instructions to love our enemies, to forgive, to avoid judging others, and to give.

The film has a strangely somber and brooding tone, a real feel of the medieval times, not only in the buildings and clothes, but also in the depiction of human misery and suffering. The often chaotic and slightly confusing activities suggest the tempo of the times, as do Francesco's own dark hours of doubt and uncertainty.

Francesco's path of transformation is merely one way to demonstrate what is the "good and acceptable and perfect" will of God. Through the centuries, many have taken the Franciscan vows of poverty, love, and chastity. St. Francis continues to be a source of inspiration for millions, although probably few follow his path quite as vigorously as he did.

In a mystical sense, perhaps Francesco serves as a symbol of the struggles that can occur when old thought meets new thought. One of his followers says: "Peace is everything. Those who are at peace with God are already in paradise." It is clear that Francesco, despite his growing spiritual awareness, is not at perfect peace throughout most of his life. He, like all of us, is a work in transformation.

Francesco's receiving of the stigmata is a visible sign of his inner transformation, of his conscious mind totally projecting itself into the Christ Presence. It is a sign of hope and personal transformation for all. As Chiara, or St. Clare (Helena Bonham Carter), says of Francesco's stigmata, "I thought that love had made his body identical to the Beloved's, and I asked myself whether I would ever be capable of loving that much." That is a question for all humankind.

YE VIEW

1. Recall the stories of how Francesco's followers come to him. Which stories are most inspiring to you?

2. Becoming a saint takes courage, Francesco says. How does he exhibit such courage?

3. Give a metaphysical interpretation of the following quotation: "He who would come with me must renounce himself and take up his cross and follow me."

IN THE SAME SPIRIT

For other views of St. Francis:

Brother Sun, Sister Moon—The youthful Francis moves with the direction of Franco Zeffirelli and the music of Donovan. (1973, Italian-British, 121 minutes, PG)

Francis of Assisi—Bradford Dillman stars as the saint in this big production. (1961, 111 minutes, NR)

GANDHI

PREVIEW

The spiritual and political evolution of Mohandas K. Gandhi (Ben Kingsley), whose peaceful movement against the British led to India's independence and who was revered as *Mahatma*, or "Great Soul," is traced in director Richard Attenborough's epic, which is awesome in scope and beauty. (1982, British-Indian, 200 minutes, PG)

META VIEW

He speaks for the consciousness of humankind

The intention of this sweeping biography, stated at the beginning, is to be "faithful in spirit" to Gandhi's life and to find a way "to the heart of the man." The movie succeeds mightily by presenting many of the actions and ideas of this man who continues to be one of the most admired figures of modern times.

The movie begins with Gandhi's assassination by a Hindu fanatic on January 30, 1948, in New Delhi. Following Gandhi's death, a radio announcer offers two quotations that capture Gandhi's place in history:

"Gandhi has become the spokesman for the consciousness of all mankind. He was a man who made humility and simple truth more powerful than empires."—General George C. Marshall, United States Secretary of State

"Generations to come will scarce believe that such a one as this ever in flesh and blood walked upon this Earth."—Albert Einstein

The film follows Gandhi's career in South Africa and India. Gandhi, who was born in India in 1869 and studied law in England, journeys to South Africa in 1893 to practice law. Personally encountering discrimination and seeing how other Indians are treated, Gandhi begins a successful campaign of civil disobedience. Discrimination must be fought, he says, because "we are children of God like everybody else."

Returning to India in 1915, Gandhi joins Jawaharlal Nehru (Roshan Seth), who will become India's first prime minister, and others in working for self-rule for India. His quiet ways and sensible, direct approaches win followers among both the influential and the populace, and it is Gandhi who consistently stirs the people toward independence. He recommends peaceful resistance and a boycott of British goods, and leads a march to the sea to protest the British monopoly on making salt. He also periodically fasts to win people's support.

Throughout the periodical turmoil, viewers are treated to repeated glimpses of Gandhi's continued quest for Truth. He is seen as a person who is not always perfect but always struggling to know and do what is right.

In discussing his thoughts on the New Testament idea of turning the other cheek to attackers, Gandhi touches the core of his peaceful philosophy:

343

"I suspect he (Jesus) meant you must show courage — be willing to take a blow, several blows to show you will not strike back, nor will you be turned aside, and when you do that, it calls on something in human nature, something that makes his hatred for you decrease and his respect increase."

Gandhi advocates peace, but never cowardliness; he realizes full well, however, that peaceful protest is not the normal way of the world nor is it without pain. In South Africa, he tells supporters, "I am asking you to fight — to fight against their anger, not to provoke it. We will not strike a blow, but we will receive them, and through our pain, we will make them see their injustice, and it will hurt as all fighting hurts, but we cannot lose. We cannot."

Gandhi's methods are revolutionary and simple, although not simplistic. At a meeting with British and Indian officials, Gandhi tells the British, "In the end, you will walk out [of India] because 100,000 Englishmen simply cannot control 350 million Indians if those Indians refuse to cooperate, and that is what we intend to achieve—peaceful, nonviolent noncooperation until you yourself see the wisdom of leaving."

When asked whether his nonviolent approach could be used to fight Hitler, Gandhi says: "What you cannot do is accept injustice from Hitler or anyone. You must make the injustice visible and be prepared to die like a soldier to do so."

Gandhi is saddened that independence for India means a divided India— India for Hindus, and Pakistan for Muslims—but he has hope, and he gives all of us hope in facing division and violence today:

"When I despair, I remember that all through history the way of truth and love has always won. There have been tyrants and murderers, and for a time they can seem invincible, but in the end, they always fall. Think of this, always."

YE VIEW

1. What experiences influenced Gandhi as a child and led to his adult viewpoints?
2. Discuss Gandhi's statement: "An eye for an eye only ends up making the whole world blind."
3. What other spiritual and political leaders and movements have been influenced by Gandhi? Why do such movements meet resistance, and what can be done to overcome resistance to them?

THE INN OF THE SIXTH HAPPINESS

PREVIEW

Against considerable odds, English parlor maid Gladys Aylward (Ingrid Bergman) in 1932 becomes a missionary in China, where she opens an inn for mule drivers, makes friends with a Eurasian colonel (Curt Jurgens) and a mandarin (Robert Donat), stands up for her adopted people's human rights, and leads 100 homeless children across country during Japanese-Chinese confrontations. (1958, 158 minutes, NR)

META VIEW

Love in action converts

Imagine actually living a life "dedicated to the simple, joyful and rare belief that we are all responsible for each other"! Gladys Aylward (1902–1970) did just that, viewers are told at the beginning of this movie based on her life.

All of her actions in the movie stem from a sincere devotion both to God and humanity. In answering what she considers to be God's call to be a missionary in China, Gladys does not wave her Bible about or preach of converting the heathen. She responds to people's human needs, and they love and respect her for doing so. Hers is very much a practical approach to Christianity: putting Jesus' teachings about loving and helping one another in practice. She is a dynamic example of Love in action.

Winning converts, Gladys tells Colonel Lin Nan, is not like collecting pretty stones for a particular religion. "To me it's making each man know that he counts, whether he believes in Christ or Buddha or nothing," she says.

Gladys never shirks opportunities to assist people, no matter how afraid she may be on a human level. Like Daniel going into the lion's den, Gladys knows that God is always with her and that her actions reflect her faith.

A dramatic example is when she volunteers to stop a dangerous prison riot. A Chinese guard, saying that Gladys has her God to protect her, taunts Gladys to go to the prison. Gladys says, "It is the safety of the soul that my faith promises, not of the body." She acknowledges, however, that if her religion loses faith in the eyes of the people at such a time, her services in China will not be of value.

Standing at the entrance to the prison, Gladys says simply: "I am afraid. Open the gate." Gladys is showing us a way to face any perceived difficulty: If need be, acknowledge a human fear and let it go; then "open the gate" of consciousness to allow spiritual power to take over. Say out loud to your inner Self, "Open the gate," and proceed without fear.

The mandarin admires Gladys and calls her forceful. Beginning to be enticed by her vision, the colonel, however, notes that Gladys is also gentle and trusting. "She walks through a world full of evil and sees only children—not complicated or cruel, just untidy ones needing to be washed and fed and loved."

Again, Gladys shows us a way to approach life: View whatever "evils" we name as simply untidy children or creations of human thought that need to be "washed and fed and loved" with a cleansing awareness of Spirit.

The inn that Gladys runs in a remote northern China town was named by Mrs. Lawson, the woman with whom Gladys begins her work in China. The name is derived from the five happinesses that one person wishes another in China: good health, wealth, virtue, longevity, and a peaceful death in old age.

"What is the sixth happiness?" Gladys inquires.

"*That* you will find out for yourself," Mrs. Lawson responds. "Each person decides in his own heart what the sixth happiness is."

The "sixth happiness" concept requires that a person look within, into the heart or feeling consciousness, for ultimate meaning. It is suggestive of Jesus' invitation to discover the kingdom of God within.

YE VIEW

1. Cite some specific examples to show why Gladys receives the Chinese name "the one who loves people."
2. What does the mandarin do in honor of Gladys' strength? In what way is his announcement a vindication of her missionary approach?
3. What do you think is the "sixth happiness" for Gladys Aylward? What would you identify as your own "sixth happiness"?

THEME MATES

Biographies of other women who epitomize Love in action:

Blossoms in the Dust—After her son dies, Edna Gladney (Greer Garson) founds a noted orphanage in Fort Worth, Texas. (1941, 100 minutes, NR)

Entertaining Angels: The Dorothy Day Story—This film traces the spiritual growth of Roman Catholic activist Day during the 1920s and '30s. Day worked extensively on behalf of the poor. (1996, 110 minutes, PG-13)

JOAN OF ARC

PREVIEW

The life of Saint Joan of Arc, the Maid of Orleans who brought France to victory during the Hundred Years' War with the British, is faithfully told in this film starring Ingrid Bergman and based on Maxwell Anderson's play *Joan of Lorraine*. (1948, 100 minutes, NR)

META VIEW

"Forward!" with faith

The political and religious feuds of fifteenth-century France and England are murky history to most people now, but the life of Joan of Arc is still stirring because it is a testimonial to and a symbol of something always sorely needed in human life—faith.

Joan makes it unmistakably clear that she is completely guided by faith in God. What is faith? The Bible says that faith is "the assurance of things hoped for, the conviction of things not seen" (Heb. 11:1). Faith is a consciousness which knows God's presence, an inner awareness which sees God in all situations and conditions.

In answering the call of her voices to be the savior of France and to bring Charles VII (Jose Ferrer), the dauphin, to the throne, the young Joan doesn't know what to do, but acts on faith that God is leading. "Then I must go and do what I can without knowing how," she asserts.

To the dauphin she stresses the necessity for faith: "What you need is faith in God. When you have that, you'll have faith in yourself. Put aside your doubts and fears."

The choice whether or not to have faith, however, rests with the individual. Unfortunately, the dauphin, whom the film's narrator describes as "spineless" and at the mercy of "unscrupulous advisors," is more interested in money and idle pursuits than in faith in God. He catches a glimmer of faith himself when looking into Joan's eyes, but he's too weak to sustain faith on his own.

To her army and followers, Joan fares better in preaching faith. "Our strength is in our faith," she tells her soldiers, and urges them to put aside all thoughts and activities that are not in line with God's goodness.

During her trial on charges of heresy and witchcraft, Joan is asked how she knows that her voices came from God. She replies, "I knew that they came from God because what they commanded me to do was only good." Faith in God leads only to what is the highest good for all concerned—but often that highest good isn't discernible to mortals. Joan's voices tell her not to fear her martyrdom, and she says to her accusers, "I have faith in them [voices]. I have _none_ in you."

"To live without faith is more terrible than the fire, more terrible than dying young," she says. "I have nothing more to do here. Send me back to God, from whom I came."

YE VIEW

1. How would you describe Joan's personality? Do you find her admirable? Why or why not?
2. What were the religious and political reasons for Joan's trial? Discuss whether or not the charges against Joan had merit.
3. Joan tells her army, "It is not enough that God is on _our_ side; we must be on _His_ side." What does she mean? How might this advice be applied to everyday life? How does this outlook show faith?

IN THE SAME SPIRIT

A retrial:

The Passion of Joan of Arc—Maria Falconetti stars in this focus on Joan's inquisition and trial. (1928, French, 77 minutes, NR)

Also famous for seeing visions:

The Song of Bernadette—The story of the French girl Bernadette Soubirous (Jennifer Jones), who said that she saw visions of the Virgin Mary at Lourdes during the 1800s, is told in this filming of Franz Werfel's novel. The Roman Catholic Church declared Bernadette a saint in 1933. (1943, 156 minutes, NR)

KUNDUN

PREVIEW

The early life of the fourteenth Dalai Lama, the spiritual leader of the Tibetan people who was the 1989 recipient of the Nobel Peace Prize, is told in this magnificent tribute from director Martin Scorsese. (1998, 128 minutes, PG-13)

META VIEW

The jewel shines brightly

"The wish-fulfilling jewel will shine from the West."—Tibetan oracle, before the Dalai Lama's departure from Tibet in 1959

One of the most visible and eloquent spokespersons for peace in the world today is the Dalai Lama. The prophesy of the oracle has been fulfilled, because the Dalai Lama's name and cause are well known in the West.

His pleas to "Free Tibet" have garnered much support in the United States. Still living in exile in India with thousands of other Tibetans, the Dalai Lama has traveled extensively in the West and elsewhere throughout the world to speak for freedom for his people and peace for all humankind.

In accepting the Nobel Peace Prize, he said, "Because we all share this small planet earth, we have to learn to live in harmony and peace with each other and with nature. Live simply and love humanity."[1]

How this remarkable man became the Dalai Lama and was forced to leave his beloved country, situated in the mountains between India and China, following the takeover of Chinese Communists is the focus of *Kundun*. All of the story precedes the Dalai Lama's emergence on the world stage as a peacekeeper.

However, the Dalai Lama's training and youthful ideas were clearly of peace.

The movie gives an accurate and spellbinding account of the Dalai Lama's discovery. After the death of the thirteenth Dalai Lama in 1933, monks begin searching for his successor. Four years later they are led to a remote Tibetan village, to a two-year-old boy named Lhamo. He is tested, declared to be the reincarnation of the thirteenth Dalai Lama, and taken to the temple in Lhasa to begin his training.

A regent tells the young boy, "You are here to love all living things . . . care for them, have compassion for them."

The Dalai Lama is known as "the Buddha of compassion, the wish-fulfilling jewel."

Of his own role, the Dalai Lama says: "I think I am a reflection like the moon on water. When you see me and try to be a good man, you see yourself."

The Dalai Lama, whose name means "Ocean of Wisdom," advocates nonviolence instead of war. "Violence is never good," he says flatly. When he finds out that monks carry guns and that there is a prison at the temple, he is calmly appalled at the betrayal of how he has thought things were.

He tells a Chinese general, "Wisdom and compassion will set us free." He adds: "*You* cannot liberate me. . . . I can only liberate myself."

During one training session, the young Dalai Lama recites part of the Buddha's teachings about the Four Noble Truths: "First, one understands that he causes much of his own suffering needlessly. Second, he looks for the reasons for this in his own life. To look is to have confidence in one's own ability to end the suffering. Finally, a wish arises to find a path to peace, for all beings desire happiness, all wish to find their purer selves."

Before the Dalai Lama leaves Tibet to travel to a sanctuary in India, he pauses and then says: "I see a safe journey. I see a safe return."

His journey was safe. One wonders, after all the years that he has spent in exile and with all the political strife between China and Tibet, if the second part of his vision will come true.

352

YE VIEW

1. What adjectives would you use to describe the young Dalai Lama? In what ways is he like a typical boy?
2. Before he is forced to leave, what are the Dalai Lama's plans for Tibet? Do you think he would have made a wise leader of Tibet? Why or why not?
3. Research the current state of affairs in Tibet and the Dalai Lama's activities. Discuss what is happening and possibilities for the future.

IN THE SAME SPIRIT

More on the Dalai Lama's formative years:

Seven Years in Tibet—When his attempt to scale a Himalayan peak goes awry, Austrian mountain climber Heinrich Harrer (Brad Pitt) finds himself in Tibet and getting acquainted with the young Dalai Lama in this story based on real events. (1997, 131 minutes, PG-13)

LITTLE BUDDHA

PREVIEW

The Buddha's teachings span the centuries as two stories unfold in this rich film directed by Bernardo Bertolucci: the search of Prince Siddhartha (Keanu Reeves) for enlightenment 2,500 years ago, and the contemporary search of a group of Tibetan monks for the reincarnation of a spiritual leader. (1993, 123 minutes, PG, *)

META VIEW

Enlightenment is a continuing story

353

The monks headed by Lama Norbu (Ying Ruocheng) give a copy of the book *Little Buddha: The Story of Prince Siddhartha* to the young Seattle boy, Jesse (Alex Wiesendanger), who they think may be their teacher returned to Earth. Jesse, who clearly has an affinity for the monks, becomes absorbed in the book. As the book is read throughout Jesse's involvement with the monks, the life of the future Buddha is brought to the screen with lavish and spectacular detail.

Legend has it that Buddha's birth around 563 B.C. in present-day Nepal was an event resplendent with miraculous signs, as the story begins. His father, ruler of one of the kingdoms of India, named him Siddhartha, meaning "he who brings good." It is said that Siddhartha was born fully conscious, with open eyes. He could stand on both legs immediately after birth, and lotus blossoms grew in his footsteps. An astrologer predicted that Siddhartha would be "the master of the world."

The king tried to keep knowledge of human suffering from Siddhartha. The handsome prince grew up in luxury and pleasures. He had a desire to see the world for himself, however, and soon learned about sickness, suffering, aging, and death. He tells his father, "I must find an answer to suffering."

Siddhartha's father replies that all people must suffer and die and be re-born countless times. "No man can ever escape that curse."

"Then *that* is my task," Siddhartha says. "I will lift that curse."

The movie dramatically depicts Siddhartha's protection by a giant cobra, his years of meditation in the woods as an ascetic, and his eventual realization that "the path to enlightenment is in the middle way. It is the line between all opposite extremes."

Even more impressive, from cinematic and spiritual perspectives, are the depictions of Siddhartha's temptations by Mara, lord of darkness, and his enlightenment under a *bodhi* tree. Mara sends the spirits of pride, greed, fear, ignorance, and desire to tempt Siddhartha. Talking to his reflection, Siddhartha says, "O lord of my own ego, you are pure illusion. You do not exist." Siddhartha is enveloped in a gold light.

The book states: "Siddhartha won the battle against an army of demons just through the force of his love and the great compassion he had found. Then he achieved a great calm that precedes detachment from illusions. . . . He had seen the ultimate reality of all things. . . . He knew there was no salvation without compassion for every other being. From that moment on, Siddhartha was called the Buddha, 'the awakened one.'"

The fusion of Siddhartha's story and Jesse's story during the scene of temptations and enlightenment is a masterful work of art that underscores the timeless spiritual Truth of the Buddha.

Lama Norbu says to remember how important it is "to feel compassion for all beings, to give of oneself, and, above all, to pass on knowledge like the Buddha."

Ye View

1. How, according to both stories in the movie, might one achieve enlightenment today?
2. Compare the temptations of Buddha with those of Jesus in the desert.
3. What are your thoughts about reincarnation?

In the Same Spirit

For another story inspired by the founder of Buddhism:
Siddhartha—The young Indian in Herman Hesse's novel meets the Buddha, but then seeks his own enlightenment. (1973, 95 minutes, R)

MALCOLM X

Preview

Denzel Washington stars as Malcolm Little (1925–1965), a good-timing hustler and convict who has a change of heart and name when he accepts Allah and the antiwhite sentiments of Elijah Muhammad, and becomes an influential spokesman for the Black Muslims in this Spike Lee film of *The Autobiography of Malcolm X.* (1992, 201 minutes, PG-13)

Meta View

Consciousness expands to Allah

Sentenced to a Massachusetts prison in 1946, Malcolm is insubordinate and put in solitary confinement. A visiting chaplain tries to tell Malcolm what a friend he has in Jesus.

"What has he done for me?" Malcolm snaps back. "He ain't done nothing for me."

As a child, Malcolm came in contact with religion, because his father was a preacher who advocated that black people should go to Africa for a decent life. His father was hounded by the KKK and later murdered. His mother was forced to allow Malcolm and her other children to go to detention homes.

On the Boston streets during the war years, when the movie opens, Malcolm hasn't had time or taken time to think much about religion. His interests run to much less lofty pursuits, and he hasn't seen religion make life easier for anyone.

In prison, Malcolm understandably doesn't relate to Jesus as friend, or to society's usual depiction of Jesus as white.

356

What Malcolm needs to help him connect with God is a religion that addresses his needs and the perceived needs of his people. Indeed, our culture partly dictates in what ways we relate to God, as well as in what ways we serve a higher purpose.

Malcolm finds his point of God reference when a fellow prisoner, Baines (Albert Hall), begins talking to him about the prophet Elijah Muhammad (Al Freeman, Jr.). Here at last is a religion that speaks to Malcolm personally. Two focuses of the religion especially appeal to him—the power to use his mind for release and the philosophy that blacks are righteous and whites are wicked.

"Elijah Muhammad has come to bring you into the light," Baines tells Malcolm. "Elijah Muhammad can get you out of prison, out of the prison of your mind."

Baines further tells him that "God is black."

The ideas set Malcolm afire, and when he is released from prison, Malcolm becomes an energetic and fanatic speaker for Black Muslims. He tells listeners:

- "The hereafter is here and now."
- "You're black and you're beautiful, because black *is* beautiful."
- "Some of you are still in prisons right now—prisons of your minds."
- "He's [Elijah Muhammad's] not teaching us to hate the white man. He's teaching us to love ourselves."

The submission to the power and will of God (or Allah or any other name for the Infinite), the use of thoughts to create our experiences, the importance of the now in our existence, and the value of personal pride are all standard spiritual beliefs for many people.

To these, however, Malcolm and the Black Muslims at that time added white-bashing. While such a stand certainly does not foster a feeling of unity with all people and with God, it nevertheless was useful to help rally many blacks to stand up for their own integrity. The position can be seen as a *means* to an end brought about by certain conditions in society, and not the end itself, which is more along the lines of Dr. Martin Luther King, Jr.'s dreams.

Malcolm's consciousness continues to expand, however. That evolving consciousness is at the core of this movie. Malcolm begins with virtually no thought of God, then a narrow view of a God for blacks, and then a comprehensive understanding of a God for all people.

After breaking with the Black Muslims, Malcolm goes on a pilgrimage to Mecca, where he is changed by being with all races and levels of people worshiping one Supreme Being for all humanity. Malcolm says he has had a "spiritual rebirth" and no longer subscribes to sweeping indictments of one race.

"I wish nothing but freedom, justice and equality, life, liberty, and the pursuit of happiness for all people," he proclaims, although his first concern, as always, is still with the welfare of his own race. He believes that Islam "can remove the cancer of racism from the hearts and the souls of all Americans."

357

Spirituality, Malcolm asserts, is the hope of the future:

"As racism leads America up the suicidal path, I do believe that the younger generation will see the handwriting on the wall and many of them will want to turn to the spiritual path of the Truth, the only way left in this world to ward off the disaster that racism must surely lead to."

Ye View

1. What part do jealousy and betrayal play in Malcolm's break with Elijah Muhammad?
2. The narrator says: "Malcolm was our manhood, our living black manhood. This was his meaning to his people, and in honoring him, we honor the best in ourselves." Comment on this estimation of Malcolm X.
3. Discuss whether or not you think younger generations are seeing "the handwriting on the wall" in regards to racism, as Malcolm X says, and are turning to "the spiritual path of the Truth."

A MAN CALLED PETER

Preview

A Scotsman who has a "close friendship with God," Peter Marshall (Richard Todd) follows "orders from the Chief" to enter the ministry and becomes a noted Presbyterian minister in Atlanta, Georgia, and Washington, D.C., and in the U.S. Senate as chaplain. (1955, 119 minutes, NR)

META VIEW

God opens the doors

As a boy in Scotland, where he was born in 1902, Peter desperately wants to go to sea, but isn't allowed to do so. His mother suggests that God may be guiding him in a different direction. Sure enough, according to narration by his wife Catherine (Jean Peters), one foggy evening Peter, now a young man, is walking by himself when God suddenly tells him to be a minister and go to America.

He works a variety of jobs after arriving in the United States. When all seems futile, "God opened a door," Catherine says. And God keeps opening doors for Peter. He graduates summa cum laude from Columbia Theological Seminary in Decatur, Georgia, and accepts a small church in Georgia. He then moves to an Atlanta church that eventually has to build a balcony and add outside speakers to accommodate the crowds that come to hear him speak. From there, Marshall is summoned in 1937 to Washington, where he soon packs the historic New York Avenue Presbyterian Church.

A continued theme of the man called Peter is God's desire to open doors for one and all.

"There are men and women in the world today who say that God orders their lives, guides them in making decisions, provides for their needs, answers their prayers, in ways which are often strange and unexpected. That is the testimony of my own experience," Peter says during a Sunday sermon.

Another time, he preaches: "God plants his own lovely dream in the human heart and . . . when the dream is mature and the time is right for its fulfillment, well, to our astonishment and delight, His will becomes ours and ours His. Now who but God could have thought of anything as perfect as this?"

At many times in his life, as seen in this biography based on Catherine's book, Peter seems indeed directly in touch with God. Peter has prepared a speech to give at the Naval Academy on December 7, 1941, but senses that

359

he needs to scrap it and speak what is on his mind. He delivers a powerful sermon on the theme "For what is your life?" He discusses death, "the shining mercy of God," and eternal life. Later that day, Pearl Harbor is bombed.

Other gleanings from Peter's always moving talks or sermons:

- "Who ever said that Christianity can't be fun or that fun can't be Christian? Who ever said the Lord likes a long face? He likes us to laugh and enjoy ourselves and enjoy living."
- "Marriage is a oneness—divine and indivisible."
- "Religion is not for sale. It's *given* away."
- "Millions of people in America live in moral fogs. They move in a sort of spiritual twilight."

Peter died in 1949, a year after becoming Senate chaplain.

Ye View

1. Discuss Peter's statement: "The great things by which we really live are not proven by logic but by faith."
2. What spiritual discoveries do Peter and Catherine make during their own health challenges?
3. Would you say that God has opened doors in your own life? If so, discuss those occasions.

MEETINGS WITH REMARKABLE MEN

Preview

"Like a hungry dog," Gurdjieff (Dragan Maksimovic) chases for an answer to the meaning of life through Central Asia and the Middle East, and finally finds his truth in the monastery of an ancient secret brotherhood in this intriguing movie based on the autobiography of the spiritual teacher and beautifully filmed in Afghanistan. (1979, British, 108 minutes, G)

META VIEW

Let's hear it for direct experience!

"In 1920 an unknown man appeared in Europe having lived through some extraordinary experiences in the East. His name was George Ivanovitch Gurdjieff. This is the story of his early years."

That's all the explanation the movie provides about Gurdjieff, but just who *was* this remarkable man who encountered so many other remarkable men and experiences? Gurdjieff was a spiritual seeker with a following and an influence that continue today. He founded experimental research centers to study consciousness, such as one in France called the Institute for the Harmonious Development of Man. He was born in the late 1860s or early 1870s between Greece and the Caspian Sea. Outside of Gurdjieff's memoirs, little can be substantiated about his life until he arrived in Moscow at the start of World War I. He died in Paris in 1949.

Watching the movie of Gurdjieff's search for answers about existence, I was struck with the thought that viewing another's quest for Truth, while interesting and enjoyable, doesn't really get one very far. It's like being a spiritual couch potato. The desire swept over me to dash off to a faraway monastery for direct experience.

Indeed, twice during his cinematic quest, Gurdjieff receives instruction in the importance of direct experience and direct knowledge.

When Gurdjieff tells Prince Lubovedsky (Terence Stamp) that he wants to know, learn, and understand, the Russian prince replies: "Be careful. What do you call learning? . . . Knowing happens directly. When not even a thought stands between you and the thing you know, then you see yourself as you *are*, not as you would *like* to be."

361

Later in his search, Gurdjieff is told by Father Giovanni: "Faith cannot be given to men. Faith is not the result of thinking. It comes from direct knowledge. . . . Thinking and knowing are quite different. One must strive to know. This alone can lead to our lord God."

Since childhood, Gurdjieff has longed to know the meaning of existence. "I had a feeling that something is missing in me," he said. "I felt that apart from my ordinary life, there is another life, a life which is calling me, but how to be open to it? This question never gives me any peace. I've become like a hungry dog chasing everywhere for an answer."

Some remarkably interesting people help Gurdjieff toward his goal, and provide fascinating glimpses into Eastern spiritual practices, beliefs, and use of life energy.

Although direct experience and knowledge are most important, the decision to begin a quest to experience and to know is itself very important. The discoveries and choices on the quest are themselves meaningful and can lead toward ultimate knowledge. Gurdjieff and his friends Prince Lubovedsky and Professor Skridlov voluntarily place themselves in positions to reach higher states of consciousness. Each purposefully opens himself to new spiritual awakenings. The teachers and guides are there when the students are ready to go to class—or to go exploring within.

Ye View

1. What is Gurdjieff told at the monastery? Why does he return to civilization?
2. What scenes do you find most fascinating in the movie? What characters do you consider most remarkable? Why?
3. Who are some people you would consider to be remarkable in your life? Discuss the reasons.

THE MIRACLE WORKER

PREVIEW

Young Helen Keller (Patty Duke), blind and deaf from a childhood illness, is completely untrained and undisciplined when Annie Sullivan (Anne Bancroft), a graduate of the Perkins Institution for the Blind in Boston and herself sight-impaired, comes to Alabama in 1887 to be Helen's governess and teacher in this powerful adaptation of William Gibson's Broadway play. (1962, 107 minutes, NR)

META VIEW

They made the world see beyond handicaps

YE VIEW

Spirit was the true miracle worker giving Anne Sullivan the determination and insight she needed to teach Helen Keller, filling Helen with the desire to learn and communicate despite her physical impairments, and spreading the story of these two women throughout the world so that their lives could serve as inspirations to millions.

Throughout America's schools, children still read about Helen Keller (1880–1968) and her dramatic breakthrough to knowledge: her graduation from Radcliffe College; her successful career as an author, social reformer, and supporter of the American Foundation for the Blind; and her friendship with writers and scientists and noted people all over the world. She received the Presidential Medal of Freedom in 1964.

The pairing of Helen Keller and Annie Sullivan was divine. Both of these remarkable women were enthused with life and an innate appreciation for discovering life's many blessings, and this energy comes across loud and clear in the movie.

A saucy, opinionated Irish woman, Annie Sullivan has just graduated with honors from the Perkins Institution when she comes to the Keller farm outside Tuscumbia. She has had nine eye operations, but her eyes remain extremely sensitive to light. She is still haunted by her own childhood memories of life in an asylum and her brother's death. But uppermost in her mind is meeting and helping her first pupil.

What she finds is an extremely bright mind trapped in several ways. Annie tells Helen's mother: "I don't think Helen's worst handicap is deafness and blindness. I think it's *your* love and pity." Annie knows that Helen must be disciplined before she can start learning, and she knows that Helen, like herself, is strong.

"That little head is dying to know—anything, any and every crumb in God's creation," Annie says of Helen. "I've got to use that appetite too."

Saying that her idea of original sin is "giving up," Annie immediately begins disciplining Helen and trying to make her understand sign language and word-object associations.

"It has a name," Annie says while Helen holds a bird's egg. "The name stands for the thing. Oh, it's so simple—simple as birth to explain."

Annie encourages her student: "Helen, the chick has to come out of its shell sometime. You come out too."

In human form, a miracle worker is one who serves as an instrument to bring another out of some kind of shell—whatever it may be that is keeping one from knowing and experiencing his or her natural wholeness and oneness with the joy of life.

Annie seeks guidance from one of her booklets and is reminded that she needs both zeal and patience to disinter a "human soul" from its physical entrapment. Annie recognizes her work as awakening Helen "to a consciousness of her immortal nature."

A miracle worker recognizes the shell as only a perceived limitation and holds firmly to the Truth, or wholeness of God, within. "I treat her like a seeing child because I ask her to see—I *expect* her to see," Annie says.

Ye View

1. How does Helen's family react to her blindness and deafness before Annie's arrival? After Annie begins working with Helen?
2. Describe the reaction of Helen, Annie, and Helen's parents when Helen finally understands the association between words and objects.
3. What do you find most inspirational about the story of Helen Keller and Annie Sullivan?

SCHINDLER'S LIST

365

Preview

In Nazi-occupied Poland during World War II, German businessman Oskar Schindler (Liam Neeson) makes a fortune by exploiting Jewish workers in his enamelware factory, but then has a change of heart and willingly spends all his money to save more than one thousand Jews in this gripping film directed by Steven Spielberg and based on Thomas Keneally's book. (1993, 195 minutes, R)

Meta View

He does the extra-ordinary

Although he doesn't know it, Schindler is mixed up about people and priorities as he begins his business. Referring to his sharp money-making abilities and talents for profiteering and presenting himself with panache, he says: "They won't soon forget the name Schindler here; I can tell you that. 'Oskar Schindler,' they'll say. 'Everybody remembers him. He did something extra-ordinary. He did something no one else did.'"

He also says that war "brings out the worst in people—never the good, always the bad. Always the bad."

Schindler is off about the first statement and wrong about the second, as he himself proves. People still remember the name of Schindler, as he predicted, but not for the reasons he expected at the time he made the statement. He does indeed do something "extra-ordinary," but it is in valuing and honoring life, not in making money. And he is an impressive example that war *can* bring out the good in people.

It is interesting to watch the change that occurs within Schindler as he witnesses more and more of the senseless persecution of the Polish Jews. With the quiet assistance of his accountant, Itzhak Stern (Ben Kingsley), Schindler gradually begins helping Jews by saying that they have necessary skills for his factory, which turns out pots and pans for the German war effort.

A woman who wants Schindler to employ her parents says to him: "They say that no one dies here. They say your factory is a haven. They say you are good."

"*Who* says that?" Schindler demands.

"Everyone," the woman replies.

Schindler is at first uneasy with his new reputation, and is torn between a desire to make money and support the German establishment and a desire to give what assistance he can to the Jewish people.

He cleverly works within the system to achieve the maximum good, and even attempts to influence the fierce Nazi camp commandant Amon Goeth (Ralph Fiennes). Schindler tells Goeth, "Power is when we have every justification to kill, and we don't." The idea intrigues Goeth, but he rejects it.

Schindler is more successful with his efforts to persuade Goeth to let him take his factory workers to his hometown in Czechoslovakia in order to prevent their relocation to Auschwitz and sure death.

Stern calls Schindler's list of his workers "an absolute good" and says, "The list is life." Later Stern tells Schindler, "There are eleven hundred people who are alive because of you. . . . There will be generations because of what you did."

Indeed, at the time the movie was made there were more than 6,000 descendants of the Schindler Jews.

Schindler, who died in 1974, is still very much remembered for the extraordinary good he did through his compassion and his life-saving actions.

YE VIEW

1. List some of the specific instances in which Schindler shows his growing concern and compassion for the Jewish plight.
2. What is the significance of Stern finally having a drink with Schindler? What does the act tell you about the two men?
3. At the war's end, why is Schindler not entirely pleased with his accomplishments? What is your reaction to what he does accomplish?

THEME MATES

Another kind of courage during the Holocaust:

The Diary of Anne Frank—The dreams and fears of a Jewish family, particularly those of daughter Anne (Millie Perkins), forced to hide in Amsterdam during World War II are movingly detailed, based on Anne's actual diary in this production of a Broadway play. Here is also another celebrated case of non-Jews helping Jews. (1959, 156 minutes, NR)

THE SOUND OF MUSIC

PREVIEW

In Austria as Nazis prepare to take over the country in the late 1930s, Maria (Julie Andrews), a free-spirited, song-loving novice, becomes governess to the seven children of widower Captain Von Trapp (Christopher Plummer) and brightens the lives of the children and the captain. (1965, 174 minutes, NR)

META VIEW

"Climb every mountain"

Since childhood, Maria has wanted to be a nun, but the sisters aren't so sure she's cut out to be one. They ask the musical questions about her, "How do you hold a moonbeam in your hand?" and "How do you catch a cloud and pin it down?"

Maria says she prays and tries to learn the ways of the convent, but admits that she sings everywhere she goes and says whatever she thinks and feels.

The wise Mother Abbess (Peggy Wood) asks Maria what is the most important lesson Maria has learned during her time at the convent. Maria replies, "To find out what is the will of God and to do it wholeheartedly."

To discover God's will for Maria and to help Maria discover what she expects of herself, Mother Abbess sends Maria out into the world. Maria is shocked at the prospect of caring for so many children and is scared, but she characteristically keeps a good attitude.

"When the Lord closes a door, somewhere He opens a window," she says.

New opportunities and experiences are ahead, Maria realizes, and sings:

"I'll do better than my best . . . I have confidence in me. With each step I am more certain everything will turn out fine. I have confidence the world can all be mine."

Such confidence succeeds, and part of God's will for Maria quickly becomes apparent. Maria discerns that the children have been terrors to past governesses because they want attention from their father, who has run the house like a solemn, disciplined ship since his wife's death. Maria introduces music and warmth back into the house, and opens the captain's eyes to the fact that he has been neglecting his children. "Oh, please, Captain, love them," Maria urges.

She finds out more about God's will for her when the Nazis demand that the captain, who remains loyal to Austria, join the navy of the Third Reich. The pieces of Maria's life fit together—her association with the convent, her love of music, her faith in God, and her confidence in herself— when the family is forced to flee Austria.

This enormously popular, uplifting Rodgers and Hammerstein musical presents a glowing portrait of the matriarch of the famed Von Trapp Family Singers, who came to the United States and opened a lodge in Vermont.

The story also gives direction on how we all can fill our lives with the sound of music, with the music of truly satisfying love: by discovering God's will for us—the same as our heart's desire—and having confidence in ourselves to be able to carry out that will and desire.

As is Maria, we're often confused about what we really want, and feel conflicted in allegiances. Maria, for example, at first has trouble reconciling her devotion to God and her feelings for Captain Von Trapp.

Mother Abbess says: "Maria, the love of a man and woman is holy too. You have a great capacity to love. What you must find out is how God wants you to spend your love. . . . If you love this man, it doesn't mean you love God less."

Beginning the inspiring song "Climb Every Mountain," Mother Abbess says, "You have to live the life you were born to live."

"Climb every mountain, search high and low. . . . Follow every rainbow till you find your dream," she advises.

The key to making our hills and hearts alive with soul-satisfying music is to identify how we can best be the instruments of God to extend divine goodness and love.

YE VIEW

1. How does Maria respond to the children's personal needs?
2. What do you think Captain Von Trapp regards as God's will for him?
3. What are some of the attributes that make Maria a good role model for all children?

Conversations With <u>Oh, God!</u>

Years before Neale Donald Walsch published his *Conversations With God* books, Jerry Landers (John Denver), an assistant manager at a grocery store in Burbank, California, began having conversations with God (in the form of George Burns, no less) in *Oh, God!* (1977, 104 minutes, PG)

God appears because He wants Jerry to be His messenger to tell people that He exists. The messages that God has for the world are, as one might expect, enlightening. Perhaps surprising to many, they are also very much in line with much modern spiritual thought.

Here's a sampling of the movie God's spin on life:

- "You know, Voltaire may have had me pegged right. He said I was a comedian playing to an audience who was afraid to laugh."
- "I'm tired of all the talk that I may be dead, that I never was at all, or that God was just particles of cosmos—gas. I'm not gas. I find that very insulting."
- "I set the world up so it can work. Only it's up to you. You can't look to me to do it for you."
- "People have to decide on their own what's to be done with the world. I can't make a personal decision for everybody."
- "*I* don't permit the suffering. *You* do. Free will. All the choices are yours . . . You can love each other, cherish and nurture each other, you can kill each other."
- "The heart is the temple wherein all Truth resides."
- "Jesus was my son; Buddha was my son; Mohammed, Moses, you, the man who said there was no room in the inn was my son, and so is the one who charges $11 for steak in this one [hotel]."

371

✻

- "I'm not sure how this whole miracle business started—the idea that anything connected with me has to be a miracle. Personally, I'm sorry that it did. It makes the distance between us seem greater."
- "I know how hard it is in these times to have faith, but maybe if you could have the faith to start with, maybe the times would change. You could change them. Think about it. Try. And try not to hurt each other. There's been enough of that."
- "If you find it hard to believe in me, maybe it would help you to know that I believe in you."

Conversations with God are continued in the sequels *Oh God! Book II* (1980) and *Oh, God! You Devil* (1984).

Charlton Heston in *The Ten Commandments,* Paramount Pictures
Photo: The Museum of Modern Art Film Stills Archive

Chapter 9

The Old Hollywood Testament

. . . .

Ah, those biblical epics—they're in a movie class by themselves. They have a look, tone, and acting style unlike any other kind of film. To be sure, these epics derive their inspiration from Scripture, but they definitely project their own New Revised Standard Hollywood Version of the Bible. The characters whose stories are told in the films in this chapter—including Noah, Abraham, David, Moses, Esther, Samson, and Ruth—are among the most prominent men and women of the Old Testament. The characters' cinematic stories may not always bear much semblance to the biblical narratives, but they nevertheless tell us much about our understanding of God, ourselves, and each other.

THE BIBLE

PREVIEW

Director John Huston's spectacle, filmed in several countries during five years, highlights the early events in the Bible, from creation through Noah (Huston) and the Flood to the lives of Abraham (George C. Scott) and his wife Sarah (Ava Gardner). (1966, U.S.-Italy, 174 minutes, NR)

META VIEW

These stories have staying power

Signing up for a five-day course in the Bible, I laughed to myself. How could the entire Bible possibly be studied in that short a time? That seemed almost on an amazing par with God creating the world in seven days. The instructor did it, though, with three days devoted to the Old Testament and two days to the New Testament.

The crash course brought the Bible alive to me as it never had been before. Why? Because for the first time, I appreciated the storytelling value of the Bible, especially the Old Testament. Most of the stories cannot be taken literally, and even the historically verifiable stories have true value beyond the facts. The stories, fables, myths, accounts—call them what you will—are people's efforts to understand life, and their reactions to it. Storytellers throughout history have "sat around the campfires" of one kind or another and spun tales to give meaning to existence and motives for their actions.

Famed mythologist Joseph Campbell writes in *Myths to Live By* that such Bible stories as the Garden of Eden, the "Fall," the worldwide Flood, and Noah's Ark (all impressively depicted in the movie) are universal "themes of the imagination" and represent "features of the human spirit."

"In short, these holy tales and their images are messages to the conscious mind from quarters of the spirit unknown to normal daylight consciousness," Campbell asserts, adding that it is important to listen to the messages to truly know ourselves.[1]

What is especially apparent in the movie is the story of humankind's evolving consciousness regarding God. The God of the Old Testament is into vengeance and favoritism, as contrasted with the loving, inclusive God of the New Testament. The pure energy of Spirit, which is love and goodness, does not change, but humankind's view of Spirit changes according to individual awareness.

For example, there are those, at the time Genesis was written and now, whose level of awareness seeks an outside source (the serpent) to blame for their own perceived weaknesses. Others, reflected most clearly by Jesus' consciousness, accept that individual perceptions determine our experiences but know that we are always one with Spirit, whatever the appearances.

God tells Abraham, "Lift up now thine eyes and look from the place where thou art—northward and southward and eastward and westward, for all the land which thou seest to thee will I give it and to thy seed forever."

That is, our place in consciousness determines what we receive, and our conscious utilization of God energy is planted in our experiences.

In the movie and in its source, God is repeatedly making covenants with people, who promptly break them. Actually, humankind makes the covenants depending on its understanding of spiritual awareness. We still create tempters, divisions, and floods according to our consciousness, and we may label them "good" or "bad" according to our consciousness and blame them on God or not—again, according to our consciousness.

However, through humankind's shifting perceptions, God remains constant. God is always, as Abraham recognizes, our "refuge and strength," because we are one with the very energy that is God.

YE VIEW

1. Do you like the movie's artistic rendering of the creation story? Why or why not?
2. What are the lessons to be learned from the stories of the Garden of Eden, Noah's Ark, and the Tower of Babel?
3. What is your reaction to the nature of God, as revealed in the movie? How does this God correspond to your own beliefs about a higher power?

DAVID AND BATHSHEBA

PREVIEW

The illicit love affair between King David (Gregory Peck), second king of Israel, and Bathsheba (Susan Hayward), wife of army captain Uriah, is embellished from 2 Samuel. (1951, 116 minutes, NR)

META VIEW

Here's how to destroy sin

The passions and mistakes of the high and mighty, so newsworthy in our own times, have their counterparts in the Bible. The story of David and Bathsheba, for example, is one of lust, adultery, murder, revenge, and guilt; the movie tells all—and then some.

The story is so much more than the sum total of its juicy details, though. The film is a marvelous example of the divine law of cause and effect in regards to sin and punishment. David says: "With our people the law is everything. It is in their bones." While he meant Mosaic law, in metaphysical

Truth, the laws of God are being applied in our minds and to our lives all the time.

The word *sin* is an archery term that means "missing the mark."[2] It does not mean a mistake that leads to everlasting punishment from a wrathful God. An individual, through personal thought and desire, is responsible for missing the mark—that is, falling short of an ideal of divine perfection, love, and goodness. When a person misses the mark, he or she can choose another way of thinking and feeling, and thus begin *hitting* the mark. With an increased consciousness, sin is effectually canceled within the person. The old arrow of a person's ways has been retrieved. Sin is simply destroyed with new thought. As Christian Science founder Mary Baker Eddy writes: "The destruction of sin is the divine method of pardon. . . . Truth destroys error. . . . Being destroyed, sin needs no other form of forgiveness."[3]

In *David and Bathsheba*, the principle is perfectly illustrated. David makes the initial choice to secure Bathsheba's affections. He may be a king and chosen by God, but he's also human. He tells Bathsheba: "I'm only a man. I need someone to understand that. I need the kind of understanding that only one human being can give to another. I need someone to share my heart." David also makes the decision to have Bathsheba's husband killed so that they can be married.

The effects of the sinful union of David and Bathsheba are the death of Bathsheba's husband in battle, unrest in the country and within David's household, and, so the prophet Nathan (Raymond Massey) says, famine and drought in the land.

"You cannot escape the punishment of the Lord [which can be read *law*]," Nathan tells David.

"I have not escaped it. My son is dead," David says, very much mentally and physically feeling the effects of his deeds.

Both David and Bathsheba recognize their part (cause) in the unhappy events. "My guilt is as great as yours, because I let you bear the burden of it alone," Bathsheba says. "God sees into our hearts."

379

✳

How can David's sins be righted? They must be destroyed with an increased consciousness and sincere turning to God. David realizes this Truth. Nathan says that David has turned away from God, but reminds David that there was once a time when he drew his strength from God and prayed to God. He says if *that* David still lives, God will not deny him mercy. In other words, if David turns his consciousness to God once again, his new awareness will result in (cause) a feeling and knowledge of freedom (effect).

Recalling Nathan's words and his boyhood, David admits his shortcomings and prays to God, "Let the boy live again . . . and take this David's life." Scenes from David's boyhood—his shepherding, his selection to be king, and his slaying of the giant Goliath—are shown. The prayer—the new consciousness—is answered on the outer with rain and on the inner with David's sense of peace, love, and freedom.

YE VIEW

1. Do you sympathize with David and Bathsheba? Why or why not?
2. Where does David say that, as a boy, he found God? In later years, why couldn't he find God again?
3. Discuss the Twenty-third Psalm, recited in the movie by David and sung by a choir, as it could apply to the story of David and Bathsheba.

THEME MATES

Another notorious woman from the Bible:
Salome—Rita Hayworth stars as the dancer pivotal to the beheading of John the Baptist in this story generously adapted from accounts in Matthew and Mark. (1953, 103 minutes, NR)

ESTHER AND THE KING

PREVIEW

In this story based on the book of Esther, a Jewish woman (Joan Collins) becomes queen of Persia and uses her influence to persuade King Ahasuerus (Richard Egan) to spare her people from the annihilation ordered by Haman, the king's scheming, ambitious chief minister. (1960, U.S.-Italian, 109 minutes, NR)

META VIEW

Gentleness breaks the sword

"This happened in the days of Ahasuerus, the same Ahasuerus who ruled over one hundred twenty-seven provinces from India to Ethiopia." So begins the book of Esther (just before the more famous book of Job).

One suspects that the happenings during the king's time were filled with a lot more excitement than depicted in the movie. This is a poorly acted, elaborately but not necessarily authentically costumed biblical drama that would not deserve attention except that it *does* generally reflect Esther's story. And that story is a rich lesson in faith and courage.

King Ahasuerus is a good man who has been betrayed and deceived, says his counsel Mordecai (Denis O'Dea), who is also Esther's guardian. Mordecai senses the king's unhappiness and tells him: "Mighty power is a burden. I know but one way to lighten it: By lessening the burdens of others, one removes his own."

The king is given a chance to lessen his burdens when he selects Esther to be his queen. He doesn't know that Esther is a Jew. Esther isn't pleased about the union because the king has been hard on her people, but Mordecai persuades her that she might be able to change conditions for the Jews. "Gentleness can break the sword of evil," he says.

Esther has a positive effect on the king and opens his eyes to injustices in taxation and treatment of people. Remaining loyal to her religion and displaying considerable courage, Esther does indeed have an opportunity to "break the sword of evil" when she intercedes after Haman orders the Jews killed.

"The night of the deliverance of our people must live in memory," Mordecai says.

It has. The Jews' rescue from Haman's orders is joyously celebrated each year during the observance known as Purim. Carnivals, dances, costumes, and food gifts are a part of the merriment. To this day, the mention of Haman's name is met with noises. The Hebrew word *pur*, which means "lot," is probably the source of the name of the observance. Lots were used by Haman to decide when the Jews would be killed.

Theatrically, the movie has many problems, but where else can one find such an elaborate dramatization of the origins of Purim?

Ye View

1. What is the king's attitude about the God of the Jews?
2. Mordecai says, "There's always hope." What is the basis of his hope? Is his hope justified by events in the movie?
3. Select a prominent modern-day woman who has used her married position to further a worthy cause, and discuss her contributions to humanity.

KING DAVID

PREVIEW

Fresh, bold realism and a script that remains extremely faithful to biblical texts propel this telling of the life of King David (Richard Gere), from psalm-singing shepherd boy to giant slayer to legendary warrior and king of ancient Israel. (1985, 114 minutes, PG-13)

META VIEW

The Lord is his shepherd

The young David plays his harp and sings what we know as the Twenty-third Psalm to soothe a troubled King Saul. For Saul, as they must have been for David in the fields with his sheep, and as they have been to thousands of people for centuries, the words of the psalm, beginning with "The Lord is my shepherd, I shall not want," are inspiring and comforting.

The words are reminders that God is always a guiding, caring presence, but the reminders are constantly needed. As the movie vividly shows, an awareness of the Lord as shepherd is necessary before the fact makes any difference in an individual's life. The Lord has made, or created, us to lie down in green pastures, but we have to claim our bed.

First, take the case of King Saul (Edward Woodward), who is tormented because he thinks God has forsaken him. Actually, Saul has turned away from God through his jealous thoughts and actions.

Next, consider the plight of David. As a youth, he is in tune with God and lives with the knowledge that God is his shepherd. Concerning God's selection of David as the next king of Israel, the prophet Samuel (Denis Quilley) says: "The Lord does not see as man sees. Men judge by outward appearances, but the Lord judges by the heart alone."

383

✳

Clearly, David has a heart pleasing to God. In serving Saul and later escaping Saul's persecution, and in the early days of his forty-year reign, David lives in the consciousness of God's presence. "As a boy I could feel His presence all around me," David recalls. Once king, however, David becomes sidetracked in more earthly and domestic affairs. Like Saul, David begins thinking that God has forsaken him.

"It is you who have forsaken Him," the prophet Nathan tells David. When David acknowledges the truth of this remark, he turns again to God and to the once-more dynamic realization that the Lord is his shepherd. With the Lord as his shepherd, David becomes "a lamp unto his people."

YE VIEW

1. What do you admire in David's personality? What do you find less than admirable? Consider his relationships with Jonathan, Absalom, and Bathsheba.
2. David tells Solomon, "Be guided by the instincts of your own heart . . . for it is through the heart, and the heart alone, that God speaks to man." Do you think that this is true? Why or why not?
3. Compare and contrast the depictions of key scenes from David's life in *King David* and *David and Bathsheba*.

THE PRINCE OF EGYPT

PREVIEW

With state-of-the-art animation and 3D-computer graphics, DreamWorks adapts the Exodus story to concentrate on the brotherly friendship of Moses (voiced by Val Kilmer) and the future Pharaoh Rameses (voiced by Ralph

Fiennes) and on God's selection and use of Moses to bring the Israelites out of Egyptian bondage. (1998, 99 minutes, PG)

META VIEW

"Let my people go!"

The Prince of Egypt is a royal feast for the eyes and the soul.

The film is stunning in its depiction of the wonders and wealth of ancient Egypt, its development of believable characters, and its special visual effects—most notably a wild chariot race, God speaking to Moses through the burning bush, the infamous plagues on Egypt, and the parting of the sea.

Foremost, however, the film is a moving story of individual freedom and faith. Much is behind the proclamation of Moses to Rameses, "Let my people go!"

Moses says that he wants a life of freedom and dignity for his people. He himself has experienced an early life of privilege in the royal palace but has also seen and felt the suffering of his people. He truly knows the value of both freedom and dignity.

"God saved you to be our deliverer, and you are," his sister Miriam (voice of Sandra Bullock) tells Moses.

From the beginning of the movie, when the baby Moses is placed in a basket of bulrushes and floated down the river toward the Pharaoh's palace, the music establishes the theme of Moses as deliverer. "Deliver us to the promised land," the slaves sing.

After God identifies Himself to Moses as "I Am that I Am" and the God of his ancestors, Moses asks what God wants of him. God tells Moses that he is to be the deliverer of His people to "a land flowing with milk and honey."

Although Moses is at first unsure of himself, God says that He will be

385

with Moses and teach him what to say. A sincere reliance on God and a genuine desire to free his people propel Moses to his destiny. "No kingdom should be made on the backs of slaves," he says.

Jethro (voiced by Danny Glover), a high priest and Moses' father-in-law, bolsters Moses' conviction by telling him to "look at your life through heaven's eyes," that is, to keep centered on God's will for him.

"You must learn to join the dance," Jethro says, even though you may not know all the steps.

Tremendous faith is required of Moses and all of the Israelites. Actually, they become aware of their inner, God-given strength. In the song "When You Believe," the people sing: "We were moving mountains long before we knew we could. . . . Who knows what miracles you can achieve when you believe somehow you will? You will when you believe."

The Exodus story, as modern Truth seekers often interpret it, represents all people's deliverance, through belief and faith in God, from the bondage of world thought and of physical and mental limitation. Moses stands for the consciousness that recognizes unity with God rather than separation from God, and the complete dominion of Spirit over matter.

In his book *Finding Yourself in Transition: Using Life's Changes for Spiritual Awakening*, Robert Brumet refers to the Exodus story as a "a very powerful lesson in letting go of the past and stepping forward into our life."

Brumet explains, "The teaching consists of two parts: first, stand firm in knowing that the Lord, the I AM of your being, will work for you today—be still and know; and the second part is to step forward in faith and courage."[4]

A metaphysical interpretation also is required to make peace with the wrathful God of the Old Testament, as presented so graphically in the movie. The killing of the firstborn throughout the land of Egypt is especially chilling (effective, but chilling). The God who inflicts such killing surely is not Jesus' God of love of the New Testament!

The Bible chronicles humankind's change in spiritual consciousness. Therefore, the God of the Old Testament is properly seen not as an accurate portrayal of an eternal God, but as an expression of humanity's primitive concept of its relationship to God. That concept has been considerably refined and softened over the years so that unconditional love is now the highest conceptualization of our relationship with God.

YE VIEW

1. Compare and contrast Moses' personality as the prince of Egypt and as deliverer of the Israelites.
2. Do you feel a sympathy for Rameses as well as Moses? Why or why not?
3. Discuss someone in the news today whom you admire for his or her efforts to bring freedom and dignity to people.

387

SAMSON AND DELILAH

PREVIEW

Strong man Samson (Victor Mature) has been chosen by God to free the Israelites from the rule of the Philistines, but he's no match for the beautiful Delilah (Hedy Lamarr), who schemes for the Philistines to have Samson reveal the secret of his strength to her, in this Old Testament spinoff. (1949, 128 minutes, NR)

META VIEW

Strength comes from God

A visual treat opens this Cecil B. DeMille story inspired but by no means limited to the account of Samson in Judges 13–16. As the world turns through clouds of time, a narrator begins talking: "Before the dawn of history, ever since the first man discovered his soul, he has struggled against the forces that have sought to enslave him."

Those forces, we're told, are fear, superstition, and tyranny. Always, however, "Deep in man's heart still burned the unquenchable will for freedom." And always, there have been individuals whose brave deeds have changed the course of human history.

Such a one is Samson, the narrator says, a mighty man in whose character is blended greatness and weakness, strength and folly.

An aged storyteller warns Philistine soldiers who are harassing him, "The power of the Lord is in Samson, and one day you shall feel it."

With much spectacle, color, and action, Samson is shown flaunting his strength to win women and seek revenge against those who have wronged him and his people. Delilah, in a role much enhanced from the biblical tale, is (to use Samson's description) a "wildcat" who at first seeks to capture Samson for herself and then, feeling scorned, vows to destroy him.

Samson always credits God as the source of his strength and appeals to God before exercising his strength.

"O Lord, my God, hear me," he prays before an encounter with the Philistines. "Gird me for battle against the swords of mine enemies. Forsake me not, O Lord, but strengthen my arm to destroy the lions who scattered thy flocks."

Samson's prayer to be girded by divine strength in order to overcome his enemies is one that still has great power today. Whatever our perceived enemies, whether of physical or mental origins, God's strength can give us power to face them and to overcome them.

When Delilah questions Samson about God, he tells her: "He's everywhere . . . in your heart if you believe in him. His is the only power in the world that can break open a seed and raise it into that great tree."

Delilah asks if *she* can share God's power.

"Anyone can share it," Samson says. "It's a gift that makes men greater than themselves. With it, some can stir the soul with music. Others can read the truth in men's hearts and then forgive them. To me, it's a strength to break any bonds that can be put upon me."

Samson wisely recognizes that the strength of God takes many forms and works in an endless variety of ways to help guide people to a realization of their oneness with God. With a firm sense of our divine strength within, like Samson, we can "break any bonds."

Then Delilah asks if Samson will always have strength from God.

"As long as I keep faith with the Almighty," he says.

As reflections of God, rays of divine energy, we always have the strength of God within, but we must realize it to effectively use it in our lives. When Samson is in tune with the strength of God within him, he is indeed strong; when he loses sight (figuratively and literally) of his divine source, he is weak. The choice is always his, as it is always ours, whether or not to access the divine strength at the core of being.

YE VIEW

1. Do you think Delilah really loves Samson and sincerely wants the two of them to go to Egypt? Why or why not?
2. According to Samson, why has he been blinded? What does Samson mean by speaking of being able to "see again more clearly"?
3. How would you say that the gift of God's strength manifests in you? Explain your answer.

389

THE STORY OF RUTH

PREVIEW

In this considerably embellished Old Testament story, a Moabite priestess named Ruth (Elana Eden) is widowed moments after marrying an Israelite, Mahlon (Tom Tryon), and gives up her homeland and pagan religion to go with her mother-in-law Naomi (Peggy Wood) to Bethlehem and later marry a kinsman, Boaz (Stuart Whitman). (1960, 132 minutes, NR)

META VIEW

Faith in God endures

The book of Ruth tells a short, simple story of a loving, brave, and bold woman, apparently of no exceptional background, sustained by faith in God.

The movie, however, fleshing out the biblical account with Hollywood and soap-opera contrivances, makes Ruth into a priestess of the Moabite god of stone that must have human sacrifices, fabricates a dangerous relationship between Ruth and Mahlon, involves Naomi's husband and two sons in a fatal involvement with the priestess, and gives Boaz a rival for Ruth's affections. All exciting, to be sure, but not in the book of Ruth.

Still, Ruth's new-found faith and loyalty, as well as Naomi's goodness, manage to endure all of the elaborate additions to the beloved story.

Mahlon's earnest character serves to introduce Ruth to a merciful God who is felt within the individual. "We believe in a merciful God," he says, whose name "matters not, so long as one knows He exists."

Discussing the Israelite's invisible but ever-present God and comparing Him with the Moabite stone god, Mahlon asks Ruth, "How can a god whose own head gets broken mend the broken heads of his soldiers?"

Ruth is disturbed and confused by Mahlon's descriptions of God, but she readily and instinctively feels that they are right.

When Mahlon dies, Ruth decides to cross the Jordan with Naomi. In a variation of her famous words from the Bible, Ruth says: "Where you go, I will go. Where you lodge, I will lodge. Your people shall be *my* people; and your God, *my* God."

When asked why she chose to accompany Naomi to Bethlehem, Ruth says "because I saw a new light in her beliefs and in her God."

Naomi is told in response to a prayer that Ruth's descendants will include a great king of Israel (David) and a prophet whom many will worship as the Messiah (Jesus).

YE VIEW

1. Why do you think Ruth accepts God so quickly and retains such strong faith?
2. How do the Israelites receive Ruth? How does Ruth react to the reception?
3. A stranger who appears to Naomi after prayer says, "We are *all* holy in the eyes of God." Discuss your response to the statement.

THE TEN COMMANDMENTS

PREVIEW

This most magnificent and star-studded of all Old Testament epics, from legendary director Cecil B. DeMille, chronicles "the story of the birth of freedom" as represented in the life of Moses (Charlton Heston), including his birth and royal upbringing, his deliverance of the Israelites out of Egypt, his receiving of God's laws on Mount Sinai, and his glimpse of the Promised Land. (1956, 220 minutes, G)

META VIEW

Thou really canst not

There's a lot to think about (not to mention all the glorious spectacles to *see*) in this lengthy movie before Moses even receives the titular commandments.

First, there is the introduction, in which the relevancy of Moses' life to modern sociological-political conditions is firmly established and the picture's theme is stated: whether people ought to be ruled by God's laws or by the whims of a dictator like Rameses. "Are men the property of the state, or are they free souls under God? This same battle continues throughout the world today." So it was in 1956, and so it is now.

Second, there is the quest of Moses to find out "why a Hebrew or any man must be a slave."

Even when he thinks that he is an Egyptian, Moses has sympathy for those in servitude.

The Hebrew slave Joshua (John Derek) is said to have committed treason by saying: "God made men. Men made slaves," but Moses says, "It is not treason to want freedom." He recognizes what would later be referred to as an inalienable right of humankind.

Moses tells Pharaoh Rameses (Yul Brynner), "Man shall be ruled by law, not by the will of other men."

Third, there is the nature of God. After Moses hears God speak from the burning bush, Moses offers a description of God that could have come from the New Testament:

"He revealed His word to my mind and the word was God. . . . He is not flesh but Spirit, the light of eternal mind, and I know that His light is within every man. . . . It is not by the sword that He will deliver His people, but by the staff of a shepherd."

Finally, the Ten Commandments are given, and Moses proclaims, "There is no freedom without the law."

Emmet Fox, who was an eminent metaphysical writer, says that the Ten Commandments are not only valid at face value but also extremely important for their profound psychological ramifications. Fox says that the laws actually address individual states of consciousness which make it possible for people to do or not do something. He writes:

"Now, there is one great fundamental law, the Law of Being, the summing up of all laws in life, and it is this: whatever comes to you, whatever happens to you, whatever surrounds you, will be in accordance with your consciousness, and nothing else; that whatever is in your consciousness must happen, no matter who tries to stop it; and whatever is not in your consciousness cannot happen. People do not know that, but it means, in other words, 'Thou canst not steal.'"[5] (This "thou canst not" consciousness, of course, applies to all ten commandments.)

Our goal then is to raise our consciousness to an awareness of God's love and peace and to an appreciation for all life as God energy, and it will no longer be in our consciousness to do anything that does not reflect the will of God, which is always for the highest good of all life.

The earlier ideas presented in the movie actually prepare us for a higher state of consciousness revealed by Fox's understanding of the Ten Commandments. To be in the state of consciousness of "thou canst not," it is necessary to realize that we are "free souls under God" and that God's light "is within every man."

393

YE VIEW

1. Do you think the characterization of Moses in this movie or in *The Prince of Egypt* is closer to the biblical accounts and descriptions? Explain your answer.
2. Other than Moses, what characters in the movie do you admire? Why?
3. Do you agree with Emmet Fox's meaning of the Ten Commandments? Why or why not?

IN THE SAME SPIRIT

DeMille's practice run:

The Ten Commandments—In this silent film, Cecil B. DeMille not only tells the traditional story of Moses, but also spins an updated tale about two brothers with extremely different personalities. (1923, 146 minutes, NR)

THEME MATES

Bringing about their fate through consciousness:

Sodom and Gomorrah—Stewart Granger stars in this Genesis tale of twin cities destroyed by fire because of lack of righteousness. Consciousness must be purified before the Christ nature can be revealed. (1963, Italian, 154 minutes, NR)

::: **FEATURE PRESENTATION**

The Ten Commandments of Movie Watching

1. You shall not talk once the movie starts. Golden idle words are frowned upon; save them for after the movie. This includes talking back to characters on-screen and commenting to your best friend that so-and-so looks better with long hair. You shall also kindly not talk on cell phones during the movie (or even bring their ringing presence into the theater).

2. You shall not endlessly unwrap crinkly cellophane from little candies. If you must unwrap cellophane, do it quickly. Unwrapping slowly—as if no one knows what you are doing—prolongs the agony and slows down the ecstasy of your first bite.

3. You shall not munch noisily on popcorn. Let the kernels melt in your mouth. (You shall do the same for ice, and not crunch.)

4. You shall not wear large hats or large hair-dos. Don't even covet them. Frizzy curls that take up two seats also are frowned upon.

5. You shall not put your feet on the back of the seat in front of you, or cross your legs and keep time by kicking the seat in front of you.

6. You shall not steal another person's pleasure of a surprise ending. If you have seen the movie before, you shall not tell your companion everything that is going to happen just before it happens.

7. Honor the starting time of the movie and make every effort to be on time so as not to disturb others once the movie has started.

8. You shall not sit directly in front of other people if there are good seats elsewhere. You especially shall not sit in front of children or other short people unless the theater is too full to do otherwise.

9. Remember refreshments before the movie starts, and keep refills (and thus popping up and down) to a minimum.

10. You shall not leave trash on the floor and otherwise make sticky messes for the next audience. Remember the old saying that cleanliness is next to godliness.

(Note: As with all commandments, people have the personal option of taking them seriously or disregarding them entirely. But it will be easy to spot who does which!)

Alastair Sim with Marley's ghost in *A Christmas Carol,*
Renown Film Productions
Photo: The Museum of Modern Art Film Stills Archive

Chapter 10

Have Yourself a Super Natural Christmas

• • • • • • • • • • • •

Visions and images of Christmas naturally spin around in our heads whenever there's talk of peace, goodwill toward men, and true brotherly love and affection. At its best, Christmas is a heavenly state of mind in which we manifest our highest nature, the Christ. In all of the Christmas movies in this chapter, Christ Love and an imaginative extension of that love, the legend of Santa Claus, are especially infectious and transformative. Note: *It's a Wonderful Life* and *The Bishop's Wife* (and its remake *The Preacher's Wife*) are among films with Christmas connections, but are spotlighted in Chapter 1 because of their all-important angel involvement.

ALL I WANT FOR CHRISTMAS

PREVIEW

After asking a department store Santa to have her parents remarry, Hallie (Thora Birch) enlists her older brother Ethan (Ethan Randall) to help make the wish come true. (1991, 92 minutes, G, *)

META VIEW

Santa has many helpers

Santa, the spirit of Christmas, uses human elves to fulfill wishes. We can think of the Christmas spirit as an aspect of God, or Universal Spirit. And Spirit is always willing, whether people are believing or unbelieving, because It is an energy that continually flows and in which we "live and move and have our being" (Acts 17:28). What causes Spirit to manifest is the *intention* of love, and what actually creates the manifestation of Spirit is the *action* of love.

Hallie believes in Santa's ability to bring her parents back together; Ethan doesn't. "He's a jolly fat guy and not a marriage counselor," Ethan says. Both, acting out of love for their family, recognize that they must be Santa's helpers, and divine energy flows freely through them.

After she gives her request to Santa (and realizes she should have been more specific), Hallie asks her brother, "What are we going to do?" Ethan has a plan "to help things along." That sounds like a good idea, since Hallie's department store Santa says he usually specializes "in stuff you can wrap."

Expressing the importance of action to accompany beliefs or desires, Ethan says, "You can dream about things and they may not turn out, but you have to at least try."

YE VIEW

1. What is the premise of Ethan's Operation Desert Island?
2. Why does Ethan consider his father a role model?
3. Identify a personal Christmas wish and make a list of what you can do to make it come true.

A CHRISTMAS CAROL

PREVIEW

Spirits from the past, present, and future take miserly nineteenth-century English businessman Ebenezer Scrooge (Alastair Sim) on soul-searching forays one Christmas Eve and help him appreciate the holiday he has spurned as "humbug" in this riveting, highly regarded adaptation of the Charles Dickens classic. (1951, British, 86 minutes, NR)

401

META VIEW

God bless Scrooges, every one!

Scrooge has gotten a bum rap. What do you think when someone says "Scrooge"? What is the dictionary entry for *scrooge*? What does it mean to call someone "Scrooge"?

That's right. The image of Scrooge is a skinflint or, as Mrs. Cratchit says, a "hard, stingy, unfeeling man." The dictionary definition is "a miserly person."[1] He's thought of as one who scorns Christmas and all its goodwill and charitableness.

Such a view of Ebenezer Scrooge is not being very Christian, however, nor is it reflecting the true Spirit of the Christ. Rather than being famous for losing his way for a while, Scrooge should be remembered for *finding* it. As Scrooge says to his clerk, Bob Cratchit: "I haven't taken leave of my senses, Bob. I've come *to* them." Rather than being remembered for not giving, he should be remembered for having a change of heart, a change of consciousness that starts him giving wholeheartedly. Rather than being remembered as a person who wrongs others, he should be remembered as a person who asks and receives forgiveness, who sees the errors of his narrow ways, repents, and then makes up for lost loving. The converted Scrooge says to his niece, "Can you forgive a pig-headed old fool for having no eyes to see with, no ears to hear with, all these years?" She comes to him with open arms. He's the Prodigal Uncle.

Scrooge's story is our own any time we are reborn or transformed in consciousness and begin living from the perspective of our divine Self rather than our human self. His should be a story and a remembrance of resurrection, rather than crucifixion (as should Jesus'). Scrooge's is a story of waking up to the unconditional love that is always there awaiting our awareness, every day of the year.

The Spirit of Christmas Present tells Scrooge: "Mortal, we spirits of Christmas do not live only one day of our year. We live the whole 365. So is it true of the child born in Bethlehem. He does not live in men's hearts only one day of the year, but in all of the days of the year. You have chosen not to seek him in your heart. Therefore, you shall come with me and seek him in the hearts of men of goodwill."

Scrooge's nephew extends unconditional love to Scrooge. "I ask nothing of you," he says when visiting Scrooge the day before Christmas, but adds that he merely comes in the spirit of goodwill. He later says of his uncle, "I'm sorry for him. . . . Who suffers worse from his humors? Himself always." It is true that when we deny ourselves the experiences of love, we cause our own suffering.

Love given from the heart with no earthly cause also comes to Scrooge from Bob Cratchit, who toasts his boss on Christmas Day, and from his former business partner, Jacob Marley, whose ghost personally arranges for Scrooge to be visited by the spirits—in hopes that Scrooge might be saved from his own fettered fate for neglecting the welfare of others.

When the spirits that be (within and/or without) help him see the love and good hearts of people, Scrooge is "born again" to an awareness of his oneness with unconditional, universal love—a change that makes him "light as a feather" and "happy as an angel."

God bless Scrooge, a marvelous example of the power of transformation and forgiveness (especially, as so expressively played by Sim), and (in later years) a superb example of the Christmas spirit of caring and loving. And as the Cratchits' child Tiny Tim says, "God bless us, every one!" as we follow Scrooge's lead.

403

Ye View

1. What circumstances of his youth and young manhood contributed to Scrooge's callous ways?
2. What shadows from the past and future have the most effect on Scrooge? How does he react to them?
3. Have you known anyone like Scrooge whose personality changed to become more giving and loving? Share your remembrance of the person.

In the Same Spirit

Adaptations and spinoffs to bless, every one:

A Christmas Carol—A solid Hollywood version, with Reginald Owen as Scrooge. (1938, 69 minutes, NR)

The Muppet Christmas Carol—Kermit the Frog, Miss Piggy, and other Henson favorites join Michael Caine as Scrooge in an enjoyable retelling. (1992, 85 minutes, G, *)

Scrooge—Albert Finney plays Scrooge in a rousing musical (1970, British, 118 minutes, G, *)

Scrooged—The times, situations, and humor are modern in this excuse for Bill Murray to be a scrooge. (1988, 101 minutes, PG-13)

EDWARD SCISSORHANDS

PREVIEW

The gossipy, nosey neighbors of Suburbia really have something to talk about when Peg, the Avon Lady (Dianne Wiest), brings home a man-made lad (Johnny Depp) who has scissors for hands in this satiric social fable from the imagination of director Tim Burton. (1990, 100 minutes, PG-13)

META VIEW

Give from your own talents

It's easy to get caught up in the Christmas rat race of buying presents and running frantically around from mall to strip mall as the Big Day approaches. While there's nothing wrong with store-bought presents, all presents do not come from stores. That may be a surprising revelation to many commercial-oriented shoppers today, but others know that some of the best presents in life are those made by the givers themselves, from their own natural, God-given talents and abilities. It's always been true. Our ancestors during the pioneer days and the Depression, for example, whittled, sewed, and baked presents that were as loved and cherished as if they had come from Tiffany's—perhaps more so, because so much of the giver's spirit is in such gifts.

From personal experience, I know the joy of giving and receiving home-made presents. Other family members and I have used such talents, hobbies, and interests as writing, photography, sewing, needlework, cooking, pottery, and woodworking to create wonderful and wonderfully appreciated presents. Some difficult-to-wrap talents have been given via coupons. For example, coupons "good for five free dish washings" or "good for a favorite home-cooked meal" are highly valued.

Christmas giving from one's own talents is magically illustrated by Edward Scissorhands. His inventor (Vincent Price) dies before replacing cumbersome scissors at the ends of Edward's arms with human hands. When Peg brings Edward from the mansion where he has lived alone and into her home and neighborhood, Edward, a kind sort who seeks to please, begins giving to people in the only way he can: by using his scissorhands in creative ways. He turns shrubs into fantastically shaped topiaries, and gives women and dogs elaborate, personal hairdos.

During Christmas, Edward gives Peg's daughter Kim (Winona Ryder), with whom he has fallen in love, his greatest gift. In the family's yard, Edward sculpts an angel out of an enormous block of ice (a heavenly iceman must have cometh). As Edward speedily sculpts, flakes of ice are scattered everywhere. This event, according to the fable, is the origin of snow, which has become an integral part of our idyllic vision of a "White Christmas."

"Before he came down here, it never snowed, and afterwards it did," says the elderly Kim, referring to Edward. "If he weren't up there now, I don't think it would be snowing."

405

Ye View

1. What is Peg's attitude about life? How is that attitude reflected in her treatment of Edward?
2. What Christmas gifts do you think Edward himself would most like?
3. Think about your own special talents and abilities. How have you or could you turn these talents into presents for others?

HOLIDAY INN

PREVIEW

Entertainer Jim Hardy (Bing Crosby) turns a farm into a country inn open only on holidays, and vies with former partner Ted Hanover (Fred Astaire) for women and attention in this musical that shines with holiday songs by Irving Berlin. (1942, 101 minutes, NR)

META VIEW

We're all dreaming of a "White Christmas"

The great psychologist Carl Jung is a guest, in theory, at Holiday Inn. That is, Jung's concept of universal archetypes is very much in evidence. According to Jung, archetypes are inherited ideas that arise from the collective unconscious and are born within each individual; they are dynamic patterns that help code the human experience.

Our collective Christmas unconscious includes the archetype of an ideal condition and place of purity, peace, and perfection (an idea explicit in the story of the Garden of Eden and in traditional images of heaven). There are several Christmas versions of this archetype, including the North Pole and that cozy abode of peace suggested by the phrase "home for Christmas." The most evocative perhaps is the version made famous in the Irving Berlin song "White Christmas" in *Holiday Inn*.

The Oscar-winning song's immense popularity and appeal for decades is proof that it touches the archetypal foundation of our psyche. It speaks to our collective longing to reconnect with our natural state of perfection in much the same manner as the song "Over the Rainbow." The words "I'm dreaming of a white Christmas" (especially, when sung by Crosby) recall an ideal picture of sparkling white snow (symbol of purity) and delighted children (symbol of innocence). Whether we live in an area that regularly experiences immense snowfall at Christmas or in an area in which snow rarely or never falls in late December, we can dream, and our collective dream is always for an inner condition of harmony and wholeness that we call a "white Christmas." The associations of a "white Christmas" are ones of beauty, external and internal.

This much-loved song even offers humanity a prayer to continue its collective remembrance of purity, peace, and perfection: "May your days be merry and bright, and may all your Christmases be white."

Ye View

1. What are Jim's values about work and time?
2. What are some patriotic archetypes found in songs from the movie?
3. Discuss the meanings, connotations, and importance of a "white Christmas" to you.

In the Same Spirit

The song goes on:

White Christmas—In this adapted remake of *Holiday Inn*, Crosby is joined by Danny Kaye at a winter resort. It's all an excuse for more good Irving Berlin music, such as the positive reminder to "Count Your Blessings (Instead of Sheep)." (1954, 120 minutes, NR)

MEET JOHN DOE

PREVIEW

To save her job and to bolster circulation, a newspaper columnist, Ann Mitchell (Barbara Stanwyck), creates a phony story about an average man who is so disgusted with the world's conditions that he intends to commit suicide on Christmas Eve, and the whole country rallies around the man the newspaper hires to be John Doe (Gary Cooper). (1941, 123 minutes, NR)

META VIEW

Spread the Christmas spirit year-round

Despite the insincerities and the insecurities found in daily existence, life is worthwhile and offers an abundance of goodness and love. It is director Frank Capra's hope that people will come to appreciate life. Capra's hope is a central message of *Meet John Doe*, as it is in another one of his films often identified with Christmas, *It's a Wonderful Life* (discussed in Chapter 1).

There are shady dealings and ulterior motives in back of the John Doe hysteria that sweeps the country. Ann wants to milk the story for all it's worth so that she will have more money to support herself, her mother, and her two children. The tramp hired to impersonate John Doe wants to have his arm mended so he can play baseball again. D. B. Norton (Edward Arnold), the owner of the newspaper, sees a power base from which to run for president.

None of that matters. When people read about John Doe and all of the social ills that he protests and when they hear him speak about hope for the future, they identify with him, they believe in him, and they rush to his defense and to his cause. The John Doe movement becomes a powerful force for good that has a life far beyond its beginnings. It even engulfs Ann and the pseudo John Doe, who come to truly believe in what they are writing and saying.

With simple warmth and conviction, John Doe reads Ann's homespun words of truth, and galvanizes the country by calling for brotherly love and cooperation to overcome social problems: "Your teammate, my friends, is the guy next door to you, your neighbor. . . . You're going to need him and he's going to need you, so look him up. If he's sick, call on him; if he's hungry, feed him; if he's out of a job, find him one."

He urges people to tear down the figurative fences that separate them from their neighbors: "Tear down the fence, and you'll tear down a lot of hates and prejudices. Tear down all the fences in the country, and you'll *really* have teamwork."

It would not take a miracle for such teamwork to occur, John Doe maintains. People are capable of changing from thoughts and feelings of separation, he says, because they do so every year at Christmastime:

"Why can't that spirit, that same warm Christmas spirit, last the whole year round? Gosh, if it ever did, if each and every John Doe would make that spirit last 365 days out of the year, we'd develop such a strength, we'd create such a tidal wave of goodwill that no human force could stand against it. Yes, sir, my friends, the meek can *only* inherit the Earth when the John Does start loving their neighbors. . . . Wake up, John Doe, you're the hope of the world."

People are eternally hungry for such a message of hope, and from time to time wake up to their greater potential and rise en masse above human conditions. Both the fictional character of John Doe and the man chosen to portray John Doe symbolically represent such an awakening and renewed hope. John says that he has heard platitudes before, but that he and others are beginning for the first time to see what they mean. No matter what people may try to do to them, the ideas themselves are still good, John says.

Ann herself says of the John Doe image, "If it's worth dying for, it's worth living for."

YE VIEW

1. How do people respond to John Doe's speech? Discuss specific examples, such as the story of Sourpuss.
2. Who does Ann say is the first John Doe? Compare the ideas offered by both.
3. How do you think people today would respond to John Doe's message? Would they support John Doe Clubs such as the ones organized in the movie? Would *you*?

MEET ME IN ST. LOUIS

PREVIEW

Excitement over plans for the St. Louis World's Fair of 1904, marital prospects of the two oldest sisters, Esther (Judy Garland) and Rose (Lucille Bremer), and the antics of youngest sister Tootie (Margaret O'Brien) fill the Smith household in this enduring musical based on a Sally Benson story. (1944, 113 minutes, NR, *)

META. VIEW

"Have Yourself a Merry Little Christmas"

Director Vincente Minnelli's masterpiece of American nostalgia is divided into seasonal vignettes leading up to the opening of the World's Fair. The "Winter 1903" segment contains many of the trimmings of what has come to be regarded as an ideal Christmas image of the early 1900s. The dramatic and romantic events are set against scenes of snow, holly, sleighs, sledding, Christmas trees, a gala Christmas dance, colorful red and green dresses, and present exchanges.

Even the child's longing for the arrival of Santa Claus is charmingly depicted. "Did he come yet?" Tootie asks anxiously. "I've been waiting such a long time, and I haven't seen a thing." In true parent or older-sister fashion, Esther replies, "Now, you know he's not going to come until you're asleep."

Running throughout the segment, and indeed throughout the movie, is one of the principal themes of Christmas—family togetherness. As Esther tells Tootie, who is distraught over the prospect of leaving their beloved city and moving to New York: "The main thing, Tootie, is that we're all going to be together, just like we've always been. That's what really counts. We could be happy anywhere, as long as we're together."

Trying to calm Tootie's fears about moving, Esther sings the beautiful Christmas ballad "Have Yourself a Merry Little Christmas," advising at the beginning to "let your heart be light. Next year all our troubles will be out of sight."

411

Interestingly, the Hugh Martin-Ralph Blane song originally struck a rather pessimistic chord, with lyrics such as "Have yourself a merry little Christmas, / It may be your last; / Next year we may all be living in the past." Garland insisted that more optimistic lyrics be added to dispel the gloom.[2] As a result, we have a classic song of hope and promises of happy times with family and friends to come, but also a reminder to celebrate the Christmas spirit *now* by accepting our blessings, regardless of the present circumstances, and by having faith in a joyous future.

YE VIEW

1. What are some specific challenges that arise for the Smith family during the Christmas season? How are they solved in the Christmas spirit?

2. "Oh, Papa, you've given us the nicest present anyone could ask for," Esther says. To what is she referring? What does the present mean for the various family members?
3. To "have yourself a merry little Christmas," what do you like to do?

MIRACLE ON 34th STREET

PREVIEW

Kris Kringle (Edmund Gwenn) insists that he isn't just playing a role as Santa Claus at Macy's in New York City, and tries to make a realistic store employee, Doris Walker (Maureen O'Hara), and her daughter Susan (Natalie Wood) believe in him and what St. Nick represents. (1947, 96 minutes, NR, *)

META VIEW

It's not childish to believe in Santa Claus

In this classic story by Valentine Davies, a New York City court is asked to rule on a question that would seem absurd to millions of children: Is there or is there not a Santa Claus?

You can decide for yourself whether or not the man who calls himself Kris Kringle in the movie is truly Santa, but the fable gives a clear metaphysical answer to the question and explains why the belief in Santa Claus is important.

Yes, the movie asserts, there *is* a Santa Claus, and we *must* believe in him, if *by Santa Claus* is meant the spirit of Christmas—the kindness, joy, and love at the heart of Christmas.

Such intangibles are what Kris Kringle stands for, says his friend and attorney Fred Gailey (John Payne), and constitute "the only things that are worthwhile."

Society, however, places increasing interest on commercialism, Kris notes. Saying that he has been fighting against the commercialization of Christmas for years, Kris laments, "Christmas and I are sort of getting lost in the shuffle."

"Christmas isn't just a day," he says. "It's a frame of mind, and that's what's been changing."

For example, he deplores Macy's procedure of trying to convince parents to buy whatever toys the store needs to clear out. Kris wants only to make children happy, and starts directing parents to other stores—an approach that the public genuinely appreciates. Store officials finally appreciate the approach too—but only as a marketing tool to increase sales and popularity; they don't "get" Kris's motivation.

Kris becomes discouraged when he is called abnormal because he sincerely wants only to make people happy, while those who are dishonest, vicious, deceitful, and selfish are called normal. Can you blame him? But Kris realizes that his concerns mean people need all the more to believe in him and his values.

The movie makes the point that a belief in a value system of happiness, love, optimism, imagination, and faith—and a symbol of that value system—is needed in the commercial, realistically oriented world.

Doris represents the skeptics who discount imagination and faith. She has raised Susan to view the world only through realistic lenses.

"I think we should be realistic and completely truthful with our children, and not have them growing up believing in a lot of legends and myths like Santa Claus," she says.

Kris considers Doris and Susan "a couple of lost souls" who need help, and he sees them as a test case for his efforts to improve society. "If I can win you over, there's still hope. If not, then I guess I'm through," Kris says.

Doris eventually learns that there is more to life than meets the senses.

413

She recognizes the need for faith, and echoes Fred's words to her: "Faith is believing in things when common sense tells you not to."

YE VIEW

1. What are some signs that could lead people to think Kris Kringle might really be Santa Claus?
2. Does Susan learn to believe in Santa Claus? If so, how? At the end of the movie, what advice does Doris give her?
3. What does Santa Claus mean to you?

IN THE SAME SPIRIT

Worth retelling:

Miracle on 34th Street—Here's a remake that is almost as good as the original. Richard Attenborough as Kris Kringle and Mara Wilson as Susan are captivating. (1994, 114 minutes, PG, *)

More converted disbelievers:

One Magic Christmas—An angel helps a struggling wife and mother (Mary Steenburgen) regain her Christmas spirit in this Disney story. (1985, 88 minutes, G)

The Santa Claus—Scott Calvin (Tim Allen) hasn't been a model father, but he becomes more loving and giving when circumstances turn him into Santa Claus. Scott initially has trouble accepting his new North Pole surroundings, but Judy the elf teaches him, "Seeing isn't believing. Believing is seeing." Adults denying their inner child don't easily believe Scott is Santa, but children readily do. As Bernard, the chief elf, says, "Children hold the spirit of Christmas within their hearts." (1994, 97 minutes, PG, *)

NATIONAL LAMPOON'S CHRISTMAS VACATION

PREVIEW

Clark Griswold (Chevy Chase) is determined to give his family a dream Christmas, but nightmares from visiting relatives and an insensitive boss threaten the jolly vision in this amusing satire. (1989, 97 minutes, PG-13)

META VIEW

Deck the halls with zeal

Clark is the epitome of the Christmas spirit and as such is brimming over with yuletide zeal. He is truly passionate about Christmas and all the joy, love, and togetherness that it has come to mean as a holiday. He is equally zealous and passionate about spreading those good feelings to his family with festive decorations and events.

The words of the song "Christmas Vacation" are truly Clark's theme: "Everybody knows there's not a better time of year."

The wholeheartedness with which Clark throws himself into the holiday is admirable: he leads the family on an expedition to cut their own Christmas tree (he pictures his chosen tree aglow in heavenly light), he sings carols, he lights the outside of the homestead with 25,000 twinkle lights, he is enthralled while watching home movies of past Christmases, he presides over the Christmas Eve dinner, and he keeps the Santa Claus tradition alive for the family children.

There's no doubt he truly believes that "Christmas is about resolving differences and seeing through the petty problems of family life."

While Clark's spirit craves a merry, merry Christmas, he's still not completely immune to human frustrations. His reactions to a tailgater, to his neighbors, and to his stingy, insensitive boss are not filled with peace or goodwill. Clark becomes a symbol of the need to integrate the Christmas spirit into all of our affairs and at all times of year.

However, Clark is extremely patient and tolerant with his in-laws, including the free-loading, out-of-work Cousin Eddie (Randy Quaid), who shows up with his family and dog in an old RV to stay a month. Sincerely loving and giving, Clark offers to see to it that Eddie's children have Christmas presents (and Eddie just happens to have a list).

Because Clark is such the spirit of Christmas and loves the holiday so much, the viewer aches, in spite of the laughter, when Clark is repeatedly foiled in his attempts to have a happy holiday.

YE VIEW

1. How do Clark's wife, children, and parents support him in his efforts to spread Christmas cheer?
2. What is Cousin Eddie's motive for kidnaping Clark's boss? Do you admire his action? Why or why not?
3. Think about your Christmases past. Have there been occasions when your attempts to create a merry Christmas were spoiled? Share those memories.

IN THE SAME SPIRIT

More zaniness:

Mixed Nuts—The staff of a suicide hotline service (presided over by Steve Martin) have some rather bizarre antics on Christmas Eve, but there's a lot of genuine caring and loving behind it all. (1994, 97 minutes, PG-13)

PRANCER

PREVIEW

Eight-year-old Jessie Riggs (Rebecca Harrell) rescues a wounded reindeer that she believes is Santa Claus's Prancer, and the results have marvelous effects for her, her widowed father (Sam Elliott), and the townspeople. (1989, 102 minutes, G, *)

META VIEW

"Make glad the heart of childhood"

A girl the same age as Jessie wrote to the editor of the *New York Sun* in 1897. Virginia O'Hanlon of New York City wanted to know the truth: "Is there a Santa Claus?"

"Yes, Virginia, there is a Santa Claus," wrote Francis P. Church in a response that became as famous as Virginia's letter.

The world would be a dreary place without Santa Claus, Church wrote, and the fact that Santa Claus isn't seen does not mean he doesn't exist.

"The most real things in the world are those that neither children nor men can see," Church said.

Santa Claus lives forever, he concluded. "A thousand years from now, Virginia, nay, ten times 10,000 years from now, he will continue to make glad the heart of childhood."[3]

Obviously, Church believed that Santa is no mere human but is a spirit of infinite goodness.

Church's editorial is Jessie's favorite section of her favorite book about Christmas. It sums up her beliefs about Santa Claus.

Jessie finds herself in Church's position of defending Santa Claus to her

417

friend Carol, who says she doesn't believe in Santa Claus because she's never seen him.

"Well, you've never seen God, either. Does that mean there's no God?" Jessie asks, refusing to give up her belief in either Santa Claus or God.

Jessie is, in fact, the type of person who actually lives and breathes the wonder of Christmas all year. She plays Christmas songs year-round. She has absorbed the various legends and myths about Christmas and made them a part of her framework for life. For example, Jessie takes quite seriously the myth that a Christmas Eve during a full moon is a magical time of peace. Magical things are bound to happen at that time, she says with conviction and excitement which are themselves magical.

It's comforting and reassuring to think that there are still young and young-at-heart Virginias. A newspaper editorial in Jessie's town of Twin Oaks, Michigan, reads, "It is inspiring to see that some children are able to hold on to their dreams and innocent spirit."

The newspaper says that Jessie is "nursing the spirit of Christmas back to health," and the paper praises such a sense of wonder and belief: "We *need* that belief. The world needs it. May it live forever."

YE VIEW

1. How do you explain Prancer's appearances and behavior? What do you think happens to him?
2. Jessie thanks Prancer "for everything." To what is she referring? What people are changed directly or indirectly by Prancer's presence?
3. Write your own editorial to answer the question: Is there a Santa Claus?

REMEMBER THE NIGHT

PREVIEW

When the court recesses until after Christmas, a New York City district attorney, John Sargent (Fred MacMurray), takes a woman he is prosecuting for shoplifting, Lee Leander (Barbara Stanwyck), home with him to Indiana for the holidays, with heartwarming results. (1940, 94 minutes, NR)

META VIEW

Hearts are especially open at Christmas

During the pervasive Christmas atmosphere of goodwill, hearts are likely to open and give love chances to work its magic like no other time of year. Take John Sargent, for example. He's a genuinely nice man, but he probably would not have given second thoughts to a shoplifter's spending several days in jail if it weren't during Christmas. He bails Lee out, and one kind act leads to another. That's how the true Christmas spirit works.

Taking Lee home to his mother and aunt on the family farm, John becomes aware of the forces that drove Lee to a life of crime. John tells his mother (Beulah Bondi) about Lee's criminal record, but adds, "That doesn't mean that she wasn't unhappy, lonely, and a human being like the rest of us."

John's mother replies: "Oh, the poor thing. She probably didn't get enough love as a child." John's mother sees the best in Lee.

His mother remembers the time John stole her egg money and then had to work to repay it when he understood what he had done wrong. John says that his mother made him understand, but *she* says, "No, dear, it was *love* that made you understand."

It *is* the love—the love of a happy, close family and community—that Lee sees and experiences during her time with the Sargent family which lets

419

Lee understand about the true richness of life. Without hesitation, the family makes Lee a part of all the activities and celebrations. Lee dries dishes, cooks, helps at a fund-raiser, shares in the family's gift exchanges on Christmas morning, and goes to the New Year's Eve dance.

Lee says that she will always remember her wonderful Christmas season with the Sargent family, but the time provides her with more than memories. Her real Christmas gift is a sampling of genuine love, and her life will never be the same.

YE VIEW

1. Contrast Lee's experience taking money from her mother with John's experience taking money from *his* mother. What conclusions can you draw about Lee's early home life?
2. When her trial is resumed, why does Lee plead as she does? What is your opinion of her for doing so?
3. What do you think becomes of the relationship between Lee and John?

SANTA CLAUS

PREVIEW

A toymaker who loves children (David Huddleston) becomes the legendary gift-giver, and goes on his merry way quite nicely for centuries, until threatened by a greedy toy manufacturer (John Lithgow). (1985, 112 minutes, PG, *)

META VIEW

Here comes Santa Spirit

Will the real Santa Claus please stand up and say, "Ho, Ho, Ho"? Who would that be? St. Nicholas, born in Asia Minor c. 280 A.D., who threw bags of gold into a poor man's house? The Roman god Saturn, who ruled over a winter feast? The Swedish elf Jultomten, who sported a red cap and white beard and traveled in a goat-pulled sleigh to deliver presents on Christmas Eve? Father Christmas, usually pictured in a fur-lined scarlet robe? Black Peter of Dutch tradition, who delivered presents through the chimney to good children? Or the amalgamation of the above whom Clement Clarke Moore fashioned into his 1822 poem "A Visit From St. Nicholas"? Or others?

The point is that one story of Santa Claus's origin is just as good as another, because Spirit is at work in each one and in combining all of them into the embodiment of certain ideals which are cherished throughout the world—happy giving, caring, and loving.

The myth of Santa's origin presented in the first part of *Santa Claus*, sometimes titled *Santa Claus: The Movie*, beautifully and imaginatively draws upon the Moore view of Santa. The North Pole and its toy shop have never looked so inviting and enchanting.

Also woven into the story is a strong suggestion of heavenly intervention in the creation of the Santa Claus legend. The special effects capture this connection. A star resembling the Star of Bethlehem shines above the land. The elves appear like messengers from heaven, and tell Santa that he and Mrs. Claus (Judy Cornwell) will live forever and, though childless, now "have all the children in the world." A reverend Father Christmas character (Burgess Meredith) appears among the elves, proclaims that a prophecy has been fulfilled with Santa's coming, and tells Santa that he can distribute gifts to all the world's children in one night because: "Time travels with you. The night of the world is a passage of endless night for you." The centuries

421
✳

indeed testify to the timelessness of Spirit manifested as the myriad spirits of Christmas.

YE VIEW

1. In your opinion, what is the movie's position on the commercialization of Christmas?

2. Santa Claus says, "The world is a different place now. . . . People don't seem to care about giving a gift just so they can see the light of happiness in a friend's eyes. It just . . . it just doesn't *feel* like Christmas anymore." Do you think the observation is reflected in the movie? Is it an accurate statement about society today? Why or why not?

3. What stories about Santa Claus or other Christmas symbols or traditions most appeal to you? Why?

Happy Merry Hallothanksmas! or Welcome to The Nightmare Before Christmas

'Tis the holiday season, with the coming of fall, to be—what? Frightened? Thankful? Jolly?

Yes. All of the above: Fall signals Hallothanksmas!

Hallothanksmas is the cultural and commercial snowball of Halloween-Thanksgiving-Christmas. It rolls in right after Labor Day in September and lingers until New Year's Day, when the heart-shaped boxes appear in stores for Valentine's Day in February.

The last quarter of the year has almost become a national holiday. We must need it.

Each year the Halloween displays in their orange-and-black majesty of the macabre and the mountains of pumpkins outside grocery stores overlap briefly with posters of turkeys and pilgrims, which in turn quickly blend with the multitudinous sights and sounds of Christmases past, present, and future, of Santas and creches and carols and lights and general joy to the world.

Spiritually, Hallothanksmas is a period of honoring and appreciating creation and creativity. What is most appealing about Halloween is the creative and imaginative costumes and the fun people have thinking up ways to playfully trick and treat themselves and one another. Thanksgiving not only commemorates an important event in the creation of the United States, but also recognizes the importance of offering thanks to Universal Spirit for all creative blessings. Christmas is a glorious time of celebrating the birth of Jesus Christ and of the Christ, the ever-creating essence of God, within each person.

423

A most creative, inventive movie that captures the seasonal blur of Hallothanksmas is Tim Burton's *The Nightmare Before Christmas* (1993, 75 minutes, PG, *). The movie uses stop-motion animation to tell the story of Jack Skellington, the Pumpkin King of Halloween, who has grown discontent and unfulfilled with his ghoulish reign and senses "an empty place in my bones."

Transported to Christmas Town, Jack is delighted and charmed by all the yuletide merriment and preparations. "What's this?" he sings. "The streets are lined with little creatures laughing; everybody seems so happy. Have I possibly gone daffy?"

Perhaps, but he notes, "In my bones I feel the warmth that's coming from inside."

Back in Halloween Town, Jack tries to understand the mystery of Christmas through science and mathematics, but to no avail. He finally realizes this about the Christmas spirit: "Just because I cannot see it, doesn't mean I can't believe it." The nightmare develops when Jack attempts to usurp Santa Claus and bring his own form of Christmas to the world.

The movie's treat and gift is the message that we can be thankful there is a time for Halloween and for Christmas, even though in the movie and in actuality they tend to mesh in the collective mind. Still, each holiday has its own character and each reflects during Hallothanksmas different aspects of our creative energies as hallowed, thankful, Christed children of God.

Notes
· · · · · · · · ·

INTRODUCTION

1. Geoffrey Hill, *Illuminating Shadows: The Mythic Power of Film*, Shambhala, Boston, 1992, p. 4.

2. *Merriam-Webster's Collegiate Dictionary, Tenth Edition*, Merriam-Webster, Inc., Springfield, Massachusetts, 1993, p. 731.

3. Charles Fillmore, *The Revealing Word*, Unity Books, Unity Village, Missouri, 1997, p. 132.

4. Francis Bacon, *The New Organon and Related Writings*, Bobbs-Merrill, Indianapolis, 1981, p. 129.

CHAPTER 1—ANGELS (AND OTHER MESSENGERS) IN OUR MIDST

1. Charles Fillmore, *Atom-Smashing Power of Mind*, Unity Books, Unity Village, Missouri, 1995, p. 45.

2. *Emmanuel's Book III: What Is an Angel Doing Here?*, compiled by Pat Rodegast and Judith Stanton, Bantam Books, New York, 1994, p. 43.

3. Edgar Allan Poe, "Annabel Lee," *Selected Prose and Poetry*, Rinehart & Co., Inc., New York, 1954, p. 419.

4. Jim Rosemergy, *The Quest for Meaning*, Unity Books, Unity Village, Missouri, 1999, p. 131.

CHAPTER 2—THE FORCE IS WITH AND WITHIN US

1. Thomas F. Crum, *The Magic of Conflict*, Simon & Schuster, New York, 1987, p. 47.

2. Confucius, quoted in *Bartlett's Familiar Quotations*, John Bartlett, Little, Brown & Co., Boston, 1980, p. 68.

3. Ken Keyes, Jr., *The Hundredth Monkey*, Vision Books, St. Mary, Kentucky, pp. 5–6.

4. Robert Browning, "Paracelsus," Part I, from *Masterpieces of Religious Verse*, Harper & Brothers, New York, 1948, p. 431.

5. George Lucas, quoted in "George Lucas, the Force and God," Terry Mattingly, Gospel Communications Network, gospelcom.net, 1998, p. 1.

6. Dale Pollock, *Skywalking*, quoted in "George Lucas, the Force and God," p. 2.

7. George Lucas, quoted in *The Kansas City Star*, April 27, 1999, Section E, p. 1.

8. Neale Donald Walsch, quoted in *The Edge*, November 1998, p. 9.

9. William Shakespeare, *Hamlet*, Act III, Sc. i, Ln. 56.

10. Charles Fillmore, *Jesus Christ Heals*, Unity Books, Unity Village, Missouri, 1996, p. 50.

CHAPTER 3—JESUS CHRIST — SUPERSTAR

1. Marianne Williamson, *A Return to Love: Reflections on the Principles of A Course in Miracles*, 1992, HarperCollins, New York, pp. 61–62.

2. Eric Butterworth, *Discover the Power Within You*, HarperCollins, New York, 1989, p. 10.

CHAPTER 4—SEEING THE BIG PICTURE

1. Franklin Delano Roosevelt, quoted in *Bartlett's Familiar Quotations*, p. 779.

2. *A Course in Miracles*, Foundation for Inner Peace, Glen Ellen, California, 1992, Introduction.

3. Rosemary Ellen Guiley, *The Encyclopedia of Dreams*, Berkley Books, New York, 1995, Preface.

4. Ernest Holmes, "The Divine Search," *Science of Mind*, October 1998, p. 7.

5. Christopher M. Bache, *Lifecycles: Reincarnation and the Web of Life*, Paragon House, New York, p. 9.

6. Jane Roberts, *Seth Speaks: The Eternal Validity of the Soul*, New World Library, San Rafael, California, 1994, p. 226.

7. Richard and Mary-Alice Jafolla, *The Quest: A Journey of Spiritual Rediscovery*, Unity Books, Unity Village, Missouri, 1993, p. 26.

CHAPTER 5—AFFIRMIN' IN THE RAIN

1. Deepak Chopra, *The A-to-Z Steps to a Richer Life*, Barnes & Noble, New York, 1994, pp. 32–33.
2. Charles Fillmore, *The Twelve Powers of Man*, Unity Books, Unity Village, Missouri, 1995, p. 130.
3. H. Emilie Cady, *Lessons in Truth*, Unity Books, Unity Village, Missouri, 1995, pp. 61–62, 66–68.

CHAPTER 6—LIGHTS, CAMERA — UNITY AND PEACE

1. George Orwell, quoted in *Bartlett's Familiar Quotations*, p. 858.
2. William Shakespeare, *Hamlet*, Act I, Sc. v, Ln. 15.
3. Ernest Hemingway, quoted in *Bartlett's Familiar Quotations*, p. 844.

CHAPTER 7—LOVING ONE ANOTHER

1. Swami Muktananda, *Play of Consciousness*, SYDA Foundation, 1994, p. 281.
2. Thomas Moore, *Soul Mates*, HarperCollins, New York, 1994, p. 96.
3. Florence Scovel Shinn, *The Game of Life and How to Play It*, DeVorss & Co., 1925, pp. 7, 26, 93.
4. Patricia Einstein, *Intuition: The Path to Inner Wisdom*, Element, Rockport, Massachusetts, 1997, p. 1.
5. St. Francis of Assisi, quoted in *Bartlett's Familiar Quotations*, p. 138.

CHAPTER 8—MEETINGS WITH REMARKABLE PEOPLE

1. The Dalai Lama, quoted in *The Dalai Lama*, Demi, Henry Holt and Co., New York, 1998.

CHAPTER 9—THE OLD HOLLYWOOD TESTAMENT

1. Joseph Campbell, *Myths to Live By*, Bantam Books, Toronto, 1988, p. 24.
2. Charles Fillmore, *The Revealing Word*, p. 179.
3. Mary Baker Eddy, *Science and Health with Key to the Scriptures*, The First Church of Christ, Scientist, Boston, 1971, p. 339.

4. Robert Brumet, *Finding Yourself in Transition*, Unity Books, Unity Village, Missouri, 1995, pp. 78–79.

5. Emmet Fox, *The Ten Commandments: The Master Key to Life*, Harper & Row, New York, 1953, p. 42.

CHAPTER 10—HAVE YOURSELF A SUPER NATURAL CHRISTMAS

1. *Merriam-Webster's Collegiate Dictionary, Tenth Edition*, p. 1050.

2. Stanley Green, *Encyclopaedia of the Musical Film*, Oxford University Press, New York, 1981, p. 123.

3. James Cross Giblin, *The Truth About Santa Claus*, Thomas Y. Crowell, New York, 1985, pp. 60–61.

Index

∙ ∙ ∙ ∙ ∙ ∙ ∙

Following is a list of all *Reel Spirit* movies. Main Attractions and those films that are sole subjects of Feature Presentations are in boldface.

A

431

435

✦

About the Author

· ·

Raymond Teague is an award-winning journalist, a popular speaker, a successful author and editor of spiritual publications—and a lifelong movie buff.

For almost thirty years, Raymond was associated with one of the leading newspapers in Texas, the *Fort Worth Star-Telegram,* as a writer and editor. He served the paper as children's book editor for twenty years. He won reporting and writing awards from the Society of Professional Journalists, Sigma Delta Chi; the Texas Associated Press Managing Editors Association; the Texas Historical Commission; and the Texas State Teachers Association. In addition, his three travel guidebooks of Texas published by the *Star-Telegram* were best-sellers.

A native of Fort Worth, Raymond began studying and writing about movies at Texas Christian University, from which he graduated with degrees in journalism and English. He began his career with the *Star-Telegram* with an historical look at movie ratings. He has written many entertainment and art reviews. His review of the 1970s hit movie *Love Story,* in which he took umbrage at the then-popular line "Love means never having to say you're sorry," is included in the book—*30—A Journalistic Approach to Freshman Composition.*

He has written magazine articles and contributed, as editor and writer, to some of the leading educational anthologies and textbooks.

For the last several years, Raymond has enjoyed combining his love of movies and writing with metaphysical interests. Since 1997 he has served as associate editor of Unity House.

Raymond is a graduate of the Unity Continuing Education Personal Development Program, and is former spiritual leader of Unity Chapel in Eureka Springs, Arkansas. He is a regular speaker at Unity churches and centers. In addition, he writes frequently about metaphysical issues, and is author of the Unity 2000 pamphlet *The Christ Within.*

His wife of twenty-eight years, Sylvia, is also a writer and editor, and their daughter Alexandra is a published poet who teaches composition at the University of Miami.

More Reel Spirit Movies

Blank pages are provided for you to make notes on about additional movies that inspire, explore, and empower—perhaps other personal favorites, new releases, or ones you would like to see when the Spirit moves you.